The Priesthood of the Plebs

A Theology of Baptism

Peter J. Leithart

Wipf and Stock Publishers
Eugene, Oregon

Wipf and Stock Publishers
199 West 8th Avenue, Suite 3
Eugene, Oregon 97401

The Priesthood of the Plebs
A Theology of Baptism
By Peter J. Leithart
Copyright © 2003, Peter J. Leithart
ISBN: 1-59244-404-0
ISBN: 978-1-49824-710-8
Publication Date: October, 2003

TABLE OF CONTENTS

TO JAMES B. JORDAN

ὅστις ἐκβάλλει ἐκ τοῦ θησαυροῦ αὐτοῦ

καινὰ καὶ παλαιά

ACKNOWLEDGEMENTS

Many more have contributed to this project than I can know, but I wish to thank some of those whose help has been most evident. For financial support, I thank the Sessions of Cherokee Presbyterian Church, Woodstock, Georgia, USA, and of Covenant Presbyterian Church, Nashville, Tennessee, USA. Tom Singleton of the Nehemiah Foundation also provided a substantial grant, for which I am very grateful. Special thanks to the Session and people of Reformed Heritage Presbyterian Church, Birmingham, Alabama, USA, whose financial support, prayers, and friendship have meant much to me and my family. We are thankful also for the prayers and encouragement of the members of the Cambridge Presbyterian Church.

Gilbert and Cindy Douglas and their family deserve special thanks for their extraordinary selflessness in handling many practical necessities "back home." Thanks also to my parents, Dr. Paul and Mildred Leithart, who took on several tasks that made our life immeasurably easier. I am grateful to my wife, Noel, and my sons, Jordan, Sheffield, Christian, and James, who curbed my almost infinite capacity for error by helping to check bibliography, citations, and Scripture references. Beyond that, Noel has long embodied true Christian sacrifice by her continual willingness to put others ahead of herself. May her good works ascend as fragrant incense.

My intellectual debts are likewise more than the hairs of my head. Thanks to my supervisor, John Milbank, whose enthusiasm for my work was encouraging and astonishing in equal measure. Early on, Tim Jenkins and Stephen Buckland navigated me through the uncharted seas of cultural anthropology. Dr. Graham Davies and

Professor Robert Gordon read and made helpful comments on the material in chapter 2, and Dr. James Carleton Paget read and commented upon a draft of chapter 3. Jim Rogers, Joel Garver, Rev. Jeff Meyers, and Rev. Rich Bledsoe read substantial portions of the thesis; I appreciate their encouragement, insight, and advice, even when I, unwisely, did not take it. Interaction with Mark Horne has helped clarify a number of issues, and more general discussions with Michael Hanby and David Field were refreshing and challenging. Over a longer term, my theological imagination, such as it is, has been decisively shaped and reshaped by the work of James B. Jordan, who also commented extensively on an earlier draft of this work. As a small token of my debt and gratitude, I dedicate this thesis to him.

PREFACE TO THE PUBLISHED EDITION

Though *The Priesthood of the Plebs* was originally written to fulfill one of the conditions for a doctoral degree in Divinity at the University of Cambridge, my more fundamental inspiration came from elsewhere: from an historical model, a biblical passage, and an ambition.

The historical model, as I note in the preface to the thesis, was the scholastic habit of examining the sacraments of the "Old Law" as a preface to the theology of the Christian sacraments. In this approach, the scholastics were building on the patristic and early medieval habit of exploring sacramental theology in a typological framework, so that Old Testament signs and seals provided the basic categories for sacramental theology. Even though scholastics raised technical and philosophical questions about the sacraments (causation, efficacy, validity, etc.), the nod to the Old Testament sacraments meant that sacramental theology was redemptive-historically qualified; sacramental theology was a central issue in understanding the transition from old to new. Since the medieval period, that procedure has largely gone into abeyance, with consequences that are, to my mind, nothing short of disastrous. *The Priesthood of the Plebs* is only the slightest beginning of the work that needs to be done, but it is, I hope, a useful beginning. Among the many projects that need to be done is a thorough Christian treatment of the Levitical system, with a view to grasping its significance for Christian liturgy and sacraments (as well as other areas of Christian theology). The explosion of interest in Levitical ritual, inspired equally by exegetes such as Jacob Milgrom and anthropologists such as Mary Douglas, provides a wealth of material for this work.

The Biblical passage that occupied a prominent place in the back of my mind was 1 Peter 3:21, where Peter, having compared baptism to the flood, wrote, "correspond to that, baptism now saves you." Peter himself qualified that statement, and theologians and exegetes have busily and sometimes anxiously added further qualifications. However hedged in with qualifications, though, Peter's statement is disturbing for many Protestants, especially Reformed and evangelical, who would never, ever say what Peter said. For much Protestant sacramental theology, it is in *no* sense true that "baptism now saves you." Yet, there it is in the text. One can either qualify the statement out of existence, or repeat Peter's statement in a whisper, or let the text challenge assumptions and provoke revisions. I chose the latter course: My goal was to provide a baptismal theology that would make it seem perfectly natural to speak, in an offhand way, about the salvific power of baptism. This served as a test for the success of my project, and, by emphasizing the corporate, historical, and bodily form of "salvation," I believe I have gone some way to passing that test. In a sense, the thesis is an exercise in systematic theology done "back to front," starting from sacramental theology and working back to refine soteriology.

As I formulated it during my research, my ambition was to write "a great cathedral of a book." Cathedrals impress because of their sheer size, the audacity of the engineering, the breath-taking heights and lengths, and I aspired to write a book on baptism with analogous reach and scope, one that reflected a cathedral's grandeur, one that would leave readers awed (as I myself was) that God can throw down nations and plant new ones with a few drops of water. Cathedrals are also incredibly intricate in detail; every nook and cranny has a story and often a story that stretches over centuries, the visitor treads over the tombs of famous men and women buried under the floor stones, doorways and stained glass windows are allegories in stone and glass. One could literally spend years studying the details of any single cathedral, and I aspired to write a book whose contours and lintels and cornices would delight and stimulate. Whether I have come anywhere close to achieving this ambition, I leave to others to judge.

I had hoped to revise the thesis extensively before publication, but the pressures of teaching and the distractions of my theological attention deficit disorder have prevented that. My second option was to work carefully through the whole thesis and write a kind of *retractiones*, interacting with my earlier opinions and highlighting weaknesses in the argument, but the pressures of teaching and the distractions of my theological attention deficit disorder prevented that too. So, I have opted to publish the thesis virtually unchanged from its original form, and to include only this briefest and most superficial of prefaces. As the years have passed and I have turned to other projects and topics, I have concluded that I will never revise the thesis with the attention that it would require, and I have concluded that it is better to put it before a wider audience as is, since the alternative seems to be leaving it dormant forever.

As a slight bow in the direction of a *retractiones*, I should note certain sections where the argument is opaque, weak, or strained. First, the vignettes from the history of sacramental theology in chapter 1 are far too compressed to make much sense to anyone unfamiliar with the debates. I trust the main point will be plain enough, and readers who need more background to grasp my point are urged to look up the secondary sources cited in the footnotes. I believe the discussion of Augustine in chapter 1 is useful, but I should have made it plainer that Augustine would not necessarily press the grammatical and musical metaphors in the ways that I have done.

Chapter 2 is generally strong, I think, but the use of a kind of algebraic notation now strikes me as odd. At the time, it was an effort to make the structure of my argument more explicit, but I see now that explicitness is directly proportional to tediousness; the skeleton of chapter 2 shows through the flesh in an unseemly, not to say grotesque, manner. The thrust of the argument in chapter 3 still seems airtight to me, but some of the exegesis of particular passages could have been stronger. As in chapter 1, portions of chapter 3 suffer from an excessive compression of the argument and perhaps too large an element of fancy. Chapters 4-5 represent my effort to offer a baptismal theology that meets the test of 1 Peter 3:21, and also offers a framework for retrieving patristic language about baptism without falling into late medieval or Tridentine errors. A great deal more research would be needed to justify some of the claims, especially my account of the Greek city as a priestly organization (chapter 5). By and large, however, I still find these chapters persuasive.

Durham's Andrew Louth, the external examiner for my thesis, found chapter 6 the weakest of all. After five chapters in which I took nothing for granted and believed nobody without scrutiny, Louth observed, chapter 6 looks like the work of a credulous amateur (not Louth's words, exactly). He complained about some of my sources, calling le Goff's books "potboilers." Far be it from me to argue with someone with

Louth's extraordinary erudition. He is quite right; chapter 6 is a far-too-impressionistic survey of a highly complex development, and one that does not make any use of the massive and massively important recent work on Gregory VII and the medieval papacy. Yet, this edition includes chapter 6, unrevised, and that reflects my conviction that, however much I am mistaken in detail, *something* of extraordinary importance happened to the structure of the church and the understanding of baptism around the time of the Investiture Struggle, and that these developments determined for centuries the position and role of "laymen" in the church. And I continue in my suspicion that this extraordinary something had enormous implications for the development of modern society, philosophy, and social theory.[1] Thoroughly defending that conviction and justifying that suspicion would require at least a book -- a book on the interactions of sacramental theology, philosophy, ecclesiastical structure, and political thought in the late medieval period, and the relevance of those interactions for the development of modernity --, and that is a book I do not expect to write for some time to come, if indeed I ever write it. Perhaps a reader will find the claims of chapter 6 worthy of further study, and my thesis can be vindicated or corrected.

I am sure that plenty of other weaknesses and errors are there to be found, and I hope for readers attentive enough to spot them and charitable enough to correct me. As Augustine observed in the preface to his *de doctrina Christiana*, "there would be no way for love, which ties people together in bonds of unity, to make souls overflow and as it were

---

[1] Besides, James Jordan, to whom this book is dedicated, *loved* chapter 6.

intermingle with each other, if human beings learned nothing from other human beings."

* * *

Since submitting the thesis for my degree, I have published chapters or sections of chapters in various journals. My treatment of Augustine from chapter 1 was published as "Conjugating the Rites: Old and New in Augustine's Theology of Signs" in the *Calvin Theological Journal* 34 (1999), and the early sections of chapter 2 were published as "Servants of the Sanctuary: Priesthood in the Old Testament" in the *Journal for the Study of the Old Testament* (September 1999). Chapter 3's exegesis of Hebrews may be found in "Womb of the World: Baptism and the Priesthood of the New Covenant in Hebrews 10:19-22" in the *Journal for the Study of the New Testament* 78 (2000) 49-65, and sections of chapters 1 and 5 appeared under the title "Modernity and the Merely Social" in *Pro Ecclesia* 9:3 (Summer 2000). A portion of my discussion of "poetic causation" may be found in "Making and Mis-Making: Poesis in Exodus 25-40" in the *International Journal of Systematic Theology* 3:2 (November 2000), along with additional material treating Milbank's concept of "poesis." Portions of chapter 6 appeared in "The Gospel, Gregory VII, and Modern Theology," *Modern Theology* 19:1 (January 2003), published by Blackwell Publishers which retains copyright. In addition, I have published several other articles that deal with related themes: "Marcionism, Postliberalism, and Social Christianity," *Pro Ecclesia* 8:1 (Winter 1999); "Christs Christened into Christ: Priesthood and Initiation in Augustine and Aquinas," *Studia Liturgica* (1999); and "'Framing' Sacramental Theology: Trinity and Symbol," *Westminster Theological Journal* 62 (2000).

Finally, in addition to those thanked in the acknowledgments, I wish to express my gratitude to Jonathan Barlow, who typeset this book, handled discussions and negotiations with the publisher, and did everything else necessary to make this a reality.

Peniel Hall
Trinity Season, 2001

ORIGINAL PREFACE TO THE THESIS

This is a thesis about baptism, written in the tradition, if not of Thales or Coleridge's Ancient Mariner, at least that of Tertullian, who called the waters that encompassed the primeval creation a *figura baptismi* and inferred from the gospels that *nunquam sine aqua Christus* (Evans 1964: 9, 21; *De baptismo* 4, 9). I will suggest that baptism covers the earth as the waters cover the sea.

This is also a book about priesthood, among the most despised concepts in modern theology, where priests are frequently brought to public view only to serve as targets of ridicule and slander. That is no matter: I take so firmly anti-modernist a stance as to suggest that together baptism and priesthood furnish an exhilarating vantage point from which to survey significant features of the topography of Scripture and history.

My strategy for reaching this location requires some explanation. The range of literature relevant to the study of Christian baptism is astonishingly wide. In its three monumental volumes, the *Sacramenta Bibliographia Internationalis* lists tens of thousands of entries, most from the past half-century, and for nearly two millennia before that every branch of theology had something to say about baptism. More recently, sociologists and cultural anthropologists have studied Christian sacraments. In the face of this overwhelming mass of material, I have the audacity to maintain that something important is missing: serious attention to the rituals of Old Testament Israel. Preachers, catechists, and mystagogues have always indulged in luxuriant meditation on sacramental types, but theologians have frequently looked outside the typological *lectio* for answers to their *quaestiones*. Against this, I propose to revive, as a prolegomena to understanding Christian sacraments, the venerable but underappreciated and underdeveloped scholastic treatise on the *sacramenta veteris legis*.

To be specific, typological connections between Old Testament priestly ordination and Christian baptism have been recognized since patristic times, and I offer an exegetical defense of this typology. Patristic commentators stressed that, by joining to Christ, initiation confers participation in Christ's royal and prophetic ministries as well as His priesthood. Though I agree with this, I am not satisfied with the "weak" argument that the New Testament occasionally employs ordination imagery in connection with baptism. I argue instead for the more rigorous thesis that baptism fulfills and replaces the ordination rite and therefore has the same role in the church as ordination had in Israel, namely, consecrating priests for ministry in God's house. My "strong" thesis also entails the contention that the priestly typology illumines many issues, including the form and historical origin of Christian baptism, New Testament baptismal imagery, patristic and medieval liturgical elaborations, and the socio-political cutting edge of Christian initiation.

Let me give a blueprint of what is to follow. Chapter 1 shows that the relation of Old and New has always been a crucial issue in sacramental theology and that a practical Marcionism has fettered theologians in conundrums of their own making. What I call "semi-Marcionite sacramental theology" has framed debates concerning the real presence, definitions of sacrament, *opus operatum*, infant baptism, the Eucharistic *anamnesis,* and the place of signs and rites in the church. As an alternative, I draw on various texts from Augustine that characterize the transition from Old to New as a "tense shift" in a "root word," the Logos, and this leads to the conclusion that New Testament sacraments are "conjugations" of the sacraments of the Old. Baptism specifically can be understood properly only against the background of Hebrew rites and events, one of which is priestly ordination.

A full theology of baptism thus requires a theology of priesthood (as well as a theology of royalty and prophecy). In chapter 2, I argue from several lines of biblical and comparative evidence that Hebrew priests were "personal attendants to Yahweh in His house," and I also examine some of the features of the ordination ritual. Then, in chapter 3, exegesis of several New Testament texts leads to the conclusion that Christian baptism fulfills the Aaronic ordination. Chapter 3 also begins to reveal discontinuities between Old and New Covenant priesthood, which are unraveled in later chapters to discover the "grammar" of the New Testament's conjugation of the Old.

In chapter 4, I apply the typology of baptismal ordination to liturgical and theological questions. Ceremonies of anointing and investiture in Christian initiation, though based on the typology I am defending, are unwarranted and potentially damaging. On the other hand, the priestly typology establishes an unbreakable connection between baptism and Eucharist, and I argue that baptized infants ought, as members of the priesthood, be given a share of the priestly meal. Regarding the theology of initiation, I argue from the priestly typology that baptism effects what it symbolizes *ex opere operato* and defend a form of "baptismal regeneration."

With the tabernacle texts in the background and drawing on John Milbank's work, I develop a "poetic" account of sacramental causation, in which baptism is a human participation in the divine act of making new men and women.

Chapter 5 broadens the discussion to examine the sociological significance of baptismal induction to priesthood. Just as the Aaronic ordination distributed priestly privilege and configured Israelite socio-religious space, so baptism is an effective sign transforming antique priestly order. The church's baptismal polity challenges not only the Israelite ordering of human society around the pairs "priest/non-priest" and "Jew/Greek," but also the shape of the Greek city, whose dualism of patrician/plebeian was also a gradation in priestly rank. Baptism, in short, announces the formation of a *polis* that offers priesthood to the plebs. Destruction of the archaic system of graded priesthood is central to the gospel of the broken wall, the rent veil, the open sanctuary, the accessible altar. In the concluding chapter, however, I suggest that, especially following the Gregorian Reform of the eleventh century, the church reintroduced the dualistic system that Paul had denounced as among the "elementary principles" of the world. As the typology connecting priesthood with baptism was smothered by a competing typology and set of practices, the church contributed to the construction of secular order.

To complete this edifice with such unpromising materials as water and priesthood is a big job. I leave to the reader to judge whether what I have built bears more than a passing resemblance to its blueprint.

* * *

Citations of the author's last name, date, and page number are included parenthetically within the text. Titles and publishing information may be found in the bibliography. In citations of patristic and medieval works, I have also cited a version in the original language. This makes for some degree of overload, but it allows the reader to choose whether he wishes to examine the translated or original version. Bible quotations are from the *New American Standard Bible*, the *Biblica Hebraica*, or the Nestle-Aland *Novum Testamentum Graece* (1981).

This dissertation is the result of my own work and includes nothing that is the outcome of work done in collaboration.

CHAPTER ONE

The Beginning of the Gospel

"The beginning of the gospel of Jesus Christ, the Son of God. . . . John the Baptist appeared in the wilderness preaching a baptism of repentance for the forgiveness of sins" (Mark 1:1, 4). So, curiously, begins the gospel of Mark. We expect John, the forerunner announcing the imminent appearance of the King. An eschatological kerygma that begins with *baptism*, though, is peculiar.

But to whom?

Apparently not to those to whom John preached, for they responded with sufficient enthusiasm to alarm King Herod and to win John an undisputed reference in Josephus. What did they think they were doing? Why was a man baptizing in the wilderness "good news"?

In the quotation from Isaiah (vv. 2-3), Mark hints at the answer. Though Isaiah's prophecy of Israel's "new Exodus" from Babylon had been fulfilled, by the first century the Jews had relapsed into a kind of exile and impatiently awaited another deliverance. And now, here is John, clearing the pathway of return (cf. Wright 1996). That he appears with water could only heighten expectations:

> The afflicted and needy are seeking water, but there is none.
>
> And their tongue is parched with thirst;
>
> I, the Lord, will answer them Myself,
>
> As the God of Israel I will not forsake them.
>
> I will open rivers on the bare heights,
>
> And springs in the midst of the valleys;

1

> I will make the wilderness a pool of water,
>
> And the dry land fountains of water.
>
> I will put the cedar in the wilderness,
>
> The acacia, and the myrtle, and the olive tree;
>
> I will place the juniper in the desert,
>
> Together with the box tree and cypress. . . .
>
> For I will pour out water on the thirsty land
>
> And streams on the dry ground;
>
> I will pour out My Spirit on your offspring,
>
> And My blessing on your descendants;
>
> And they will spring up among the grass
>
> Like poplars by streams of water
>
> (Isa. 41:17-19; 44:3-4; cf. Ezek. 36:24-27, 30).

When John's water falls on the scorched clay of Israel, it can only be a matter of time before she again crosses the sea, before Eden is restored.

In this wider perspective, Mark's opening verses reflect assumptions about the gospel shared by the entire New Testament. A gospel that begins in baptism is a *Jewish* gospel, arising within the particular history of Yahweh's dealings with Israel. Since it deals with the fortunes of a historical people, a gospel that begins in baptism refuses to be tucked safely into the mystical interstices of human life. It is a *material* gospel, public truth. A voice that proclaims baptism must reverberate with political overtones.[1] Such a gospel thus stakes a claim in the field of

---

[1]See Milbank (1990; 1997); Kerr (1986); Hauerwas (1983); Lash (1988); Lindbeck (1984); de Lubac (1950; 1956). Current Jesus scholarship has emphasized the "political" dimensions of Jesus' ministry and preaching (Wright 1996 and Borg 1984; 1993), and Pauline specialists have recently accentuated his Jewish setting and therefore the ecclesial dimensions of his theology (see Dunn 1990; Wright

history and culture, but this is ground that secular thought has claimed as its exclusive possession. A boundary dispute is inevitable.

Thus, Mark's opening verses can serve as a touchstone for competing accounts of Christianity. To avoid this touchstone, which is for modern thought a scandal, a stone of stumbling, secularism has attempted, with great success and considerable cooperation from Christians, to evict the gospel to different ground. Against Mark, modern philosophy, sociology, and theology imagine that Christianity is "internal" and "spiritual." Thus, for Nietzsche, Jesus' teaching was a flight from the real world of culture to the inner kingdom (1988: 29); for Kant, true piety was rational moralism (Kant 1960); and for the romantics and the early Hegel true religion was inner religion (Fackenheim 1967: 53-54). The evolutionary schema for religious development posited by Comtean sociology of religion cannot encompass a gospel that begins with baptism, nor can much modern, especially Protestant theology. Heralding baptism is significantly different from heralding Schleiermacher's religion of feeling, Barth's ineffable word, or an evangelicalism combining an affirmation of disputed doctrines with the inner experience of the new birth.[2]

Also against Mark, many modern accounts of Christianity, including theological ones, accept some form of Marcion's sundering of Old and

---

1991; Sanders 1977; Stendahl 1963).

[2]On liberal Protestantism, see Harnack (1958); Schleiermacher (1928; 1958); Sykes (1971; 1984); Crouter (1988). Sykes (1984: 193; 1988: 88-107) suggests that Barthian neo-orthodoxy is a species of hyperliberalism, locating the encounter with the word in an unfathomable "inwardness beyond inwardness." Evangelicalism combines, in the categories set out in Lindbeck (1984), cognitive and expressivist tendencies, and shares liberalism's refusal of a catholic "cultural-linguistic" framework.

New.[3] Modern Marcionism, like its ancient counterpart, conspires with a gnostic ambivalence to physical creation and sees Christianity as removing the husks of materialism in religion. Christianity is not merely a different religion but a different *kind* of religion from that of Israel.

Treacherously, each stumbling stone serves as foundation for the other: The Marcionite account of history supports the reading of Christianity as inwardness, and the interpretation of Christianity as inward piety sets it off from the materialism and socio-political concerns of Hebrew sensibility.

Among the "husks" of Old Testament religion supposedly discarded in the emergence of the spiritual "kernel," ritual has first place. Hebrew religion is to Christianity as empty ritualism is to heartfelt piety, as Baroque Catholicism is to Puritan liturgical minimalism. Modern Marcionism thus has, at its heretical margins, completely repudiated sacraments (Reventlow 1984). Far from proclaiming a gospel that begins in baptism, Marcionism preaches a gospel that ends baptism altogether.

Here, however, the problem is historically more intricate and challenging, for modern theology is not alone in combining an uneasiness

---

[3]Modern Marcionism developed from late medieval Spiritualism, Renaissance Humanism, and Deism (Reventlow 1984: *passim*), but came into its own in nineteenth-century liberalism. O'Neill asserts that Marcion achieved his greatest success in nineteenth-century New Testament studies (1985: 171; cf. Harris 1975: 181-184; Neill and Wright 1988: 20-30), but his comment is relevant beyond that field. See Kant (1960: 116-118); Harnack (1990: 133-142); Schleiermacher (1928: 60-62, 608-611); Lindbeck (1997: 434-437). Brunner (1964: 245) believed Schleiermacher's negative attitude toward the Old Testament was "decisive" for his entire dogmatics. Hostility to the Old Testament has been most virulent in Old Testament studies; cf. Wellhausen (1885); Weinfeld (1979); Blenkinsopp (1977: 18-22; 1992: 9-12). Milbank (1990: 92-98) indicates how the Marcionite "liberal Protestant metanarrative" structures the sociology of religion.

toward rites and signs with ambiguity toward the Old Testament. As this chapter shows, a spiritualizing semiotic theory and a semi-Marcionite account of redemptive history form sizable and mutually reinforcing eddies in the mainstream of the tradition.[4] By a "spiritualizing semiotic theory," I mean the belief that signs and rites function as more or less dispensable aids to invisible spiritual transactions, or the similar notion that signs aim primarily at achieving channeling grace to the soul. As David Jones puts it in his much-cited essay, "Art and Sacrament," defenders and opponents of a sacramental economy of grace share the assumption that interior grace is "what matters," disputing only the usefulness of external signs for achieving this internal state (Jones 1959: esp. 165-166). By "semi-Marcionite," I mean a structuring theological narrative that, while remaining within orthodox parameters, betrays reservations about Old Testament materialism or legalism, or minimizes the grace offered to Israel. I shall call the intertwining of these themes "Marcionite sacramental theology" or some variation of that label.

Marcionite sacramental theology can lead in a realist or a mystical direction. Realists construe the Old as a covenant of "mere signs," while those of the New are "effective signs," "signs that contain or confer realities," or signs that veil underlying "substance." For mystics, the rites and signs of Hebrew religion are bound up with the material and outward form of the Old Covenant, whereas Christianity begins an ascent to spirit, a descent into the heart, or both at once. From the perspective developed here, realism and mysticism are variations within a Marcionite framework,

---

[4]See Rahner (1963: 29-32) and Leeming (1956: 7-12) for discussion of the sacraments of the Old and New Law.

since both dig a chasm between Old and New and both aspire to an divine-human encounter beyond signs. Because of the influence of semi-Marcionite sacramental theology, the church has not supplied an account of either the gospel or of baptism that apprehends how the two arise together.

In the next few sections, I briefly review the Eucharistic doctrine of Paschasius Radbertus, the sacramental theology of Hugh of St. Victor, medieval formulations of *ex opere operato*, and the Reformers' criticisms of this formula, showing how Marcionite sacramental theology figures into each.[5] Even theologians who do not embrace Marcionite assumptions often implicitly rely on them. Scholastic theology detaches technical or mechanical questions of sacramental operation from patristic and early medieval typological mystagogy,[6] so that, for example, Thomas construes sacramental "causality" in the categories of Aristotle rather than according

---

[5]These examples will also illustrate persistent confusion of two senses in which the Old Testament economy is considered an economy of "signs" or "figures." In the first sense, developed in the New Testament and essential to orthodoxy, the Old Testament system is considered a figure of the future age of the New Covenant. In the second sense, the Old Testament is considered figurative because it employed symbols and rites in religious exercises. When the two senses are conflated, the New Testament writers who claim that Christ's coming has introduced an economy of "truth not figure" are interpreted as promising an escape from the economy of signs and rites that made up cultural and religious life of Israel.

[6]On the primacy of typology in patristic sacramental and liturgical theology, see Danielou (1960). On baptism specifically, see Lundberg (1942) and Finn (1992a; 1992b). I confine this discussion to Western theology; from my limited exposure, it seems that Orthodoxy, by maintaining a firmer grasp on the typological foundations of theology and by emphasizing that liturgical theology reflects on the church's practice (which is saturated with typology), avoids some of the problems that I address here.

to biblical patterns of flood, Exodus, or the ablutions of Leviticus. Answers to scholastic *quaestiones* were thus sought outside the typological *lectio* (Chenu 1968: 127). Marcionite sacramentology thus shapes method as well as content. I then move on to tell three stories of twentieth-century sacramental theology -- the question of the Eucharist *anamnesis*, Continental debates on infant baptism, and the theological use of categories from the social sciences -- to show that theologians continue to swim in these waters.

Strands in Augustine tell the story of the exodus from Old to New differently and therefore assign sacraments a different role in the New order. Augustine implies that man, made in the image of the Word, lives and moves and has his being in an economy of signs. Therefore, the transition from Old to New is not an ascent beyond semiotic processes but a transformation within the semiotic and linguistic medium that makes up the life of a religious community. In Augustine's metaphor, the New is a "conjugation" of the Old. If so, then, in scholastic terms, the "treatise on the sacraments of the Old Law" must serve as prolegomena to a "treatise on sacraments in general." Augustine's formulation thus furnishes the methodological thesis of this dissertation, that the typological *lectio* has considerable resources, largely untapped, for addressing even the most arcane of *quaestiones*.

Eventually, I hope to arrive at a vantage point from which to proclaim a gospel that begins in baptism, that is, a public gospel that grows out of Israel's history, taking a stand on the stone the builders rejected, which has, of course, become the chief cornerstone of a stable edifice.

7

Out of the Shadows: Paschasius Radbertus

The ninth-century "debate" between Paschasius Radbertus and Ratramnus produced the first treatises on the Supper.[7] Though common, it is simplistic to contrast Paschasian realism with Ratramnian symbolism (McCracken and Cabaniss 1957: 92), for on the question of *figura* and *veritas* they define their terms so differently that they were talking past each other, assuming they intended to talk toward each other at all. Both, moreover, affirm that the Supper is figure and truth.[8]

A genuine difference emerges, however, in their evaluation of Old Testament sacraments, for which 1 Corinthians 10 provides a *locus classicus*. Ratramnus insists that Christ was truly offered to and received by Hebrew saints. To deny that Israel was genuinely baptized in the Red Sea insanely contradicts Paul, and Ratramnus even claims that the cloud and sea contained (*continebant*) the invisible operation of the Spirit. Besides satisfying corporal hunger and thirst, Israel's manna and water administered the power of the word. What the church now eats and drinks in its bodily meal of bread and wine is thus the "same" as the food

---

[7]See Macy (1984: 27-31) and Jones (1994: 72-79). Portions of Paschasius' treatise and all of Ratramnus's are translated in McCracken and Cabaniss (1957).

[8]For Paschasius, *figura* and *veritas* are two aspects of a thing, corresponding roughly to outer appearance and inner essence, while for Ratramnus, they are two different ways in which something can be represented, as in literal and figurative language (Ratramnus 7-8; McCracken and Cabaniss 1957: 119-120). See Paschasius, 4.2 (McCracken and Cabaniss 1957: 102; 4.43-46 in Paschasius 1969: 29; PL 120, 1278C); Ratramnus 49 (McCracken and Cabaniss 1957: 132; PL 121, 147), for evidence that both affirm a "both/and" of figure and truth.

and drink given to Israel, since *unus idemque Christus* fed them His flesh and stood in the spiritual rock to offer His blood. Ratramnus concludes ecstatically, insinuating that the meal of Israel, in which Christ offered His flesh and blood *before* His incarnation and death, was *more* miraculous and incomprehensible than the meal of the church (*mirum, incomprehensible, inaestimabile*). Such a miracle should not be subjected to *ratio* but accepted in faith *quod factum sit* (paragraphs 20-26).[9] The Christological substance of the sacraments remains constant throughout history, as does their visible/invisible and figural/real structure. Methodologically, for Ratramnus typology controls ontology.[10]

Paschasius does not openly repudiate Paul, but a palpable aversion to identifying the sacraments of the Old and New haunts his discussion. His initial question is decisive: If Israel received the "same" food as the church, why has there been a change? The Hebrews, he concedes, received figures of the body and blood,[11] they might even have received some *virtus sacrandi*, and they lacked nothing necessary for spiritual life. Yet he remains recalcitrant: He couches the statement concerning the

---

[9]McCracken and Cabaniss (1957: 124-125; PL 121, 137-139). Cf. the strong statement of section 25: *Ipse namque qui nunc in Ecclesia omnipotenti virtute panem et vinum in sui corporis carnem et proprii cruoris undam spiritualiter convertit ipse tunc quoque manna de coelo datum corpus suum, et aquam de petra profusam proprium sanguinem, invisibiliter operatus est* (PL 121, 138-139; McCracken and Cabaniss 1957: 125).

[10]Ratramnus's theory is not perfect. As Chauvet points out, he introduced the image of the "veil" into sacramental theology, which has been the source of much mischief (Chauvet 1995: 292-293; cf. FitzPatrick 1993: 133-173).

[11]This is perhaps the sense of the cryptic phrase *in praefiguratione idem*, where the antecedents of *idem* are quite difficult to determine (5.1; McCracken and Cabaniss 1957: 104; 5.20 in Paschasius 1969: 31).

virtus sacrandi in a conditional clause, and his exegesis is shaped throughout by a sharp contrast of *figura/imago* over against *veritas*. Despite Paul's insistence that God gave the same food and drink to Israel and the church, therefore, Paschasius claims there is clearly a great difference (*patet ... multum interest*), so that the food is the same not *in re* but only *in specie ac figura*.[12] By contrast, the church enjoys the unadulterated *mysterium veritatis*, which is *sola veritas* and *non figura* (McCracken and Cabaniss 1957: 104; 1969: 33, 5.43-48). Paschasius grants that the Supper has a figural element so long as it is clear that "not every figure is shadow or falsehood," and *umbra* is to be understood in the sense used in Hebrews as a description of the foreshadowing Old Covenant.[13] Methodologically, in his discussion of 1 Corinthians 10, Paschasius is *more* rationalist than Ratramnus; unstated assumptions of ontological possibility qualify Pauline typology.

Paschasian "realism" thus turns out to be a refraction of his questionable reading of the Old-New transition. To grant that the Supper is *figura* confines the church under the economy of *umbrae*, yet to grant that Israel received Christ *in re* seems to make the incarnation superfluous. Thus, the sacraments of the New must contain or communicate some

---

[12]5.1, 3 (McCracken and Cabaniss 1957: 105, Paschasius 1969: 33, 5.64-66; PL 120, 1281C). There is a textual problem in the final line. McCracken and Cabaniss translate as "in appearance," assuming *in specie* (cf. PL 120, 1281C), while the *Corpus Christianorum* text reads *in spe*, while including a note on variant texts. While Paschasius' argument emphasizes a promise-fulfillment pattern and *veritas* is defined in terms of fulfillment, the denial that the sacraments of the Old were not the same *in re* shows that, whatever the proper reading, Paschasius was challenging the Augustinian, and, apparently, Pauline, conception.

[13]*non enim omnis figura umbra vel falsitas*, 4.2 (McCracken and Cabaniss 1957: 102; Paschasius 1969: 29, 4.46; PL 120, 1278C). Cf. 5.1 (McCracken and Cabaniss 1957: 104; Paschasius 1969: 31-32, 5.20-26; 15.77-87; PL 120, 1323C).

"truth" not found in the Old. The Old Testament was an economy of "mere signs," while the New, though it still employs signs, is an economy of "realities" beyond signs.[14] The difference between Old and New is focused on the difference in the way sacraments "work."

Vases Don't Cure the Sick: Hugh of St. Victor

Though he employs *sacramentum* in the expansive patristic sense, Hugh of St. Victor's *De sacramentis* includes elaborate consideration of sacraments more narrowly conceived. To his credit, Hugh continually takes note of the physical and material character of the sacraments and of their specific symbolisms,[15] but the dualistic structure of his theology ultimately leads, as Macy says, to a "mystical" sacramentology.[16]

---

[14]Though it is, of course, anachronistic to attribute "transubstantiation" to Paschasius, he moves in that direction, and this form of realism too depends on a radical contrast between Old and New. I could contest recent defenses of transubstantiation, such as Pickstock (1996: 421-430) and Marion (1991: 161-182), on the same basis. Schillebeeckx (1968) argues that "transsignification" lacks the "ontological weight" to provide a full account of the Eucharistic presence, and thus concludes that his theory supplements rather than displaces traditional formulations. Presumably, "transsignification" would be an adequate description of the sacraments of the Old Law. On the other hand, the Zwinglian notion of a "mere sign" is *entirely* defined by opposition to realism, and thus represents another extreme within the same framework.

[15]As explained briefly below, Hugh's claim that sacraments are given for *humilitatio* and *exercitatio* is an important move, despite the dualistic form it eventually takes (1.9.3, Hugh 1951: 156-157; cf. Asad 1993: 78-79). He notes, further, the appropriateness of circumcision, which causes physical pain, as a sign of a covenant of law, while the painless ablution of baptism is appropriate for a covenant of charity (1.11.8; Hugh 1951: 185).

[16]The following examples are drawn from many: The firmament created on the second day of the creation week represents *ratio* as the boundary between the

Sacraments are a medicinal *remedia* for sin, conferring an *invisibilium antidotum* through the visible rite. Metaphors of sacramental "medication" are patristic, but Hugh conflates them with a vague form/matter distinction, so that the sacramental rite becomes the "container" of the medicine of grace. It is only an analogy, but Hugh is willing to press the analogy: "vases do not cure the sick but medicine does."[17] "What matters," to borrow Jones's (1959) phrase, is what is inside the bottle.[18]

Containers are "medicine" only in a subtly inverted sense. According

---

sensualis natura hominis and the heavenly *puritas intelligentiae* (1.1.19; Hugh 1951: 22-23; PL 176, 200D). Though in a sense there are *vestigia Trinitatis* of power, wisdom, and love in the visible creation, these are only *signa tantum* while interior things are the very *imago* (1.3.28; Hugh 1951: 56-57; PL 176, 230C). In fact, *corporea natura similitudinem capere non potuit Divinitatis* (1.6.2; Hugh 1951: 95; PL 176, 264D). While he affirms that embodiedness was part of Adam's original good nature, sin caused something like a "fall into language"; prior to the fall, God instructed Adam *intus* but afterward *foris* through the *species rerum temporalium et visibilium* (1.7.33; Hugh 1951: 138; PL 176, 302D).

[17]*Deus medicus, homo aegrotus, sacerdos minister vel nuntius, gratia antidotum, vas sacramentum. Medicus donat, minister dispensat, vas servat quae sanat percipientem aegrotum gratiam spiritalem. Si ergo vasa sunt spiritalis gratiae sacramenta, non ex suo sanant, quia vasa aegrotum non curant, sed medicina. . . . ut peritiam suam medicus ostenderet in illo remedium praeparavit, a quo languidus occasionem morbi accepit. Quia enim homo visibilia concupiscens corruptus fuerat, coagrue reparandus in eisdem visibilibus salutis occasionem recipere debebat, ut per eadem resurgeret per quae corruerat* (1.9.4; Hugh 1951: 150; PL 176, 323). Thomas uses the medicinal analogy in denying that there were sacraments in paradise (*ST* 3a, 62, 2).

[18]A similar spiritualizing move is implicit in Peter the Lombard's general definitions of sacraments, drawn from Augustine and the *Summa sententiarum: sacra signa, invisibilis gratiae visibilis forma* (PL 192, 839). The *Summa sententiarum* adds, *in sacramento baptismatis figurabatur ablutio interior per illam exteriorem et visibilem* (PL 176, 117). If grace is *invisibilis*, and if sacraments are grace-causing signs, then by definition sacraments have as their "target" an internal transformation (cf. Macy 1984: 122-124).

to Hugh, attachment to visible things corrupted Adam, a belief that, as with Augustine, blends Christian polemics against idolatry with anxiety about physical creation. Outward and visible as they are, sacraments, *secundum se*, serve only to exacerbate sinners' unhealthy infatuation with the visible. Yet, God instituted these paradoxical remedies to show that He alone promotes health (1.9.5; Hugh 1951: 160-163; PL 176, 325-326). External rites thus become remedial when we learn that external rites cannot possibly be remedial, and so are forced to look beyond visible things for healing. Sacraments also contribute to saving *humilitatio* by subjecting the proud to insensible and visible things over which they were created to rule (1.9.3; Hugh 1951: 156; PL 176, 319-320).[19]

Hugh's sacramental theology is set in a historical narrative progressing from the *umbra* of natural law, through the *imago vel figura veritatis* of the written law, to the *corpus veritatis* of the time of grace, which looks to the *veritas spiritus* of the consummation (1.11; Hugh 1951: 182-187). In part, this is no more than an unveiling: As history moves toward the sunrise of the incarnation, spiritual realities are increasingly illumined (Schlette 1959: 163). Expiation and justification were *occulte* in the tithes and oblations of the natural law, became *vero evidentius* in circumcision, and *manifeste declaratur* in baptism. History's trajectory *also* runs, however, from *foris* to *intus*: Oblations "cut off" part of a man's wealth, circumcision "cut off" a superfluous body part, but baptism wounds more deeply, declaring "the perfect cleansing of man and the interior lustre of the soul."[20]

---

[19]See Peter the Lombard, *Sententiae* 4.1.3 (PL 192, 839-40).

[20]Baptism is a sacrament *quod perfectam hominis emundationem et interiorem animae candorem* (1.11.8; Hugh 1951: 185; PL 176, 348).

Eschatologically, humanity follows the same trajectory, eventually resuming its prelapsarian communion with God, which, like the angels', was wholly *intus*, outside a symbolic and linguistic medium.

In their structure and operation, the sacraments duplicate the mystical, inward trajectory of redemptive history. Old sacraments were "visible and signs of the visible" (*visibilia, et signum visibilium*) while the New, though "in truth visible," are *invisibilis gratiae signa et sacramenta* (1.11.2; Hugh 1951: 182; PL 176, 343). Like Ratramnus, Hugh contends that the Mosaic sacraments were effective, deriving sanctification as *signa tantum* of Christian sacraments (1.11.1, 5; Hugh 1951: 182, 184; PL 176, 343, 345).[21] Sacraments of the church, however, contain "their own" sanctification (1.11.2; Hugh 1951: 182; PL 176, 343). Thus, though *signum et figura* adequately describes the Old rites, the New are, strictly, *sacramenta*, since they contain "by sanctification some invisible and spiritual grace" (1.9.2; Hugh 1951: 155; PL 176, 317-319). Though Hugh does not draw the conclusion of some later writers that the Old Law had no sacraments, the sacraments of the two covenants have different structures and operate according to different logics.[22]

Despite Thomas's appreciation for the embodied form of Christian practice, Victorine static disturbs his arguments for the necessity of sacraments. He first roots signs anthropologically: Humans know spiritual

---

[21]Chemnitz saw Hugh's theory as the first departure from the more straightforward patristic consensus, still affirmed by Bede, that the sacraments of the Law conferred eternal life through the power of Christ (1978: 46-47).

[22]Consistent with his definition of *sacramentum*, Lombard hesitates to apply the term to the Old Covenant rites and signs, since, as Hebrews says, they were incapable of making a man just (*Sententiae* 4.1.2; PL 192, 839).

realities through the senses, which, it seems, is an unexceptionable condition of created life. Contradictorily, Thomas also explains the physical character of the sacraments as an accommodation to sin and borrows Hugh's idea that sacraments are physical to foster humility (3a, 61, 1). A similar ambivalence toward signs is evident in Thomas's denial that sacraments were necessary in Eden. Before the fall, there was a proper hierarchy, with Adam's body subject to his soul, and it therefore would have been *contra ordinem* if he had needed anything *corporale* to achieve perfection (3a, 61, 2). The New Law is, further, "intermediate" between the *figura* of the Old and the *nude et perfecte* eschatological manifestation of truth (3a, 61, 4). The church thus walks a pathway that leads out of the thicket of signs into the clean and open field of naked spiritual encounter.

Methodologically, Hugh's formulations imply that one cannot conduct an inquiry into the "how?" or even the "what?" of Christian sacraments by examining the "how?" of Old Testament rituals. Dualist anthropology, which reflects an ontological dualism, trumps typology. Aquinas implies the same methodological conclusion when he denies that the sacraments of the Old Law contained or caused grace and defines them, in very "Protestant" fashion, as *quaedam illius fidei protestationes* that *solum* signified faith in the Passion of Christ (3a, 62, 6). Thus, he explains the causality of the New Covenant sacraments by the distinction of principal and instrumental causality (3a, 62, 1) and does not refer at all to the rites of the Law. While scholastics used Old Testament ceremonies typologically and examined the fittingness of Old Testament ritual law, these considerations were not germane to their explanations of the "mechanics" of Christian sacraments.

Opus Operatum and Its Reformation Opponents

Implicit in Hugh, semi-Marcionite sacramentology became more formalized in the later Middle Ages in the distinction between *opus operatum* and *opus operans*.[23] Though often employed to underscore the Augustinian view that the moral state of a minister is irrelevant to the validity of a sacrament (cf. Augustine 1974b), this distinction also formed the boundary between the sacraments of Old and New. Jewish sacraments were not efficacious by virtue of the thing done (*opus operatum*) but by virtue of the recipient's faith (*opus operans*); in the church, by contrast, sacraments are effective simply by being rightly performed on a subject who places no *obex* in the way of grace. Behind Reformation polemics against Catholic *ex opere operato*, then, were differences concerning the relation of Old and New, and Luther, Calvin, and Chemnitz attacked Catholics on the latter point as well as the former.[24]

---

[23]Without using this technical terminology, the *Decretum pro Armenis* of the Council of Florence (1439) claimed that sacraments of the Old Law *figurabant* the passion of Christ but were not causes of grace, while those of the New *continent gratiam, et ipsam digne suscipientibus conferunt* (Denzinger 1965: 333; 1957: 220). Trent followed Florence (Session VII, Canon 6), buttressing its claims with the technical term *ex opere operato* (Canon 8; Denzinger 1965: 382; 1957: 262-263). On the development of *opus operatum/opus operans* and its relation to the Old/New distinction, see Leeming (1956: 7-12); Landgraf (1933: 241-242).

[24]Luther claims that the argument put forward in favor of the notion of "effective signs" is Paschasian one: If the sacraments of the New Testament are "mere signs," there is no difference between Old and New (Luther 1959: 64-66). Chemnitz asserts that "the man-made opinion of the *opus operatum*" was invented by scholastics following Hugh and Peter the Lombard in order to make a

In practice, however, Protestant theology continued to play a semi-Marcionite tune. Immediately after affirming that the sacraments of the Old and New are equally effective, Luther explains that the sacraments of the New Law are like those of the patriarchs, while both differ "vastly" from Mosaic "legal symbols," which did not have any promise attached to them. Reversing the scholastic *operatum/operans* distinction, he claims that the sacraments of the Mosaic order were not sacraments of justification but "only sacraments of works. Their whole nature and power consisted in works, not in faith. Whoever performed them fulfilled them, even if he did it without faith." Efficacy in Christian sacraments, by contrast, wholly "consists in faith itself" so that one may fulfill them even without enacting the rite (Luther 1959: 64-66). In spite of his vigorous affirmation of continuity both of substance and operation, Calvin's theology of baptism begins with the New Testament, and, apart from a brief typological meditation on the Exodus and an extended polemic for infant baptism from its analogy with circumcision, the Old Testament plays comparatively little role in his fundamental theology of baptism (Calvin 1960: 1303-1359; *Institutes* 4.15-16). Theoretically, Calvin overcomes scholastic Marcionism; in practice, he perpetuates it.[25]

"distinction between the sacraments of the two Testaments" (Chemnitz 1978: 47). "We must," Calvin agrees, "utterly reject that Scholastic dogma . . . which notes such a great difference between the sacraments of the Old and New Law, as if the former only foreshadowed God's grace, but the latter give it as a present reality." Israel received in their sacraments the same thing Christians do, "Christ with his spiritual riches" (Calvin 1960: 1299; *Institutes* 4.14.23).

[25]With its doctrine of the covenant and its emphasis on continuity between Old and New, later Reformed theology mitigated Marcionite tendencies to some extent (cf. Witsius 1990: 2.362-378). Yet it persisted in drawing the (very traditional but confusing) distinction between a "material" Old and a "spiritual"

Marcion and Modern Sacramental Theology

Some major liturgical works of this century, particularly studies of the Eucharist, have sought to expound Christian liturgy by explicit reference to Old Testament or later Jewish rites and institutions.[26] Yet, semi-Marcionite sacramental theology remains widespread. To demonstrate this, I tell three stories of twentieth-century sacramental theology.

Mystery Religion and Eucharistic "Re-Presentation"

Influenced by Odo Casel's "mystery" view of Christian worship, liturgists have interpreted the Eucharistic *anamnesis* ("Do this in remembrance of me") "dynamically" as "the making effective in the present of an event in the past."[27] For Casel, this means not only that "Christ himself is present and acts through the church," but also that the

---

New Covenant (cf. Calvin 1960: 1.428-464; *Institutes* 2.11-12), which was sometimes allied, as with Zwingli, with an at best ambivalent affirmation of sacraments (Eire 1986; but on Calvin cf. Wallace 1982; Gerrish 1993). For Puritan sacramental theology, see Reventlow (1984) and Holifield (1974).

[26]Wainright (1991: 55). Bouyer (1955) is in part an effort to root Odo Casel's "mystery" concept in the Old Testament, and Bouyer (1968) traces the Eucharistic prayer to the Jewish *berakoth*. See Jeremias (1966); Thurian (1960-1961); Schmemann (1986: 53-75). Gavin (1928) has much less to say about the Old Testament than about postbiblical Jewish ideas and practices.

[27]Wainwright (1980: 297), quoting from the Windsor statement of the Anglican/Roman Catholic International Commission. On Casel, see Bouyer (1955: 86-98); Jones (1994: 187-188); White (1995: 80, 83-84); Neunheuser (1976: 489-504); Worgul (1980: 205ff.).

18

God who exists outside time permits the church in the liturgy to "enter into the divine present and everlasting Today" so that at worship "there is neither past nor future, only present" (Casel 1962: 141-142).

In several respects, Casel's work is important and fruitful: He broke with both cognitive and expressivist models of Christianity, attacked individualism in Eucharistic theology, and his insistence that the encounter with mystery must be embodied in signs, rites, and gestures prepared for the "interpersonal" emphasis of Schillebeeckx (1963; 1968) and Schoonenberg (1967: 3-11; see Casel 1962: 9-13, 21-23, 30). Yet, Casel explicitly grounds his theory in supposed analogies between Christianity and Greco-Roman cults, whose mysteries were closer to Christian worship than anything in the worship of Israel. Contrary to Neunheuser's assertion (1976: 496-497), Casel argues that Passover was a memorial event but not a mystery, since it was "related first of all to human events, and human deliverance." Because of their legalism and their belief that God was "a powerful, terrible ruler, separated from mankind by an unbridgeable gap," the Jews developed no liturgical sense of "close relationship" with God, and Christ's Pasch has "no expression in the old covenant." Fortunately, outside Israel, God was preparing "certain religious forms" that "could offer words and forms to express this new, unheard-of" personal relationship. Thus, "the Hellenes sometimes found it easier to grasp and to grasp more deeply the truth of the gospel than did the Jews with their purely Semitic, imageless, legal thinking. The Christianity of the ancient world appears to us as the fulfillment and glorification of what Greco-Roman antiquity was" (Casel 1962: 31-37). Liturgical expressions of the Old Covenant are now used in

19

a "higher sense concerning the purely spiritual facts of the new," so that New Covenant worship reaches toward "a new and higher kind of reality" (1962: 40).[28]

Casel's Marcionism colludes with a semiotic theory surprisingly close to Zwinglianism. Baptismal water "can only be the exterior and visible expression of the inward, real birth from *pneuma.*" Though in itself the water has "only symbolic value," this symbolism is "absolutely necessary," since "without this exterior act we could not recognize God's act" (1962: 41). Signs as "mere signs" have no potency but only express invisible realities; "what matters" is what takes place behind the veil of symbols.

A rarity, but this story has a happy ending. Having examined the Old Testament background of the *anamnesis*, Max Thurian and Joachim Jeremias discovered that it has very little to do with Casel's time-bending speculations or "dynamic re-presentation." Biblical memorials instead present a material or enacted "reminder" to God. For Thurian, the church joins the heavenly intercession of Christ through its sacramental action, imploring the Father "to recall and not to forget, to have respect unto the covenant, to arise and plead" (1960-1961: 2.35, 40-41). For Jeremias, the Eucharist "represents the initiated salvation work before God" so that the Father will remember the Messiah and bring in the fullness of the kingdom (1966: 252-254). Both present a thoroughly anti-

---

[28]Bouyer finds it "somewhat disconcerting" that Casel, with many liturgical scholars, seeks antecedents of the Eucharist "outside of Judaism." Casel "looks for neither origin, nor explanation anywhere except in the pagan mysteries" (1968: 16-17). Schillebeeckx suggests that Casel's theory dehistoricizes and thus docetizes Christ's death and resurrection (quoted in Jones 1994: 188). On historical question of the relation of mystery religions to the New Testament, see Wedderburn (1987).

Marcionite account of *anamnesis* allied with a "pragmatic" semiotic in which rites and signs are, in their materiality and bodiliness, "instruments" in the church's liturgical transactions with God and in the realization of His redemptive purposes.

Circumcision, Nationalized vs. Spiritualized

Our second story, the Continental Protestant debate on infant baptism in the mid-twentieth century, as yet has no ending but bears all the marks of interminability. Ignited by Emil Brunner's brief comment in *The Divine-Human Encounter* that the current practice of infant baptism was "scandalous" (1944: 131), the debate was fueled by Barth's inflammatory 1943 lecture. [29] According to Barth, baptism is not a "cause" of

---

[29]For brief summaries of the subsequent debate, see Kavanagh (1991: 86-97) and Payne (1959: 15-24). Cullmann (1950) is a response to Barth, and the debate took on a historical dimension in the works of Jeremias (1960; 1963) and Aland (1963). One indication of the implicit Marcionism of modern treatments of baptism is the absence or thinness of the discussion of Old Testament backgrounds to baptism in many works of the past half-century. This is already implicit in the effort to write a "New Testament theology" of baptism. Flemington (1948) discusses first-century Jewish baptismal practice, but says virtually nothing about the Old Testament. Lars Hartman discusses Old Testament cleansings in a single page (1992: 10), Kavanagh (1991: 6-7) briefly mentions Old Testament ritual cleansings but makes no theological use of them, passing quickly on to proselyte baptism, and Beasley-Murray (1962) devotes ten pages to Old Testament washings. Markus Barth lists four theses concerning the origin of Christian baptism: Hellenistic mysteries, proselyte baptisms, John the Baptist, and Old Testament prophetic imagery (1951: 12-20). Only the last would recognize influence from the Old Testament, and limiting the Old Testament background to the "prophetic" period ignores the rich narrative and ritual significance of water to which Tertullian already drew sustained attention. Significantly, one of Barth's large aims is to subject traditional conceptions of sacrament to biblical critique; but in practice, this means subjecting sacramental theology to a "New Testament" critique. On the other hand, see the more balanced works of White (1960) and

redemption but an auxiliary rite concerned, as Calvin put it, with the *cognitio salutis*. Christ's word and work alone cause salvation but this word and work seek public recognition and therefore take on a sacramental *Gestalt* (1948: 27-28). Baptism thus enables the believer to "get sight" of his fellowship with Christ by picturing death and resurrection with Him. If this is true, candidates for baptism must *come* to it rather than be *brought*. Thus, Barth castigates infant baptism as a "wound in the body of the Church," a "hole" in baptismal practice, as "arbitrary and despotic" (1948: 40-42), turning what should be a free dialogue into an act of violence by imposing a religious identity on the baptized without his consent (1948: 47). Rhetorically, Barth is less ferocious in the fragment on baptism that closes the *Church Dogmatics*, but his rejection of infant baptism is implicit when he describes baptism as man's initial Yes to God's prevenient grace (1969: 161).

In his lecture, Barth takes note of the traditional Reformed analogy of circumcision and baptism but dismisses it with the comment that circumcision was a sign of natural birth into the lineage of Israel (1948: 43). In *Church Dogmatics IV/4*, Barth concedes that the analogy is "intrinsically correct and important" because it highlights the "unity of the old and new covenants in spite of their formal distinction." Still, this does not imply that the "definitions and meaning of the two were interchangeable," because the church, in contrast to Israel, is "not a nation. It is a people freely and newly called and assembled out of Israel and all nations," recruited not by birth but through the new birth, so that "Christian baptism, as distinct from Israelite circumcision, cannot be on

---

Schmemann (1974).

the basis of the physical descent of the candidate" (1969: 177-178).

There are several problems with this. Circumcision was never a sign of purely natural descent, since Yahweh instructed Abraham to circumcise every male member of his household, including servants and their sons (Gen. 17:12; Exod. 12:44). Even conceding that circumcision had a "national" character, it was equally a religious initiation, since the nation was religiously constituted. It would be wholly foreign to the Old Testament to dissociate covenantal faithfulness from life among God's people: Belonging to Israel meant belonging to the people belonging to Yahweh; "your God will be my God" entailed "your people shall be my people" (Ruth 1:16). Barth's contrast between Israel as "nation" and the church as freely called assembly hints that the Christian religion no longer has the irreducibly public and political character manifest in Hebrew religion. This interpretation is strengthened by Barth's claim that baptism is a public expression of Christ's work of salvation, a formulation that implies that salvation itself is hidden from public view.

Inclusion of infants in Israel was not a "formal" matter, a fact hinted at in Genesis 17:13, where household circumcision is identical to the "covenant." Redemption is the restoration and glorification of humanity, and Israel was elected as the seed and type of a redeemed race, living in Yahweh's presence as humanity was created to live. Therefore, the covenant was necessarily as wide as human life itself, embracing the whole communal practice of Israel, from worship to politics, from cradle to grave. Were infants excluded, Israel would no longer have been the initial form of redeemed humanity but an organization for the religiously mature. Barth's protest implies that, while Israel was the type of redeemed humanity, the church is a religious association, consisting of those who have made free and conscious decisions.[30] Barth's complaint is really against the Old Testament form of religion, and this radically subverts his affirmation of covenantal unity.[31]

Barth's complaint is equally against the Old Testament's view of initiation, for Yahweh not only permitted but demanded the "violence" of an imposed religious identity; to neglect this duty was to break covenant (Gen. 17:14). For the Old Testament, initiation was *not* a matter of "getting sight" of one's status, nor the echoing human Yes; for male infants of Israel, it was the prevenient sign that one was included, willy-nilly, under the Yes of God. For Barth, initiation "works differently" in the church than it did in Israel. Semi-Marcionite sacramentology is hard at work.

Eerily similar evaluations of the actual content of Old Testament religion are apparent, albeit more subtly, in defenses of infant baptism. Oscar Cullmann directly challenges Barth's "weak" treatment of circumcision, which, he insists, was not a sign of "natural racial succession" but a "seal of faith" (Rom. 4:11) that from the outset envisioned the inclusion of the nations. Even in the Old Covenant, Abraham was father of believers in a salvation-historical rather than a racial sense. Rightly understood, then, circumcision was not an outward,

---

[30]Barth's position, by implying that the church is a religious organization rather than a new creation, colludes with the secular privatization of the church.

[31]What is implicit in Barth's treatment comes to extreme expression in the work of Paul K. Jewett, whose entire argument against infant baptism turns on a highly questionable account of the difference Old and New Covenants (1978: 90-91, 234).

national sign but concerned the heart (1950: 57-59). In short, Cullmann defends what might be called the "genuinely religious" character of circumcision by insisting that it had inner, spiritual significance. Pierre Marcel likewise recognizes that the relation of Old and New is crucial (1953: 81), and he adopts the Calvinist view that the two covenants are the same in substance though different in form. To defend the circumcision-baptism connection against Barth and Leenhardt, however, Marcel's strategy is to insist that circumcision was a sign of the "spiritual" blessings of justification, adoption, glorification, and God's dwelling among His people, the "material" blessings being only secondary consequences (1953: 72-73, 87). Recent work stressing the ecclesiological concerns of New Testament theology has made it difficult to conceive of justification, adoption, etc., as purely "spiritual" blessings since they are linked with membership in the historical community of the church. More seriously, Marcel is sloppy with the Old Testament, since the promises that circumcision sealed were the earthly, material promises of land and an abundant, royal seed (Gen. 17:1-14). Marcel is thus an open target to Baptist writers who can simply quote the actual promises to Abraham to insist that those of the New Covenant are much "higher."

What Cullmann and Marcel do *not* say is that citizenship in Israel *as such* was religiously significant (though it never guaranteed Yahweh's favor). Rather than "spiritualizing," paedobaptists should insist that the promises of the New Covenant are precisely the Abrahamic promises: In the Seed of Abraham, the seed of Abraham inherits the earth (Rom. 4:13) as a multitude of kings and priests, spread out like the sand of the seashore (Rev. 1:5-6; 4:9-10; 7:9). In spite of their disagreement with

Barth, Cullmann and Marcel seem to share his ambivalence toward the religious outlook of the Old Covenant. Baptist and paedobaptist, like Eucharistic realist and Eucharistic mystic, compete on the same semi-Marcionite ground. It is hardly surprising that their debates seem impossible of resolution.

Sacramental Theology and the Social Sciences

The third story concerns the introduction of models and categories from the cross-disciplinary subject of ritual studies,[32] which, along with concepts from contemporary philosophy and semiotics, provides a welcome corrective to certain tendencies in traditional liturgics and sacramental theology. Anthropology situates rites and practices within a community's concrete social relations and power structures, which is to say, that sacramental theology is embedded in ecclesiology (Cooke 1990: 286). Moreover, anthropology often attends to the surface of a rite's

---

[32]Among the key texts are Douglas (1973; 1984); Durkheim (1976); Grimes (1995); Leach (1976); Levi-Strauss (1981: 667-684); Smith (1927); Turner (1966; 1967); van Gennep (1960). Important shorter studies include Goody (1961: 142-164; 1977: 25-35); Leach (1968: 520-526); Tambiah (1979: 113-169); and see Morris (1987: 182-263). Recent critical studies of the field are Bell (1992); Humphrey and Laidlaw (1994); Asad (1993: 55-79). From the perspective of comparative religions, see Smith (1987) and the various works of Eliade (1955; 1959; 1966). For reviews of the literature applying anthropological models to sacramental theology, see Power, et. al. (1994: 657-705) and Bourgeois (1994: 103-31; 1996: 111-140). Works in sacramental theology and liturgics that borrow from anthropology and other social sciences include Kiesling (1970: 422-432); Osborne (1974: 544-549); Turner (1976: 504-526); Worgul (1980); Power (1984); Lawler (1987); Thompson (1987: 55-102); Cooke (1990: 271-291); Hoffman (1991: 22-41); Searle (1992: 51-58); Chauvet (1995); Anderson (1995: 482-504); and the articles in *Studia Liturgica* 23:1 (1993) and *Concilium* 259 (1995).

actions, materials, sounds, and movements, and thus restores some of the patristic and medieval sensitivity to the multivalent symbolisms of washing, breaking, eating, of water, bread, wine. Sacramental theologies influenced by ritual studies have thus been able to develop Rahner's (1963) and Schillebeeckx's (1968) insistence that sacramental efficacy is an efficacy of *signs* and *symbols* rather than a quasi-physical or a moral causation.

Ritual theory, however, is not an entirely benign tool for sacramental theology. Methodologically, some theologians treat the social sciences as theologically innocent foundations upon which to build theological conclusions. Kenan Osborne claims that once a phenomenological approach to the sacraments produces an "initial understanding," *then* "biblical, historical, and liturgical approaches to the sacrament fall into place" (1974: 536-549). Similarly, Worgul borrows the "correlation" method of David Tracy to find the "real foundation for sacraments within concrete human existence" (1980: 31-33). Cooke (1990), rather old-fashionedly, repeatedly implies that theology must adjust to the certain deliverances of science. "Larger" concerns of anthropology thus position theology. If Milbank (1990) is right that the social sciences are an alternative, even heretical, theology, then these assumptions are far too credulous.

Substantively, ritual studies privilege certain biases of modernity. As Talal Asad (1993: 55-79) and Catherine Bell (1992: 69-74) have observed, there is no obvious line of demarcation between "symbolic" and "functional" acts (cf. Turner 1976: 504), a distinction that tarnishes the brilliance of Louis-Marie Chauvet's massive *Symbol and Sacrament*. For

Chauvet, liturgy takes place on the far side of a "symbolic rupture" from the everyday, and is thus "beyond the useful-useless distinction" because it "creates an empty space with regard to the immediate and utilitarian." Whatever worshipers may gain from the liturgy, "rituality functions at *another level*, the level of symbol," which permits "a space for breathing, for freedom," for "the intense experience of the *letting go* of our theoretical knowledge, our ethical 'good works,' our personal 'experiences' of God" so that we can be opened to grace (1995: 337-338). Ritual opens out a (noumenal?) "symbolic order" that is "completely different from that of immediately experienced reality."[33]

Many traditional societies do not, however, share this dichotomy. Asad points out that medieval monks understood the daily office as an intrinsic element in a program of *paedeia*, not as "expressive" or "symbolic" actions occupying a realm "beyond useful and useless." For all its flaws, Hugh of St. Victor's notion that sacraments effect *humilitatio* and *exercitatio* shows that he was not operating with a functional/symbolic dualism. By imposing changing bodily postures and movements, Hugh argues, liturgy corrects the "bad changes" that result from sin and inscribes a Christian choreography, training the worshiper to dance life virtuously (1.9.3; Hugh 1951: 156-158; Asad 1993: 77-79). On the far side of Chauvet's rupture, one trembles to ask what "everyday" life looks like, once scoured of symbol. And the closest answer seems to be, very much

---

[33]1995: 113, quoting from E. Ortigues, *Le discours et le symbole*. That this dualism is fundamental to Chauvet's work is indicated by his rigorous distinction between the logics and levels of marketplace and symbolic exchange (1995: 106-107, 111). Surely, as in the phenomenon of buying "status symbols," the two interpenetrate so complexly that talk of "levels" is misleading.

like the modern secular West.

Ritual theory privileges modern biases also in theorizing about the functions, patterns, or features of "ritual in general." Undeniable "family resemblances" exist among rites from widely varying times and places, but, working with the Kantian form/content dualism that infects sociology and anthropology generally (Milbank 1990: 64, 67, 104), ritual theory often abstracts a static form from different ritual contents.[34] This reduces the Christian interpretation of a rite to a religious gloss on more basic natural institutions or sequences of action; anthropology isolates the container, while Christianity pours in the medicine -- and the Victorine allusion is deliberate. David N. Power, for example, suggests that ritual imitates bodily acts. "Remote action" (moving away from, looking at) is the basis for rites of alienation; copulation is the natural foundation for rites of bonding; and digestion is the basis for rituals of fusion that blur individual identities (1984: 88-89).[35] Yet, these bodily actions are not

---

[34]For Durkheim (1976), whatever the specific actions done or words spoken or symbols manipulated, and whatever the participants *believe* they are doing, what is *really* taking place is the reanimation of social bondedness. Likewise, van Gennep's rite of passage pattern can become a Procrustean bed into which many different sequences of action are forced; van Gennep is explicit about his interest in the "essential significance" of rites rather than particular actions (1960: 191). Douglas warns against dismissing "ritualism," apparently without regard to the particular rituals being dismissed (1973: esp. ch. 2). Grimes notes, "Although Turner's theory is certainly not archetypalist in either a Jungian or Eliadean sense, it aims at a high level of cross-cultural, transtemporal generalization" (1995: 155). There is, to be sure, a countervailing emphasis among anthropologists on the particularities of the words, gestures, objects, colors, and so on that make up the ritual.

[35]This dual structure is of a piece with Power's claim, following Suzanne Langer, that communication and experience are lodged in bodily action prior to language, which intervenes at some second stage to "transform" experience and objectify it (1984: 68, 84). Chauvet seems to be operating with similar assumptions when he

"raw" experiences but are always already encoded and suffused with particular intentions. "Moving away" out of embarrassment or revulsion is a different act from "moving away" out of respect or deference; sex is always already infused with symbols and gestures; and every meal has to be arranged in *some* manner, so that there is no "eating *as such*" but only "eating *in this or that way.*" Similar objections can be brought against Michael Lawler, who defines sacraments as "prophetic symbols" that raise literal realities to the "representative-symbolic" level at which Christian meanings come into play. Marriage, according to Lawler, has a "natural level" meaning of "union of this man and this woman" but as a representative symbol becomes suitable to "proclaim, realize, and celebrate in representation" Christ's union with the church (Lawler 1987: 52-53) -- as if *marriage* could exist in the slightest degree outside a representative-symbolic matrix![36]

Abstract formalism is only part of the problem here. Against Power

---

says that liturgy brackets theory and discourse in favor of sheer symbol, and hints at the possibility that ritual, even though embedded in a tradition, can be performed "before any words" (1995: 338-339, 342). Rites, however, are always performed by people who have already spoken about the rites being performed, and they almost always include speech acts. Not to mention that speech is itself a bodily act. Cf. Bloch (1989: 19-45); but against Bloch's claim that formalization of speech is necessarily restrictive, see Ladrière (1984: 1.70) and Humphrey and Laidlaw (1994: 83-84).

[36]For Chauvet, rites always function in a space of "liminality," symbolically set apart from the "everyday," and thus at the level of "signifying and the pattern it forms" rather than at the "level of the signified and ideational 'contents'" (1995: 326). Even if these "levels" can be distinguished, any intelligible response to a "signifying pattern" requires some recognition of "contents"; otherwise, the pattern is no pattern but kaleidoscopic chaos. "It was lovely and moving, but I have no idea what it was about" is not, surely, the hoped-for response to the church's worship.

and Lawler, I have insisted that no pre-linguistic or pre-semiotic human life exists. If this is the case, then some language and semiosis is already encoded in the activities and institutions relevant to Christian sacraments. By introducing Christianity at a secondary level, theology collaborates with secularism in refusing to allow the Christian coding of reality to enter constitutively into the definition of bodily actions or social institutions. Sacramental theology is thus recruited into the force that "polices the sublime" and keeps religion in its proper, privatized place (Milbank 1990: ch. 5). If the gospel merely pours content into preexisting forms, it cannot trans-form, cannot burst the wineskins.[37]

Worgul goes to an unusual extreme, combining Levi-Strauss and Turner to describe the efficacy of the Eucharist. Having portrayed human life as a set of binary oppositions, he claims that ritual enables passage from the "bad pole" to the "good pole," from death to life, and that each transition passes through a moment of Buberian, egalitarian *communitas*. Strong experiences of *communitas* keep a culture stable, while weak *communitas* can lead to disintegration.[38] Worgul claims that the Eucharist is an example of this process, but though the Eucharist no doubt effects a passage from death to life, the path does not run through *communitas* (1980: 185-193; cf. Hoffman 1987: 168-169). Undifferentiated *communitas* has nothing to do with the church, which is precisely a differentiated

---

[37]Historically, the church did not merely raise marriage to a prophetic symbol, but transformed the inner dynamics of family life, destroying the Roman *paterfamilias*, the primacy of clan and blood vengeance, and the cult of the ancestors. Recoding thus took place in the basic meaning of "family."

[38]In a sense, this is the sheerest tautology: A community whose members have strong ties to one another will be more stable than one where ties are weak.

community, one *body* of many members. Be that as it may, Worgul's anthropological revision of Eucharistic theology does not provide any "deeper" insight into how the Eucharist works (Worgul 1980: 224) than theological explanations. To say that baptism is a "rite of passage" is *not* to arrive at some more basic level of description but merely to re-describe what the New Testament calls "death and resurrection with Christ," "the washing of regeneration," "crossing of the Red Sea."[39] Redescription can have the valuable heuristic function of highlighting unnoticed features of a rite, but the *theological* description must remain fundamental. In the context of the preceding discussion, anthropological redescription forces typology to the margins, so that Christian rites are interpreted without reference to Old Testament patterns; the scholastic detachment of *quaestiones* from *lectio* re-emerges, radicalized.[40] The prolegomena to Christian sacramental theology is no longer a "treatise on the sacraments of the Old Law" but a "treatise on the rites of the Ndembu."

Symphony in Two Movements

To evade the semi-Marcionism of the tradition, I take as my guide

---

[39]It is a separate question whether the category of *rites de passage* is a useful or coherent one. Milbank (1990: 122-123) sees Turner's emphasis on liminality as a secular effort to marginalize religion by confining it to sublime moments of transition. He also suggests that cultural boundaries are constituted by symbol and ritual, and therefore ritual functions more to form boundaries than to provide safe passage across boundaries that are simply "there."

[40]By vindicating the rationality of "primitive" prohibition and taboo, anthropology can also reinforce a flattened hermeneutic in which the holiness restrictions of Israel are retained in some form by the church (cf. Power 1984: 90-91).

the fountainhead of Western sacramental theology, Augustine of Hippo. In important respects, Augustine is more plight than solution, combining a suspicion of signs with misgivings about the Old Testament. Regarding "signs," the early treatise *De Magistro* serves to illustrate.[41] After persuading Adeodatus, his son and dialogue partner, that we learn nothing apart from verbal or gestural signs (10.29-30; 1968: 42-44), he abruptly veers in the opposite direction by claiming that knowledge is more valuable than signs, which implies that true knowledge is immediate and transparent perception of *res in se* rather than a knowledge encoded in signs (10.31; 1968: 45). He then poses this dilemma: "when I am shown a sign, it cannot teach me anything if it finds me ignorant of the reality for which the sign stands; but if it finds me acquainted with the reality, what do I learn from the sign?" (10.33; 11.36; 1968: 46).[42] Knowledge of reality does not come through signs after all, but the reverse. One knows a sign is a sign only when one knows the reality, so that knowledge of both signs and realities comes by opening a gap between *signa* and the world of *res* (10.33; 1968: 47), a gap that Augustine eventually fills with the *deus ex machina* of the "Interior Teacher," Christ.[43] Adeodatus concludes

[41]On Augustine's semiotic theory, see Markus (1972: 61-85; 1996); Prenter (1948: 5-26); Todorov (1982: 36-59); Rist (1996: 23-40); Milbank (1997: 88-91). Louth (1989: 151-158) highlights the Neoplatonic elements of Augustine's account but argues that he believed in the possibility of redeemed communication through love. Williams (1989: 138-150) suggests that Augustine has arrived at a more thoroughly Christian semiotic.

[42]*Cum enim mihi signum datur, si nescientem me invenit cujus rei signum sit, docere me nihil potest: si vero scientem, quid disco per signum?* (PL 32, 1214).

[43]Distinguishing *signum* and *res*, however fluidly, is necessary to any sane grasp of the world. By "gap," I mean to indicate a view that suggests one must move "beyond" the sign to grasp the naked reality, the *Ding an sich*. Among other

that human teaching does not transmit knowledge but uses *verba externa* to remind us that Christ dwells within (14.46; 1968: 60; cf. Rist 1996: 32-33).[44] The semiotic of *De Magistro* is, in Derridean terms, a radical form of logocentrism, where even the voice is secondary to the true inner word.[45] Regarding the Old Testament, Augustine admits in the *Confessions* (6.4.6; 1953: 136) that it was only Ambrose's allegorizing preaching that freed Scripture from absurdity.

These twin themes come together in *De doctrina christiana* 3.5-9 (1958:

---

things, this raises the specter of skepticism. In fact we move from one sign-encoded reality to another, and even our approach to God is through words and gestures of love and fear.

[44]That this model of signs and knowledge is not merely immature Neoplatonism is indicated, firstly, by the fact that in *Retractions*, Augustine does not revise his teaching but says that the whole purpose of *De Magistro* was to defend philosophically Jesus' statement that He alone is Teacher (*Retractiones*, 12; PL 32, 602). Secondly, Augustine's discussion in *De Trinitate* 15.10-11 of the "interior word" prior to all language is a variation of the same type of theory (1970: 473-480). In the same connection, Augustine comments in *De Genesi: contra Manichaeos* that the fall made necessary the *nubes* of external, transient words (2.4.5; PL 34, 198), and in *De catechizandis rudibus* he negatively contrasts teaching through audible words with immediate intellectual grasp (2.3; PL 46, 122-123).

[45]Both the mentalist context of semiosis and the gap between visible sign and understood thing are incorporated into Augustine's sacramental theology. Preaching before the celebration of the Eucharist, he distinguishes between what is seen in the sacrament and what is understood (*aliud videtur, aliud intelligitur*), the former having to do with corporeal things and the latter with spiritual fruit (*Sermo* 272; PL 38, 1247). In *De catechizandis rudibus* 26.50, he distinguishes between the visible *signacula rerum divinarum* and the *res ipsas invisibiles*, and compares this to the difference between the sound of Scripture (*carnaliter*) and the *spirituale* significance (PL 40, 344-345). And in his second letter to Januarius (#55), he defines sacraments as commemorative ceremonies that indicate something to be received and says that the purpose of figures is to draw away from this world to "higher and inner things" (Augustine 1951-1956: 1.260-261; PL 33, 205, 210-211).

83-87). Augustine is discussing the hermeneutical imperative to distinguish between figurative and literal language and warning against taking the figurative as literal. This was the error of the Jews, who fell into the "habit of taking signs for things," a "miserable servitude" in which they were not "able to raise the eye of the mind above things that are corporal and created to drink in eternal light" (3.5.9; 1958: 84).[46] Israel was in a superior state to the pagan world, since God appointed useful signs for her worship, while even if a pagan were to ascend from *signum* to *res*, he would not be profited since the *res* itself is an idol. Christ liberated the Jews from useful signs, "elevating them to the things which the signs represented" but destroyed pagan signs, not to lead them to "servitude under useful signs, but rather to an exercise of the mind directed toward understanding them spiritually" (3.8.12; 1958: 86).[47] Thus, just as a proper use of signs involves a *transitus* and elevation from sign to thing, so there is a *transitus* from useful signs to real thing in redemptive history. This is a classic statement of Marcionite sacramental theology.

Even in this passage, there are some countervailing tendencies. "Bondage under signs" in Augustine does not always mean that religious signs are confining *per se*; bondage results from the idolatrous *mis*use of signs.[48] Accordingly, Augustine does not hold that Christianity escapes

---

[46]*Ea demum est miserabilis animae servitus, signa pro rebus accipere; et supra creaturam corpoream, oculum mentis ad hauriendum aeternum lumen levare non posse* (PL 34, 69).

[47]*Quamobrem christiana libertas eos quos invenit sub signis utilibus. . . elevatos ad eas res quarum illa signa sunt, liberavit.* Describing the converted pagan's use of signs, he adds, *nec sub ipsis jam signis utilibus serviturae, sed exercitaturae potius animum in eorum intelligentia spirituali* (PL 34, 70).

[48]This is true, for example, in 3.9.13 (1958: 87), but other passages give pause.

signs altogether (3.9.13; 1958: 87). More generally, Augustine brilliantly and originally develops his reflections in the context of communication (2.2.3; 1958: 35) and thereby introduces the subject alongside *signum* and *res* as a fundamental component of semiotic reflection (O'Donovan 1982: 384).

Augustine eludes his vestigial Marcionism and moves toward a more satisfying theory of signs and of redemptive history in Epistle 138 to Marcellinus (1951-56: 3.36-53; PL 33, 525-535).[49] Marcellinus had been challenged to provide an explanation for the change of sacraments from Old to New, since this change seemed to imply either that God changed or that the Old rites were evil, since a thing done right ought not to be changed. After pointing out that change is the story of creation and human growth, Augustine distinguishes between the "fitting" (*aptum*) and the "beautiful" (*pulchrum*). The second is constant, but the aptness of a thing depends on connections with other things, so that as the total web of circumstances is altered, what is *aptum* changes with it. Old Testament

---

Concerning 3.8.12 (1958: 86), why does Augustine deny that pagan converts come under the "servitude of useful signs"? This apparently means they are not subjected to the condition of ancient Israelites, who were in bondage, though their signs were useful. If this is true, there is servitude in being under signs, not merely in being under them wrongly. Similarly, 3.6.10 (1958: 84-85) describes the Jewish subjection to temporal signs as a bondage, though their use of these signs was pleasing to God and therefore cannot have been idolatrous.

[49]Hints of Augustine's firmly anti-Marcionite sacramental theology are found throughout Western theology. See the theologians surveyed in de Lubac (1949) and Thomas Aquinas (*ST* 3a, 61, 1). It has been recovered and developed more consistently in this century, partly under the inspiration of de Lubac; see McPartlan (1993; 1995). See also the superb articles by Rowan Williams (1987: 32-44; 1996: 89-102).

sacraments were fitting for their time, but are no longer so. In no way does this imply change in God or His plan, however, since the Old Testament prophesied the transformation of sacraments (1951-1956: 3.38; PL 33, 527).

Though Augustine refuses to elaborate the reasons for the change in rites, he offers a brief but immensely provocative metaphor as explanation. Just as verbal signs -- the letters of a written verb and the sounds of a spoken verb -- vary according to the time the verb indicates, so the rites of the church develop to show a shift in "tense," from anticipation to fulfillment.[50] Though initially distinguished, *aptum* and *pulchrum* are harmonized by means of a musical analogy: Precisely by means of variations in what is fitting, the sovereign God orchestrates "the beauty of the entire world" (*universi saeculi pulchritudo*) that "swells ... into a mighty song of some unutterable musician" (*magnum carmen cujusdem ineffabilis modulatoris*; 1951-1956: 3.39; PL 33, 527).

By this combination of metaphors, Augustine underscores his repeated insistence that sacramental "substance," or, continuing the analogy, the "verbal root," remains the same in both Testaments. Christ is the *Verbum* spoken, offered, and received in the word and sacraments of both Old and New.[51] Moreover, just as a conjugation is not a transition

---

[50] *Verumtamen breviter dici potest, quod homini acuto fortasse suffecerit, aliis sacramentis praenuntiari Christum cum venturus esset, aliis cum venisset annuntiari oportuisse; sicut modo nos idipsum loquentes, diversitas rerum compulit etiam verba mutare. Siquidem aliud est praenuntiari, aliud annuntiari; aliud cum venturus esset, aliud cum venisset* (1951-1956: 3.41; PL 33, 528). He uses the same analogy in *Contra Faustum* 19.16 (1974a: 244-245; PL 42, 356-357).

[51] Hence, in *Contra Faustum* 19.16, he gives the following as examples of changing verb tenses, *nasciturus et natus, passurus et passus, resurrecturus et resurrexit*. The story

from language to not-language but a transformation from one linguistic form to another, so also the transition from Old to New remains within the economy of linguistic and cultural signs. The New is a radically fresh and surprising variation on the themes of the preceding movement but it is not a wholly new musical departure.[52] New Covenant rites and signs are thus not grudging concessions to the weakness of the flesh but are necessary to develop redemptive themes in the symphony of universal history. Practically, this means that words do not give place to silence, nor external rites to interior piety, nor does the New Testament open a gap between signs and realities that was not apparent in the Old. In both Old and New, Augustine implies, worship involves the performance of sacramental signs and confession in a particular form of words. The difference in wholly in the times.

Finally, in a proto-structuralist move, Augustine suggests that the New is meaningful only by virtue of its *difference* from the Old: *Resurrexit* can be understood only against the background of the prior *resurrecturus*. On Augustine's analogy, if this is true for word, it is equally true for sacraments, and this implies that the sacramental forms themselves should embody this conjugation. Augustine's insistence on the necessary relation

---

announced by the sacraments remains the same, though it develops from future to past (1974a: 245; PL 42, 357).

[52]In comparison with the polyphony of the Old, the New is a "minimalism." The sacraments of the New order are fewer and easier to perform, though most "sublime in implication," most "upright in observance" (*pauca pro multis, eademque factu facillima, et intellectu augustissima, et observatione castissima; De doctrina christiana* 3.9.13; 1958: 87; PL 34, 71; cf. *Contra Faustum* 19.13; 1974a: 244; PL 42, 355; *Epistle* 54; 1951-1956: 1.252; PL 33, 200). The Baroque of Leviticus does *not*, however, yield to the silent symphony of Philip Glass.

of Old and New has implications for the act of worship. In the music that is the liturgy, the sacraments and forms of the church pulse to rhythms set by Israel. Prayer and praise conjugate the offering of sacrifice and incense, baptism recapitulates circumcision and the crossing of the sea, the Eucharist is a fresh performance of Passover and Booths, thank offering and purification. As for theological reflection on liturgy, Augustine intimates that the "treatise on the sacraments of the Old Law" is a *necessary* prologue to Christian liturgics. Both liturgically and theologically, the melody of the New lacks the aesthetic power to raise men to *contemplationem speciei Dei* if unaccompanied by the (more darkly colored) harmonies of the Old.

The same motifs appear in *Contra Faustum*, with some important developments. According to Faustus, a Manichean, Catholics are hypocrites because they attack Manicheans for dispensing with the Old order but themselves refuse to keep Jewish rites and customs; thus, Catholics as much as Manichaeans dispense with the Old (18.1; 19.4; 22.2; 1974a: 237, 240, 272-273). Appealing to Jesus' statement that He came to fulfill not to destroy the Law (Matt. 5:17), Augustine's alternative paradigm is not so much a "spiritualization" as a "humanization" of the Old Covenant order. Preeminently, Christ, the God-Man, fulfills the rites and institutions of Israel, but for Augustine Christ and His body are inseparable. Regarding the Eucharist, Augustine claims that the Christ who is the *res* of the sacraments is the *totus Christus* comprising Head and body. In the terms developed by scholastic theology, the *res tantum* of the Eucharist is the unity of the church in and with Christ; the *res sacramenti* embraces the incorporated church (cf. Lash 1968: 66-67). Or, as

39

Augustine dramatically put it to his congregation, *vos estis quod acceptistis* (*Sermo* 227; PL 38, 1099).[53] Thus, the various figures of the Old Testament are fulfilled in the church. Christians do not continue to practice Levitical baptisms since Christ came to "bury us with Himself by baptism into death," Christ fulfills the dietary laws by refusing to incorporate any who are like unclean beasts into His body, and no architectural tabernacle remains because believers are the dwelling of God (19.10; 1974a: 243).[54] The Christian conjugation of "cleansing rites," "food laws," and "tabernacle" is "Christ," but, because Christ is *totus Christus*, the present tense is equally, "church."

And the church, like Israel, is necessarily a community constituted by rites and signs. Augustine explains that every religious society requires signs and visible sacraments, since without these no people can be "coagulated" into a unified association (*Contra Faustum* 19.11; 1974a: 243).[55] This perspective disrupts any attempt, including Augustine's, to

---

[53]The *totus Christus* doctrine is arguably the center of Augustine's entire theology. Karl Adam suggested that the "real, essential union of our humanity with the new man, Christ, is the sum and climax of Augustine's teaching regarding redemption." The "fundamental conception of Christianity [is] a vital union of all the redeemed with the new man who is Christ" (Adam 1932: 44-48). See the similar statement of Vetter, quoted by Mersch (1936: 45, fn 1): "Le mystère du corps du Christ est le mystère central dans la théologie augustinienne." Mersch (1936: 2.84-138) marshals abundant evidence of the pervasiveness of this theme in Augustine's writings and sermons. What little Augustine says about deification is connected with the basic idea of incorporation into Christ (Bonner 1986: 369-386). See also Evans (1972: 65-128); Réveillaud (1968: 67-94); Adams (1971: 17-69); Congar (1970: 11-24); Kelly (1968: 412-417).

[54]*Venit enim consepelire nos sibi per Baptismum in mortem* (PL 42, 354). *Non admittens ad corpus suum . . . quidquid per illa animalia in moribus hominum significatum est* (PL 42, 354).

[55]*In nullum autem nomen religionis, seu verum, seu falsum, coagulari homines possunt, nisi*

classify *sacramenta* as a species of *signa* in Augustine's technical sense. A *signum*, Augustine had said, is something that "over and above the impression it makes on the senses, causes something else to come into the mind as a consequence of itself" (*De doctrina christiana* 2.1.1; 1958: 34).[56] In *Contra Faustum* 19.11, however, signs have a "pragmatic" and "performative" role, not a cognitive one. Signs are not merely for raising the mind to things signified; signs *do*, and what they do is form a body from many members. Moreover, if the *res* of the Eucharist is the *totus Christus*, and if the goal of the sacrament is to unify the church in Christ, then contemplating the meal (assuming that contemplation is what one is supposed to do with food) does *not* bring some *other* underlying thing to mind: What is sensibly apparent in the Eucharist *is* what is brought to mind, and this, in turn, is what is accomplished -- the unity of the body.[57]

Augustine implies, further, that signs and rites are necessary for the achievement of redemption. If humans exist in a linguistic and semiotic medium, the sin will manifest itself *there*; as Augustine says, even false religious communities employ signs. Redemption, the restoration of man

---

aliquo signaculorum vel sacramentorum visibilium consortio colligentur: quorum sacramentorum vis inenarrabiliter valet plurimum, et ideo contempta sacrilegos facit. Impie quippe contemnitur, sine qua non potest perfici pietas (PL 42, 355).

[56]*Signum enim res, praeter speciem quam ingerit sensibus, aliud aliquid ex se faciens in cogitationem venire* (PL 34, 35).

[57]There are, to be sure, invisible and mystical dimensions to the sacramental exchange, but this does not mean that the sacramental rite is a hoop through which the church passes into a non-ritual encounter. It means that the visible action of the rite is a part of a larger whole, as the visible exchange of gifts between lovers is part of a relationship that is not completely on the surface, and yet the visible exchange *is* the relationship and not an external pointer to it.

41

to God, involves the creation of true religious community, which is coagulated through divinely instituted signs and sacraments. Sacraments are not "outside" redemption pointing "inward" but make up the reality of the *totus Christus* in its earthly manifestation, which is salvation promised and now, though pre-eschatologically, fulfilled.[58]

Conclusion

Thus, the pattern of Augustine's typology is: The Old Covenant order was a real participation in the redemption to come, yet also pointed to its fulfillment in Christ; since Christ is not only Head but body, the types of Israel's order prefigured both Jesus and the church; since no organized religious group can be united into a body without signs and rites, the rites of the Old anticipated the sacraments of the New; and conjugation of word and sacrament was necessary to attain beauty in the music of history. The following chapters are not an extension of Augustine's counter-Marcionite semiotic theory but a study in biblical theology guided by these Augustinian principles. Specifically, I shall examine baptism as a "conjugation" of Old Testament priestly ordination. If the argument of this chapter has been correct, the assertion that baptism fulfills the ordination rite, if exegetically and theologically sound,

---

[58]Hugh's "container" analogy depends on his assumption that the human disease is located, primarily if not exclusively, within. On this view, the specific external form of the church's sacraments is indifferent, since what matters is the invisible medicine poured out from the ritual container; who cares if the bottle is green or blue, conical or cylindrical? If, however, sin is embedded not only in the heart but in cultural practices, in, for example, a prideful refusal to share a common table, then the form of the sacrament is simply indistinguishable from the matter.

is not typological ornamentation but a necessary dimension of the theology of baptism.

Imaginative reading of Scripture -- something I hope to have come close to achieving -- is an art that cannot be reduced to a list of rules, yet I must make, besides these Augustinian principles, some sketchy remarks about my approach to the Bible. I affirm the orthodox view that, though human writers produced the canonical texts, ultimately, as Thomas put it, *auctor sacrae Scripturae est Deus*. This means, first, that the Bible is a single book whose many episodes and fields of imagery form an interlocking whole. It means, second, that Scripture bears the authority and truth of its Author, so that the theologian is to be mastered by not master of the text. As Thomas recognized, however, Scripture's "double authorship" introduces a hermeneutical dilemma: Since the Author's intention determines the literal meaning, and since God comprehends all things at once (*simul*), then there is no question but that *secundum litteralem sensum in una littera Scripturae plures sint sensus* (*ST* 1a, 1, 10). If this is true, how, on the one hand, can we make sure that we hear all that God intended to communicate? And how, on the other hand, can we avoid, as R.A. Markus has put it (1996: 12), "putting words in God's mouth"? I would avoid impalement on the first horn of this dilemma by admitting that the church will never hear all that Scripture says, since Scripture is as inexhaustible as its Author. Dodging the other horn requires more skillful footwork. Several exegetical controls will be operative here.

I am situated in an interpretive tradition that serves as a check on individual ingenuity, and I take confidence from the fact that the typology of priestly ordination and baptism is a truism of this tradition.[59] Though patristic and medieval exegesis yields a result I wish to defend, I am not always satisfied with the means by which the result was reached, so some further controls are necessary. Grammatical and historical considerations serve as a foundation and continual guide. Attention to the literal sense does not, however, preclude discovering a network of correspondences within the original setting; a literal sense is thoroughly infused with analogies and symbolic correlations. These correlations are of essentially two related kinds. First, with a nod to cultural anthropology, I seek to understand Scriptural statements, institutions, rites, and events within a set

---

[59]The best single collection of relevant texts is found in Dabin (1950). See also the frequent reference to this typology in Johnson (1995: 4, 66f, 182, 187, 197-98, 200, 312-314, 318), and the texts in Finn (1992a; 1992b). Among patristic writers, Tertullian, Cyril of Jerusalem, Ambrose, Prudentius, Jerome, Augustine, Leo, Salvian the Presbyter, Fastidius, Cassiodorus, Origen, Basil the Great, Gregory Nazianzus, Didymus of Alexandria, John Chrysostom, Hesychius, Theodoret, Pseudo-Dionysius, and Procopius of Gaza all make the connection in one way or another. Among Western theologians of the medieval period, we find the same set of themes in John the Deacon, Isidore of Seville, Bede, Alcuin, Leidradus of Lyons, Theodulf of Orleans, Maxentius, Amalarius, Rabanus Maurus, Hincmar of Reims, Atto of Vercelli, Peter Damien, Lanfranc of Bec, Ivo of Chartres, Rupert of Deutz, Peter Abelard, Master Simon, Honorius of Autun, Peter Lombard, Peter of Celle, Martin of Leon, Peter of Poitiers, Sicardus of Cremona, Innocent III, Helinand of Froidmont, Alexander of Hales, William of Auvergne, and Thomas Aquinas. Eastern theologians of this period likewise perpetuated the patristic view, including Anastasius of Sinai, Theodore the Studite, Photius, Arethas of Caesarea, Oecumenius, Serronius, Theophylactus the Bulgar, Germanus, archbishop of Constantinople, and Symeon of Thessalonica. Various liturgies and church orders offered similar perspectives on initiation, especially the anointing: *Didascalia Apostolorum*, 3.12 (Connolly 1929: 146); *Apostolic Constitutions*, 3.15 (quoted in Whitaker 1960: 27); *Sacramentum Gelasianum*, 1.40 (PL 74, 1099D); *De liturgica Gallicana*, 3.37 (PL 72, 277C); *Sacramentum Gelasianum, missa chrismalis*, 1.40 (PL 74, 1099D, 1100B); Gregory, *Liber sacramentorum* (PL 78, 83B, 85A); *Monumenta liturgica, benedictio olei* (PL 138, 1065B). Among modern writers, see especially Schmemann (1974: 94-99) and Kavanagh (1991; 1995: 268-272).

of cultural and social contexts. Moses' anointing of Aaron, for example, is a link in the chain of ritual actions of ordination; the ordination is a feature of the institution of priesthood; the anointing of Aaron is connected to other uses of oil in ancient Israel; the priestly office is part of the holiness system that ordered Israel's life; and so on. Second, there are textual correlations. Surrounding structures, allusions to earlier passages, repeated scenarios or sequences of action, tropes and technical terms serve to bring out theological significance. References to the priestly duty of maintaining the lamps of the Holy Place, for example, bracket the chapters in Exodus concerning the priestly garments and ordination, and this suggests an analogy between oil-burning lamps and anointed priests (cf. Exod. 27:20-21; 30:7-8).

Textually justified comparisons such as this bring together two networks of association, which can be compared and cross-compared at length (cf. Soskice 1985: 49-51). From the correlation of priest and lampstand, any number of connections may proliferate: Anointing has to do with illumination, priests are light-bearers, priests stand like the lampstand in the Holy Place, and so on. Since each term of the comparison is related to other metaphorical networks, one could extrapolate almost indefinitely. Not all possible elaborations are legitimate; some lack textual support, others run up against the claims of other portions of Scripture, others are plain weird. Yet, through attention to these social and textual contexts, I arrive at a thick exegesis of Old Testament texts on priesthood and ordination, a *sensus litteralis plenior*. The New Testament is a massive program of innerbiblical interpretation (cf. Fishbane 1985), as New Testament writers view Christ through the prism of earlier events in Israel's history. Against the background of the Old Testament *sensus plenior*, I argue that the New Testament describes baptism in terms of the ordination rite. Having established a typological connection between baptism and ordination, I develop some features of a theology of baptism by elaborating comparisons between these two fields of association. I explain these procedures in more detail as the argument progresses.

My study will of course also reveal differences between Old and New, and considering them will disclose the grammatical rules at work in the redemptive-historical "conjugation" of the rites. Thus, through typological interpretation the Bible becomes "a cross-referencing, interglossing semiotic system which can be used . . . to assimilate by redescription all the worlds and world views which human beings construct in the course of history," providing a reading of "history in biblical terms" (Loughlin 1996: 29 fn. 1). If this is not to be mere sloganizing, it demands substantial grappling with the text, as our discussion of Augustine makes clear, of both Old and New Testaments and the relations between them. In the end, I arrive at a rendition of history using the biblical themes of priesthood and baptism, which will also contribute to a theology that is social science (Milbank 1990). In this way, I hope to measure up to the Markan touchstone, elaborating a gospel that begins in baptism. I freely admit that priesthood and baptism provide only one perspective of many, and in defense I must plead simple creaturely limitation: For I can stand in only one place at a time (cf. Frame 1987).

A tree is known by its fruits: so we have it on the highest possible authority. In the end, then, I would have the value of my work judged by its fruitfulness in illuminating Scripture and edifying the church. And, beyond all, I intend this work to be a harmonious echo, however faint, of the song of the ineffable Singer whose mighty song is the history of creation.

CHAPTER TWO

Attendants in Yahweh's House: Priesthood in the Old Testament

Priests have been principal targets in the Marcionite assault on the Old Testament in modern philosophy, sociology, and theology. In *Religion Within the Limits of Reason Alone*, Kant characterizes "priest-craft" as the "oldest of all fictions" and the source of "ecclesiastical faith" that corrupts pure religion with dogma and ritual (Kant 1960: 15; cf. Reventlow 1984). Nietzsche also focuses on the dishonesty and nihilism of priestly religion, which entered Christianity through Paul's teaching and missionary efforts (Nietzsche 1988: 50, 85-86, 121, 134). Both Kant and Nietzsche loathe priesthood as a peculiarly Jewish institution, inimical to Kant's rational moralism and Nietzsche's celebration of the natural. In Weber's opposition of institutionalized priesthood and prophetic charisma, the prophets are the promoters of ethical monotheism, the good bit of the Old Testament (Milbank 1990: 83-92, 94). Much modern Old Testament scholarship similarly denigrates priestly ministry. Though occluded in the Old Testament text, the *real* story of Israel's priesthood was one of continual strife among self-interested priestly families and between temple priests jealous of their privileges and country Levites snatching at a piece of the sacrificial pie. Priests were mean and miserly, the prototypical Jews of anti-Semitic mythology. Oddly, these same priests who dominated both lesser Levites and laymen meekly acquiesced to every liturgical whim of the Davidic kings.

Not least among the problems with this account is its remarkably flimsy textual support. To a considerable extent, Wellhausen's reconstruction rests ponderously on a handful of texts (Ezek. 44:6-16; 2 Kgs. 23:8-9; Deut.18:6-8), all of which are open to plausible alternative interpretations (Wellhausen 1885: 123-124, 146-147).[1] Wellhausen argues for a late date for "P" partly by drawing attention to the contrast between the elaborate priesthood described in Leviticus and Numbers and the spontaneity of liturgical expression in the narratives of Judges. With characteristic wit, he says that the sudden appearance of the cult is matched by the suddenness of its disappearance after the conquest, so that "the Book of Judges forthwith enters upon a secular history completely devoid of all churchly character" (Wellhausen 1885: 127). The absence of priests from Judges is alarming because the Hexateuch leaves the impression that the High Priest was the central figure in Israel's amphictyony. Large historical conclusions built on the evidence of a single text are, however, exceedingly tenuous. More important, Wellhausen ignores the fact that Judges is the work of a "former prophet," not a "scientific nineteenth-century historian." With this in mind, it is significant that the Levites who appear in the long dramas at the end of Judges are little short of scoundrels (Judg. 17-21). By placing these events at the climax of the book, the author shows that the political failures of the early theocracy were the fruit of the failure of Levitical priests to guard Israel from Canaanite idolatry (Jordan 1985: 279-334). Absence of priests is a *thematic* device that underscores their practical absence from the life of

---

[1]Duke (1987: 193-201) and McConville (1984: 124-153) reject Wellhausen's equation of the rural Levites of Deuteronomy 18 with the priests of the high places in 2 Kings 23, as does von Rad in his commentary on Deuteronomy. On Ezekiel 44, see Cook (1995: 193-208); McConville (1983: 3-31); Abba (1978: 1-9).

Israel. Judges raises precisely Wellhausen's question – Where are all the priests? – without at all demanding Wellhausen's answer.

Even so sober a scholar as de Vaux somehow knows that the Zadokites were "a conservative-minded family, with little liking for innovation which might change their way of life" (1961: 375). Quite apart from the banality of this characterization – who *isn't* resistant to change? – the evidence de Vaux cites (1 Kgs. 15:12-13; 2 Kgs. 18:3-4; 23) hardly supports his conclusion. As de Vaux points out, these texts show that kings rather than priests initiated reform programs, and he implies that reactionary Zadokites headed the resistance. Yet no mention of priests either supporting or resisting can be found in the first two texts, and the Josian reform was catalyzed by a *priest's* discovery of the "book of the law" (2 Kgs. 22:8-20). Why, furthermore, would the Zadokites have resisted reforms that, to all appearances, consolidated their liturgical monopoly – unless perhaps we must add "naive" and "short-sighted" to de Vaux's catalogue of their failings? Reconstructing the struggle between the Zadokites and the descendants of Abiathar, de Vaux relies on the prophecy against Eli (1 Sam. 2:27-36) and some passages from Jeremiah (de Vaux 1961: 375-376), all denunciations of massive liturgical abuses. To say that these charges provided pious garb for what amounted to a power play unmasks the larger assumption that Israel's priests were astonishingly cynical, even to the point of deploying Torah simply to gain an advantage over the competition (cf. de Vaux 1961: 376). No doubt there were power struggles among Israel's priests, as among Old Testament scholars, but one should not assume that either community is a site of unchecked *libido dominandi*.

Richard D. Nelson's sympathetic portrayal of Israel's priesthood provides a useful corrective to the Marcionite scholarship of the past century, but his analysis is occasionally infected by perspectives he elsewhere rejects. Commenting on the difficulty that Jerusalem priests had in responding to Nebuchadnezzar's destruction of the temple, he writes, "Priestly theology on its own could offer no critique of its own ritual guarantee of Yahweh's unwavering favor to a disobedient people" (Nelson 1993: 102-3). Nelson thus treats "priestly theology" as if it existed as a discrete ideology in ancient Israel, when in fact it is a modern construct from the Old Testament (and other texts and evidence). Whether or not priestly theology "on its own" had resources for self-critique is irrelevant, for "priestly theology," assuming it existed at all, never existed "on its own" (cf. Nelson 1993: 99). After all, critical reconstructions of textual history, which Nelson largely accepts, place the "priestly literature" centuries later than other Pentateuchal material. Nelson also notes that priestly literature includes ethical components that go beyond mere external conformity (cf. 1993: 129; e.g., Lev. 19; Pss. 15; 24), but if "priestly theology" had ethical dimensions irreducible to ritual prescription, then it did possess resources for self-critique after all. Evidence for this is found in Jeremiah's devastating assault on Israel's antinomian trust in the temple (esp. Jer. 7); for Jeremiah was himself a priest (Jer. 1:1). Ezekiel, a "ritualist" if ever there was one, recorded the departure of Yahweh's glory from His temple (Ezek. 8-11), scarcely a vision that accords with a theology of ritual guarantee.[2]

---

[2]Jeremiah and Ezekiel were also heirs of earlier prophetic tradition, and it might be argued that this was the source of their critique of "priestly theology." This supports my point, against Nelson, that "priestly theology" (if it existed as a

Nelson occasionally leaves hints of a residual bifurcation of priesthood and eschatological prophecy. He asserts that "priests developed no eschatology other than one completely realized in ritual" (1993: 103), but this jars with his characterization of the Priestly Writing as a "theology of hope to a despairing nation" (1993: 105). Nelson's extended discussion of the "utopian" visions of Ezekiel 40-48 and Zechariah 1-8 (1993: 112-125), moreover, belies his previous statement that "the priestly response to exile was limited to attempts to restore everything to the way it should have been before the demolition of the temple" (1993: 103), for, on his reading, Ezekiel proposes *changes* in priesthood and liturgy (1993: 116). For Nelson, Christianity envisions a "world without culture map boundaries" with little room for priestly tasks (1993: 170-172), though he insists that the main function of Old Testament priesthood was community maintenance, which is surely relevant to the church.

Animus to priesthood has so infected modern thought that it is necessary to reassemble a theology of priestly ministry from the ground floor. With his emphasis on the priest's role in the community, Nelson has made significant progress, but his valuable work needs to be carried through more consistently. Eventually, I argue that the Christian gospel, ritualized in baptism, announces the eschatological reconfiguration of

---

discrete ideology at all) did not exist "on its own" but was open to cross-fertilization from other motifs of Israelite religion. Nelson might also stress that the priestly theology was formulated by Jerusalem priests, while Jeremiah's assault came from a priest from the discredited community of Anathoth (Jer. 1:1; cf. 1 Kgs. 2:26-27), but this assumes a Wellhausen-like history for which I find little evidence.

priesthood, but I cannot demonstrate that this is *good* news without a thoroughgoing purge of Marcionite prejudice. In the remainder of this chapter, then, I offer some rudiments of a theology of priesthood, so that, against Kant, Nietzsche, Wellhausen, and many others, I can mount a defense – in a sense to be elaborated below – of priestcraft.

Solving the Equation

Though the following discussion has value in comparative religions and relies to some extend on comparative evidence, my main goal is to describe priesthood in ancient Israel. Even with this limitation, the way forward bristles with difficulties. As described by the Pentateuch, the duties of priests can be arranged on a spectrum according to their proximity to the sanctuary. Priests alone had access to Israel's sanctuaries, and the only High Priest, on the Day of Atonement, entered the Most Holy Place to sprinkle blood before the ark (Lev. 16). In the Holy Place, priests offered incense and trimmed the wicks of the menorah lamps every morning and evening (Exod. 30:7-8; Lev. 24:1-4). Each Sabbath, the priests removed and ate the old shewbread and put out new loaves on the golden table (Lev. 24:5-9). In the courtyard, priests offered sacrifices morning and evening and at feast days on the bronze altar (Num. 28-29) and assisted lay Israelites with their private offerings. Though worshipers killed the victims (Lev. 1:4-5; etc.), priests alone manipulated sacrificial blood and turned meat and/or grain products to smoke (Lev. 1:5; 21:16-24). Priests, with the Levite clans, guarded the tabernacle (Num. 3:8, 38) and managed firstfruits, tithes, and votive offerings (Lev. 27; Num. 18).

They judged matters of uncleanness and performed some rites of cleansing to readmit laymen to the sanctuary (Lev. 12-15). In return for their service at the sanctuary, they received tithes and designated portions of the sacrifices (Lev. 7-8; Num. 18).

The duties sketched in the previous paragraph form a coherent complex of tasks but in addition priests had several functions within Israelite society. Bearer of the Urim and Thummim, the High Priest delivered Yahweh's oracles to the people (Exod. 28:30; Num. 27:21). Priests taught Torah (Deut. 33:10), especially ceremonial distinctions between clean and unclean, sacred and profane (Lev. 10:8-11; cf. Jer. 18:18; Hos. 4:4-6; Mal. 2:1-9), and in certain cases, they served as civil judges (Deut. 17:9). This set of duties, like the previous set, is internally coherent.

Acute difficulties arise when one seeks to combine the two sets of duties in a single framework. Can we find an umbrella big enough, and of the right shape, to keep the entire priest out of the rain? In asking this question, I am not searching for a hard kernel of unchanging "essence." Umbrellas can expand and contract and even, in a strong wind, be inverted. Nonetheless, I submit that "priest" has a certain "reach," such that Israelites from different periods of history would have supplied כהן ("priest") for crossword puzzle definition "x," just as we supply "priest" for a crossword puzzle definition such as "one who presides at Mass." Logically, the issue is one of abduction (cf. Eco 1984: 39-43): let "p" = priest, $\{a, b, c. . .\}$ = the set of duties of Israel's priests, and "x" = the definition of priesthood, currently unknown. I shall propose a value of x in the equation $p = x$. There are two criteria for determining the success of my calculations. First, x must be such that p = x produces the set {a, b, c. . .}, and, second, it must be true that p and only p = x.

The agnostic option is to deny such an equation exists. Resolving the problem diachronically, some scholars suppose that one or the other set of duties, or one specific activity, was temporally prior; at one time p = x, at another, p = y. Two main reconstructions have been proposed: Some claim that the original priestly function was to deliver oracles, while others suggest that early priests guarded the house of God and its treasures. On both theories, sacrifice came to dominate priestly activity later on.[3] Though the functions of priests undoubtedly changed over time,[4] neither of these solutions is persuasive. In part, the idea that early priests were solely oracular consultants depends on a doubtful etymological connection between כהן and the Arabic *kahin*, "soothsayer."[5] Neither is plausible in the context of Ancient Near Eastern religious practice: Oracles were sought, from early times, through sacrifice (cf. Num. 23:1-3, 14-16), and the earliest sanctuaries, as "houses of god," were places of sacrificial food

---

[3]Smith and Bertholet (1902: 3840-3841); Smith (1918: 308); Cody (1969: 12-13); Sabourin (1973: 99).

[4]For example, post-exilic priests had a far more prominent "civil" role than under the monarchy.

[5]Among other problems, the meaning of *kahin* is disputed. Keil and Delitzsch suggest that "The primary meaning of *cohen*, the priest, has been retained in the Arabic, where it signifies . . . to act as a mediator for a person, or as his plenipotentiary, from which it came to be employed chiefly in connection with priestly acts" (Keil and Delitzsch 1980: 2.192). Schrenk makes the same etymological connection but translates *kahin* as "seer, prophet" (1965: 260; cf. Smith 1918: 307), and for Brown, Driver, Briggs the Arabic term signifies a soothsayer or diviner who is an instrument of a jinn or god (Brown 1959: 462).

offerings.[6]

Commonly, "priest" is defined as a president of sacrificial worship (p = s),[7] and several texts are cited in support. Leviticus 21:21 describes priests as those who "offer the bread of God," and Ezekiel 44:16 confines the privilege of approaching the Lord's table to the Zadokites. Yet, this equation meets neither of the criteria set out above. Though sacrifice was apparently a priestly act, not everyone who sacrificed held a priesthood (e.g., Noah, Gen. 8:20; Abraham, Gen. 12:8). Many who did not fit under "priest" could therefore huddle under the umbrella, "one who sacrifices"; it is thus not true that p and only p = s. Nor does p = s yield the set {a, b, c. . .}. Not even all of the priests' activities in the sanctuary were "sacrificial" and their social functions dangle precariously.

Mediation has also been seen as the basic meaning of priesthood (p = m). After enumerating the duties of priests, de Vaux concludes,

> All these various functions have a common basis. When the priest delivered an oracle, he was passing on an answer from God; when he gave an instruction, a *tôrah*, and later when he explained the Law, the Torah, he was passing on and interpreting teaching that came from God; when he took the

---

[6]On temples, see Kramer (1988: 1-16) and the articles under the heading "The Significance of the Temple in the Ancient Near East" in Wright and Freedman (1975: esp. 145, 152-153, 164, 169-70, 175). Pritchard (1969: 325-326, 329-330, 338-339, 343) describes the priests' care for images in Egypt and Uruk.

[7]Payne (1980: 431); Baudissin (1889: 269); Smith and Bertholet (1902: 3838); Grabbe (1995: 52, 64, 182-183). P = s is embedded in Christian confessions and catechisms: cf. Westminster Shorter Catechism, question 25.

blood and flesh of victims to the altar, or burned incense upon the altar, he was presenting to God the prayers and petitions of the faithful. In the first two rôles he represented God before men, and in the third he represented men before God; but he is always an intermediary. . . . The priesthood is an institution for mediation (1961: 357).[8]

Again, some evidence supports this: Aaron's breastplate was adorned with stones engraven with the names of Israel's tribes (Exod. 28:15-21), which shows that the High Priest officiated as representative of the people (*pace* Haran 1988: 18). Several priestly duties were not, however, obviously connected with mediation -- guarding the house and trimming the wicks of the lampstand, for example -- or, at least, they point to a specific form of mediation. With some fudging, p = m might be made to produce the set {a, b, c . . .}, but it is not true that p and only p = m, for in several passages, prophets rather than priests "mediate." Scripture first applies "prophet" (Heb. נביא) to Abraham when he interceded for Abimelech (Gen. 20:7), and the prophet Amos acted as intermediary, speaking Yahweh's word and interceding on Israel's behalf in Yahweh's council (Amos 7:1-6; cf. 1 Sam. 12:23; Jer. 11:14; 14:11; 15:1; Heschel 1962: 1.21). De Vaux recognizes that prophets and kings were also mediators but claims that their mediation depended upon personal charisma, while

---

[8]See Bergman (1995: 70, 74); Auneau (1985: 1173); Sabourin (1973: 101).

priesthood was an "institution of mediation" (1961: 357; cf. Bergman 1995: 70, 73). Prophetic communities, however, existed in Israel (cf. 2 Kgs 2:5, 15-16; 6:1), suggesting that prophecy was institutionalized to some degree and not based on sheer untransmissible charisma. Even if one can legitimately contrast "charismatic" prophetic to "institutionalized" priestly mediation, the same distinction does not hold between king and priest, for the king's mediatorial role was as institutionalized as the priest's. In any case, if prophets and kings were mediators, mediation, though doubtless an aspect of priestly ministry, cannot define the distinct nature of priesthood.

Others suggest that sanctuary guarding was the basic priestly ministry (p = g).[9] Guarding the holy place was one function of priests and Levites (Num. 3:5-10; 18:1-7; Milgrom 1970), and this definition usefully highlights the priests' location in the Lord's house. If guarding was *the* central task of priesthood, however, it is difficult to account for the absence of any reference to guarding in many texts that describe priestly ministry (Lev. 21:21-23; Deut. 33:8-11; 1 Chr. 6:49). Guarding was at issue in Korah's rebellion (Num. 16--18), but the main dispute concerned who could "draw near" (Num. 16:5). Levites, moreover, serve as sanctuary guardians, though they are not priests; thus it is not true that p and only p = g. Finally, it is far from obvious that every priestly task fits under the umbrella of guarding; p = g does not produce the set {a, b, c . .

---

[9]James B. Jordan has suggested that "guarding is the essence of [man's] priestly task" (Jordan 1988: 134, 136). Abba offers a variation of this view in his conclusion that "the essential function of the Levitical priesthood is . . . to assure, maintain, and constantly re-establish the holiness of the elect people of God," though Abba eventually defines priests as mediators (Abba 1962: 877).

.}.

Aelred Cody's conclusion that "the earliest priests among the Israelites were essentially sanctuary attendants" is more comprehensive (1969: 29), but his diachronic emphasis vitiates Cody's insight. During the time of Samuel, Cody argues, offering sacrifice did not count as "priestly activity," since in those days "a priest was still looked upon as a sanctuary minister." Only after Deuteronomy, which Cody considers to be much later, did sacrifice become a priestly monopoly (1969: 74, 119-120; cf. 101). Undeniably, sacrifice was offered by men who were not priests in places that were not sanctuaries (though merely erecting an altar implied a mapping of sacred space[10]), but sanctuary ministry always involved sacrifice, among other things. Saying that priesthood developed "from sanctuary attendance to sacrifice" makes no sense, for the former was inclusive of the latter.

By making a clear distinction between the respective qualifications for sacrifice and temple service, Menahem Haran has offered a description of Israelite priesthood that satisfies our two conditions. Whatever the practice regarding extra-sanctuary sacrifice, from the beginning Levitical priests had a monopoly of Israel's temple ministry (1972: 1071-1073). In the sanctuary precincts, only ordained priests offered sacrifice, but this was one of a wider set of duties that can be brought under the heading of "housekeeping." Israel's sanctuary was the house of Yahweh, and priests were His personal servants who cared for His "needs" and managed His house, "just as any reigning monarch has in his palace servants and retinue

---

[10]See Christine Sourvinou-Inwood's criticisms (1993: 1-5) of de Polignac's interpretation of Homeric sacrifice.

surrounding him constantly and performing his orders" (1988: 18).[11] Priests were personal attendants to Yahweh in His house (ha = household attendant), and the cult was their personal and household service. Thus, p = ha. In the following pages, I first examine several lines of evidence to show that p and only p = ha, and close the chapter by showing how p = ha yields the set {a, b, c. . .}.

Ancient Near Eastern Parallels

Haran's description of Israelite priesthood depends in part on comparative evidence. In the Ancient Near East,

> The priests' involvement in the cult was conceived of essentially as service of the deity. This concept is rooted in the primary nature of the temple which was regarded as a 'house of the god.' . . . In this abode there are servants who attend on him and fulfill his wants, the whole cult being designed essentially to provide for the needs of the deity. This conception of the nature of the priesthood was accepted throughout the ancient world and found its expression in images and even in technical terms connected with the priesthood. For example, the Egyptian name designating priest, *hom-neter*, literally means 'servant of the god' (Haran 1972: 1069).[12]

---

[11]See Haran (1985: 218-219); Cody (1984: 257); Castelot and Cody (1990: 1254); Smith (1906: 229); Fairbairn (1870: 2.266-267, fn. 1); Youngblood (1992: 912-13); Nelson (1993: 62).

[12]See Sabourin (1973: 1-97) and the essays in Beard and North (1990: 95-174). On priesthood in Egypt, see Bergman (1995: 61) and Auneau (1985: 1175-1183).

According to the *New Jerome Biblical Commentary*, "In the ancient Near Eastern religious view, priests waited upon a god resident in his temple, with his presence focused in a mysterious, quasi-sacramental manner in his image or on a sacred object, even as earthly courtiers and retainers waited upon a king resident in his palace" (Castelot and Cody 1990: 1254). Greek conceptions were consistent with this; in Plato's phrase, Greek priests were "sacristans to the gods" (νεωκόρους . . . τοῖς θεοῖς).[13]

Haran notes the remnants of this conception in the Bible, but claims that it lost "its actual, concrete meaning as it became fossilized in linguistic usage" (1972: 1069). On the contrary, both in Levitical law and in Ezekiel, references to Yahweh's food, table, house, and the description of priests as "servants" (see below) are not "dead metaphors" but living clues to the biblical understanding of priesthood, sacrifice, and liturgy. Israel's tabernacle was מִשְׁכָּן ("dwelling place") and אהל מועד ("tent of meeting or appointment"), both terms indicating that Yahweh lived among His people (cf. Exod. 25:8).[14] In general, Yahweh is said to שׁכן ("dwell") among the Israelites, but several passages speak of His enthronement (ישׁב) between or above the cherubim attached to the cover of the ark of the covenant (1 Sam. 4:4; Ps. 80:1; 99:1; cf. Exod. 25:18-22).[15] Like gods and

---

[13]Plato (1967; *Laws* 6.759). See Woodhouse (1918: 303, 306); Sabourin (1973: 36-37); Martha (1882); Beard and North (1990).

[14]On the terminology of "dwelling" and "tent of meeting," see Davies (1962: 498); Rothkoff (1972: 679); Haran (1960: 50-65); Hendrix (1991: 213-223; 1992: 3-13). On the tabernacle as the dwelling of God, see Poythress (1991: 30-34); Haran (1985: 221-229, esp. 226); Keel (1978: *passim*).

[15]Cross (1947: 67); Clements (1965: 116); Hendrix (1991: 213-216); Rodríguez (1986: 136).

kings in other Ancient Near Eastern nations, depicted in iconography seated between or upon winged creatures (cf. Keel 1978), Yahweh reigned from the throne of cherubim wings that overshadowed the ark, which served as footstool under His feet.[16] The tabernacle was thus the "royal tent" of the divine King of Israel, appropriately decorated with rich curtains, veils, and gold-plated furniture. With Solomon's היכל, the royal connotation is more explicit, for this word can mean either "palace" (1 Kgs. 21:1) or "temple" (1 Kgs. 6:3, 5; 2 Kgs. 18:16). Israel's priests, like their counterparts throughout the ancient world, were attached to the palace of the divine King.

The ministry of Israel's priests, moreover, was like that of other ancient priests. As Milgrom has described it, the tabernacle was Israel's "picture of Dorian Gray" (1983: 75-84), which registered the nation's sin and uncleanness. Sprinkling blood at the altars was a form of "house-cleaning" that ensured the palace would remain hospitable to Yahweh. Turning sacrificial meat into smoke was "table service," and formed a central part of the priests' personal attendance upon Yahweh. Were it not for the distortions of theological debates, the fact that Old Testament sacrifice was a food rite would be obvious,[17] and the terminology

---

[16]Haran (1985: 246-259); Poythress (1991: 15); Clements (1965: 29-35); Sarna (1986: 209-212); Lewis (1977: 542-543). On the cherubim throne, see Albright (1938: 1-3); Keel (1978). Yahweh's enthronement follows His victory over Egypt (Fox 1995: 393).

[17]Sacrifice was expiatory, but expiation was one moment of a larger sequence, the goal of which was a meal. Yahweh does not need such food for His sustenance (Ps. 50:12-13), but there are, even for humans, other uses of food. Chiefly, sacrificial meals maintained covenant relations between Yahweh and Israel.

associated with sacrifice reinforces this conclusion. Ezekiel described the altar as the "table of the Lord" (Ezek. 44:16); the altar fire, which Yahweh Himself lit, "ate" the flesh (אכל; cf. Lev. 9:24); the sacrificial meat was the "bread of God" (Lev. 21:17, 21); and according to Gordon Wenham, אשה, sometimes translated as "offering by fire," means "food offering" (Wenham 1979: 56, fn. 8).[18]

Comparative philological evidence provides additional support for p = ha. Cognates of כהן are found in cultic contexts in Phoenician and other Northwest Semitic texts, but the Ugaritic evidence is particularly intriguing. The Ugaritic term *khnm* is not included in lists of cultic personnel but of administrative officials, sometimes connected with the palace,[19] and Ugaritic texts refer to "sacrificers" with other terms (Urie 1948: 45-47). Tarragon thus concludes that *khn* may refer to an administrative office, and he warns that the analogy between the Ugaritic *rb khnm* ("chief of the *khnm*") and the High Priest of Israel is not especially close, since the *rb khnm* did not have distinctively "sacerdotal" functions (Tarragon 1980: 135). Auneau compares the *rb khnm* to the Akkadian *sangu*, a general term for administrator with no necessary association with sacrifice or worship, and also cautions against a facile equation of Ugaritic

---

[18]Rendtorff (1985: 63-68) argues that אשה means "gift" and refers specifically to those sacrificial portions given to Yahweh as His property. Rendtorff admits, however, that priests delivered Yahweh's portion to Him by placing it on the altar-table, and he recognizes that the אשה is called לחם (1985: 65).

[19]Urie (1948: 42-45); DeGuglielmo (1955: 89-91); Rainey (1965: 122-124); Kraus (1966: 95); Tarragon (1980: 134-138); Auneau (1985: 1192-1193). Strangely, Payne cites the Ugaritic evidence to support his notion that the Israelite priest was a "sacrificer" (Payne 1980: 431).

and Hebrew officials (Auneau 1985: 1184; cf. Bergman 1995: 63-64). These arguments, however, assume that Israel's priests were primarily sacrificial ministers, an equation I have already contested, and this assumption gives the arguments a curious turn: The Ugaritic word that we expect to mean "priest" is not used of sacrificial and cultic personnel; therefore the Ugaritic term is *not* really parallel to the Hebrew, despite its philological identity. Why not conclude instead that priests in Ugarit and Israel were not "sacerdotal" in our post-Tridentine sense of the term? An Ugaritic *khn* had administrative charge either in the palace or the temple; this can be taken as evidence that Israel's כהנים held analogous posts in the palace of Israel's King.

What Does כהן Do?

Old Testament usage of כהן provides another line of evidence. Several etymological hypotheses have been offered,[20] but none is certain. In any case, the history of a word does not necessarily disclose its meaning at any particular time; as Nicholas Lash has put it, words pick up meanings more from the company they keep than from their ancestors. We can learn more about כהן, then, by interrogating its comrades. Two verbs are found in regular company with כהן: עמד ("stand") and שרת ("serve, minister"). Examining the usage of each in non-cultic contexts, I draw analogies between priestly and non-priestly uses to fill out a *sensus plenior*.

---

[20]Schrenk (1965: 260); Smith (1918: 307); Abba (1962: 877); Cody (1969: 26-28); Auneau (1985: 1197-98).

These verbs thus help define כהן by answering the question, What do כהנים do?

Standing to Serve

עמד has the literal meaning of "stand," "stand up," and "stand still," and is also used in a variety of metaphorical senses. Applied to priests, the word's spatial significance is never completely absent, since priestly "standing" or "status" involved physical location in holy space or at the altar (cf. Lev. 21:21, 23). In one passage, the hiphil form of עמד describes the installation of Jeroboam's "priests of the high places," who were "made to stand" in their ministry at the hilltop shrines (1 Kgs. 12:32: הבמות העמיד ... את־כהני). Joshua the High Priest "stood before the angel of the Lord" (Zech. 3:1), and the priest Phinehas "stood before" the ark (Judg. 20:28). For a priest to "stand in place" could mean to "perform assigned tasks" (2 Chr. 30:15-16; 35:10; lit. "they stood on their standing"; Heb., יעמדו על־עמדם), but this included standing at the altar or within the sanctuary. A כהן is one who has a place to *stand*.

Used of "standing" before a superior in non-liturgical contexts, the word has, besides its spatial sense, several nuances. To "stand before" can imply a one-time audience to submit a request, make a demand, or seek a favor (cf. Gen. 43:15; 47:7; Exod. 9:10; Num. 27:2; 1 Kgs. 1:28; 2 Kgs. 4:12). עמד also describes permanent personal service. Abishag "stood before" David (1 Kgs. 1:2), though her duty was to keep him warm in bed. Saul requested that David "stand before" him, and David became the king's armor bearer and played the harp when an evil spirit afflicted Saul

(1 Sam. 16:21-23).[21] Joshua's apprenticeship to Moses is described in similar terms (Deut. 1:38). Those who permanently "stood before" a ruler not only cared for his personal needs but also offered assistance in matters of state. Joseph became second to Pharaoh, a place of surpassing political "standing," to administer famine relief (Gen. 41:46). Solomon's servants and advisors "stood before" him continually (1 Kgs. 10:8; 12:6; Heb. תמיד), and Jehoiakim received Jeremiah's prophecy with princes standing beside him (Jer. 36:21). During the exile Daniel and his friends were selected for training to "stand before" Nebuchadnezzar in his palace (היכל; cf. 1 Sam. 1:9; 2 Kgs. 18:16), who consulted them concerning any matter of wisdom or insight (כל דבר חכמת בינה), to interpret dreams or advise on policy decisions (Dan. 1:4-5, 19-20; 2:2). When applied to a priest, the word implies that the כהן was to Yahweh as a member of a royal retinue was to a king.

Prophets also "stood before" Yahweh (e.g., 1 Kgs. 17:1), so to distinguish priestly from the prophetic "standing," the second of כהן's companions must be introduced. שרת (noun form משרת) means "attend to," "wait on," or "minister to." In Joel 1:9 and 2:17, priests are called "servants of Yahweh" (משרתי יהוה), and in 1:13 both "servants of the altar" (משרתי מזבח) and "servants of my God" (משרתי אלהי). Samuel, in training with the High Priest Eli, served Yahweh (1 Sam. 2:11; Heb., משרת את־יהוה). Nehemiah 10:39 speaks of "priests who are ministering" (Heb. v. 40; הכהנים המשרתים), Ezra 8:17 uses משרת in the phrase "ministers for the house

---

[21]David stood before Saul because he had found favor (חן) in the king's eyes (1 Sam. 16:22). Likewise, priests found favor in Yahweh's eyes, and were chosen to draw near to stand before Him.

of our God" (משרתים לבית אלהינו), and Yahweh made a covenant with the Levitical priests as "My ministers" (משרתי, Jer. 33:21). In Ezekiel 45:4, the objects of priestly service are Yahweh's house and Yahweh Himself: Priests were משרתי המקדש who come near to שרת את־יהוה. Several texts in Exodus demonstrate that "service" is central to priesthood: Priests "served" in the holy place (Exod. 28:35; 30:20), clothed in garments that qualified them to שרת בקדש and לכהן (Exod. 35:19; 39:1, 41). Given the parallel of the two phrases, this passage defines "priesting" as "שרת in the holy place."

Outside liturgical contexts, the word is used to describe administrative activities. Joseph found favor (חן) in Potiphar's eyes and served (שרת) him (Gen. 39:4), and this meant that Potiphar appointed (פקד) Joseph over all his house by giving everything into his hand (vv. 8-9). 1 Chronicles 27:1 lists the divisions of Solomon's "officers who serve (שטריהם המשרתים) the king in all the affairs of the divisions which came in and went out month by month." שרת can also connote more direct personal service. Seven eunuch משרתים attended Ahasuerus (Est. 1:10). The captain of the bodyguard appointed Joseph over the two servants of Pharaoh, and Joseph ministered to them (Gen. 40:4). Joshua was משרת to Moses, the עבד יהוה (Josh. 1:1; Exod. 24:13; 33:11; Num. 11:28), and Elisha to Elijah (1 Kgs. 19:21).

עמד and שרת are used together in several priestly passages. The tribe of Levi, Moses said, was separated (הבדיל)[22] to "stand, serve, and bless"

---

[22]The hiphil of בדל, used here of the separation of the Levites, also describes the separations of creation (Gen. 1:4, 6). A new creation comes into being with the separation of the Levites. See chapters 4-5, below.

(Deut. 10:8: לעמד לפני יהוה לשרתו; 17:12: העמד לשרת), chosen (בחר) to the same purpose (18:5: לעמד לשרת). Hezekiah encouraged the priests of his day by repeating this formula to explain their duties as Yahweh's משרתים (2 Chr. 29:11: בחר לעמד לפניו לשרתו). When the glory of Yahweh descended on Solomon's temple, the priests were unable לעמד לשרת (1 Kgs. 8:11), which suggests that under normal circumstances this was what they were to do. עמד and שרת occasionally combine without כהן in their company. The Queen of Sheba marveled at Solomon's court, remarking on the food and the "standing of his servants in their robes" (1 Kgs. 10:5: ומלבשיהם עבדי מעמד משרתו). Joshua stood before Moses (Deut. 1:38) to serve him (Josh. 1:1). Analogously, priests formed Yahweh's royal retinue, like the robed attendants at Solomon's banquet table, and priests were personal assistants to Yahweh, as Joshua was to Moses.[23] To say a priest was ordained "to stand to serve" meant he was literally and metaphorically positioned to attend to the One before whom he stood.

---

[23]Yahweh is also enthroned in heaven, attended by angels (Ps. 103:20-21; Dan. 7:10), and heavenly symbolism was taken up into the tabernacle, as in other Ancient Near Eastern sanctuaries. Moses built the tabernacle after the heavenly pattern revealed on the mountain (Exod. 25:9, 40; 26:30; Davidson 1981: 367-388) and its curtains were interwoven with cherubim (Exod. 26:1, 31). The writer to the Hebrews's claim that the earthly tabernacle was a shadow of heaven is thus a perfectly scientific judgment that might have been published in *Biblical Archeology* (Poythress 1991: 13-18; cf. Keel 1978: 174). In this perspective, Israel's priests were the angels of Yahweh's earthly palace. A further aspect of the heavenly symbolism is suggested by Clifford (1971: 225) who, drawing on Ugaritic texts that describe the assembly of the gods at El's tent, has suggested that "assembly, appointed meeting" in the phrase "tent of meeting" has the specific connotation of "meeting (of the divine assembly)." Clifford recognizes that monotheism radically alters the meaning of the phrase but fails to see precisely the alteration involved; for the "gods" admitted to the council of Yahweh are men. Priests were the earnest of the humanity's "deification."

According to Numbers 16:9, Levites were also brought near (קרב) to עמד and שׁרת, yet this comes in a text that censures Korah's claims to priesthood.[24] "Standing to serve" and "drawing near," then, cannot in themselves define the specifically priestly location, privilege, and task (Duke 1987: 198). Here, it is essential that we eschew the critical assumption that any complexity in the biblical text reveals diverse sources. Apparently, "draw near, stand, serve" can have various nuances, some applicable to both the Levites and priests, others only to priests. Numbers 16 itself subtly distinguishes between Levitical service and priestly ministry proper. Levites served the Lord's house by performing עבדה, the physical labor of transporting the tabernacle (Milgrom 1970), and they did not give personal service to Yahweh, but "stood to serve" Israel. In Numbers 3:6, likewise, the Levites are described as משׁרתים to Aaron, not to Yahweh. Hence, Aaron:Yahweh::Levites:Aaron or ::Levites:Israel. Both Levites and priests stood to serve the Lord's house, but only priests יעמדו in the holy place and at the altar and only they ישׁרתו Yahweh Himself.

Similarly, in Ezekiel 44:9-15 the distinction between priestly and Levitical ministry relates to proximity to and attendance on Yahweh. Because the Levites had gone astray after idols, their duties would be limited to ministry (משׁרת) of the house, defined as oversight (פקדת; v. 11) and guarding the doorways (שׁמרי משׁמרת, v. 14). Appointed as תא־הבית משׁרתים (v. 11), they would oversee all the עבדה done in the house (v. 14).

---

[24]The piling up of priestly terms in Number 16:9 is remarkable. Like the priests, the Levites were הבדיל from the rest of the congregation; they were permitted להקריב to Yahweh; their עבדה was directed to the משׁכן יהוה; and they were to עמד and שׁרת.

Yet, these Levites were not priests: They "will not come near to Me to serve as a priest to Me (לכהן לי), nor come near to any of My holy things, to the things that are most holy" (v. 13). The house of Zadok, however, "kept charge of My sanctuary when the sons of Israel went astray from Me." Because of their faithfulness, Yahweh would allow them to "priest." While Levites ministered in the house, Zadokites could "come near to minister to Me" (v. 15; יקרבו אלי לשרתני). While Levites served at the gates, the Zadokites were to perform table service, offering Yahweh the fat and blood on His altar (vv. 15-16). While the Levites stood before the people, the Zadokites stood before Yahweh (v. 11, 15). Access to Holy Place and altar was the specifically priestly privilege, and the priestly task was service to Yahweh in the inner chambers of His house.[25]

One criterion of a fruitful equation is its potential for encompassing anomalous data. P = ha fulfills this standard, helping to solve several enigmas in the historical books. In the vast majority of cases, כהן refers to sanctuary ministers, but several texts apply the title to men who were not descendants of Aaron nor (apparently) ministers of the hole place (2 Sam 8:18; 20:26; 1 Kgs. 4:5; cf. 1 Chr. 18:17). Though a variety of explanations have been offered,[26] our findings suggest that, though the word is used in

---

[25]Given that the Levitical system as a whole was a system of "graded holiness" (Jenson 1992), this distinction within the priestly tribe makes sense.

[26]Some scholars take these passages as evidence for the permission of non-Aaronite priests in the early monarchy: see Hertzberg (1964: 294); Baldwin (1988: 226); Mauchline (1971: 238). Driver (1913: 285) suggests that David's sons were something like "domestic priests" or chaplains, and Leimbach (1936: 163) cites the view that David's sons stood at the king's side during state ceremonies. Others soften the force of these passages with text critical arguments (Robinson 1993: 198; Jones 1984: 1.137; Mettinger 1971: 11; Payne 1980: 431; Wenham

an unusual context, the meaning of כהן is consistent with its more common connotation.[27] Since, as we have seen, כהן verges toward משרת, it is not surprising to find semantic influence going the other direction as well. כהן in this political context means precisely what it always means: a king's personal attendant serving in the palace.[28]

The Rite of Ordination

A few threads of evidence in favor of p = ha emerge from the rite of ordination. It is important, first, to provide an overview of the eight-day

---

1975: 79-82). Against this, McCarter finds it difficult to believe that "the surprising designation of David's sons as priests [has] arisen by corruption from an uncontroversial text," and follows "majority opinion" in concluding that the readings of the versions are attempts to avoid the implication of non-Levitical priests in David's court (McCarter 1984: 255). Others, accepting the MT as it stands, have argued that these texts provide evidence of something like the Canaanite ideology of "royal priesthood" in early monarchic Israel (Armerding 1975: 75-86, and, cautiously, Gordon 1986: 247). See also Rawlinson (1906: 209) on the "priests" of Ahab's house (2 Kgs. 10:11).

[27]See Baudissin's comment that "Die Chronik wäre also im Rechte, wenn sie jene Davidssohne (called "priests" in 2 Sam. 8:18) als 'Erste zur Hand des Konigs' bezeichnet" (Baudissin 1889:191-2). He concludes that כהן in these passages means a state official.

[28]Though it lies outside my chief concern, a word about the relation of priest to prophet and king is needed. The differences among these roles can be seen in relation to the house. Prophets were sacred architects, delivering, as Moses (Exod. 25:9, 40; 26:30) and Ezekiel (40-48) did, the heavenly blueprint (תבנית) of Yahweh's earthly house. David functioned in "prophetic" mode when he received the pattern (תבנית) for the Solomonic temple and relayed it to his son (1 Chr. 28:19). Solomon built the house, and other kings initiated its repair and reform. Priests oversaw its day to day operations and ministered to its Inhabitant.

ritual described in Exodus 29 and Leviticus 8-9. On the first day, Moses washed Aaron and his sons, anointed them, and invested them with priestly garments (cf. Exod. 28), and a series of three sacrifices followed (purification, "whole burnt," and the "ram of filling"). The ordinands then remained in the "doorway of the tent" for a week, repeating at least the חטאת, and probably the entire sacrificial series, each day (Exod. 29:35-37; Milgrom 1991: 539-540). On the eighth day, Aaron moved to the altar to offer a purification and burnt offering for himself and his sons, then the same two sacrifices for the people, and concluded with a peace offering for the people. Fire burst from the tabernacle to consume the altar portions, a sign that Yahweh accepted Aaron's offerings.

I cannot provide a full inspection of this rite but instead shall examine several technical terms associated with it and a few features of the ritual that support my proposed equation. As the exploration progresses, wider perspectives on priesthood and ordination begin to emerge. As it becomes necessary to my argument, in later chapters I shall reintroduce components of the rite for more detailed dissection.

Filling the Hand

To ordain is, in Hebrew, to "fill the hand" (מלא יד), an expression also used in this technical sense outside the Bible (Jenson 1995: 335). Though in some passages the phrase describes priestly or quasi-priestly ministry, it normally refers to the rite of ordination itself. By the rite, Yahweh "fills their hands in order to priest" (Num. 3:3: מלא ידם לכהן) or "fills his hand in order to put on priestly garments" (Lev. 21:10: צת-הבגדים

72

מלא את־ידו ללבש).

Some scholars have suggested that the term originally referred to payments given to the priest in return for religious services.[29]   Stated in baldly mercenary terms, this conclusion is misleading and the textual proof unconvincing. Judges 17:5, 12, where Micah is said to "fill the hand" of his son and the Levite, is frequently enlisted as evidence. Since Micah enticed the Levite to serve at his idolatrous shrine by offering silver, clothing, and regular maintenance (Judg. 17:10), "filling the hand" means "filling the hand with fees" (Noth 1962: 231). A more doggedly prosaic reading of Judges 17, which is sharply ironic, is difficult to imagine. That the Levite was willing to serve anyone who would "fill his hand" indicted him as one who shared the cultural ethos in which "every man did what was right in his own eyes" (Judg. 17:6; 21:25).[30] His hands were not really filled precisely because he was intent only on filling his hands.

Nelson likewise argues that the expression refers to "a priest's rights to the sacrificial portions upon which he lived" and cites Exodus 32:29, where Levites "filled their hands" with swords to execute idolaters, as a "rather grim pun on this phrase" (1993: 49-50; cf. Gray 1925: 249-250). A pun there is, for the Levites' reward for resolutely performing this sacrificial slaughter was the privilege of helping in another form of slaughter in the future. Yet, the passage is evidence against Nelson, since

---

[29]Gerstenberger (1996: 111); Noth (1966: 232-233; 1962: 231); de Vaux (1961: 346).

[30]Occurrences of this refrain frame the priestly "appendixes" to Judges. Levites above all "did what was right in their own eyes," a description that originally had to do with liturgical rather than social anarchism (Deut. 12:8).

73

the Levites' hands were not filled with payment but with weapons. A similar sense is found in 2 Kings 9:24, where Jehu "filled his hand" with a bow as he wreaked vengeance on the house of Ahab. In both passages, the phrase denotes not only grasping a weapon but also implies the execution of Yahweh's wrath (cf. Ps. 149:6-9). Filling the hand means zealously taking in hand the task at hand, even if that task demands enmity toward son and brother or the destruction Israel's royal house.

The conclusion that hands were ritually filled with responsibilities is supported by two late texts. David asked for Israelites willing to "fill the hand" to Yahweh, and the leaders responded with contributions of gold, silver, brass, iron, and precious stones (1 Chr. 29:1-9). Hezekiah, another Solomon, urged those who had filled their hands to Yahweh (2 Chr. 29:31: מלאתם ידכם ליהוה) to bring offerings into the restored house. Whether members of the Levitical choir or the assembly brought שלמים, in both passages non-priests function in quasi-priestly fashion, and in both cases "filling the hand" literally involved bringing contributions to the house of God. Hands were consecrated by giving; the people "filled their hands" to empty them in homage.

The ordination rite included a literal act of "filling the hand." Portions of the ram of "filling" were placed, with several grain offerings, on the palms (כף) of Aaron and his sons, lifted to Yahweh, and then taken from their hands (יד) to be turned to smoke on the altar (Lev. 8:26-28). During his initial ministry at the altar on the eighth day, Aaron again "filled his palm" (ימלא כפו), this time with a grain offering (Lev. 9:17). Priests' hands were filled *not* with the portions they received as payment but with the fat, flesh, and entrails of their table service (Kurtz 1980: 337-

74

338). With "hands filled," Israel's priests were enrolled as household servants and personal attendants to Yahweh. As Potiphar placed the management of his house in Joseph's hands (Gen. 39:8-9), so Yahweh filled Aaron's hands to take oversight of His palace.

In several senses, priests were also recipients in the ordination, so "fill the hand" has a double connotation. Priestly standing was itself Yahweh's gift (cf. Num. 16:5), and Yahweh provided the materials for His own service as well. An exchange occurred, but Yahweh remained the primary and in a sense the sole Giver, since the priestly *redditio* depended entirely on Yahweh's prior *traditio*. Moreover, the rite of ordination climaxed in a meal (Lev. 8:31), and portions of the ram of filling were sanctified as priestly food (Exod. 29:27-28). Aaron's hands were thus filled both with the bread of Yahweh and with food for his own consumption. To see this as a purely economic arrangement, however, is to read modern conceptions of exchange into the ancient text. As Mauss showed, in many societies gift-giving has as much to do with forging social bonds and allocating power as with economics (1990). Several details suggest that the ordination is an example of Maussian gift exchange or, in biblical terms, of covenant-making. The preparatory sequence of washing, clothing, and anointing is found elsewhere in the Old Testament in covenant-cutting ceremonies.[31] Israel's preparations for the Sinai covenant did not include anointing but anticipated the ordination rite in

---

[31]Ruth prepared for her midnight tryst with Boaz on the threshing floor by bathing, changing clothes, and anointing herself (Ruth 3:3). If this sequence was commonly associated with marriage, it perhaps suggests that Aaron and his sons, as representatives of Yahweh's bride, adorn themselves for the consummation of their "marriage" (cf. Isa. 61:10, where the groom is invested).

other respects (Exod. 19:10-14; cf. Gen. 35:2-3):

Sinai Covenant	*Ordination Rite*
Purify and wash clothes, Exod. 19:10-14	Washing, investiture, anointing
Series of sacrifices, 24:1-8	Series of sacrifices
Feast on the mountain, 24:9-11	Feast in holy place

This parallel suggests that within the covenant with all Israel, Yahweh entered, through the ordination rite, into a priestly covenant with Aaron and his sons (cf. Mal. 2:4).[32]

The sequence of offerings underlines the point. As in other sacrificial rituals (Num. 6:16-17), the offerings progressed from a חטאת to an עלה to a form of שלם.[33] As Milgrom has argued, the חטאת was a "purification offering" (1983: 67-69) that cleansed the altar and worshiper in preparation for entry into Yahweh's presence. Purified, the altar might be used as a table for His bread. As King and Master of the house, Yahweh received the first and best portions, so the fat of the חטאת and the entire עלה were placed on His table to be eaten (אכל) into His fire (cf. Lev. 9:24). Fat from the "ram of filling" was also given to Yahweh, but the

---

[32]Keil (1980: 343); Kellogg (1988: 220, 223); and Harrison (1980: 102) all refer to a "covenant of priesthood."

[33]Kellogg calls this the "invariable order" of sacrifices (1988: 232); cf. Harrison (1980: 105).

priests shared the flesh of this sacrifice. Through this elaborate multi-course meal, Aaron and his sons were bound to Yahweh as His personal משרתים.[34]

By "filling their hands" with food, Yahweh invited Aaron and his sons to be table companions; priests thus might eat flesh forbidden to strangers (זרים; Exod. 29:33; Lev. 22:10-16). Thus, because of the rite, Aaron and his sons were no longer considered זרים -- but to what were they no longer strangers? Attention to the spatial progression of the rite answers this question. Aaron and his sons began at the "doorway of the tent of meeting," where they remained throughout the seven-day incubation (Lev. 8:33). On the first day of a new week, Aaron passed from the doorway to the altar and then into the house itself. Moving from the courtyard through the curtain, the ordinands were installed in a kind of "naturalization" ceremony as residents of Yahweh's tent, members of His household, sharers in the bread of God (cf. Gorman 1990: 111-112). The rite forged a personal bond between Yahweh and His priests. "Priest" verges toward "son," "ordination" toward "adoption."

Consecration

---

[34]Kellogg (1988: 221) writes: "This sacrificial feast most fitly marked the conclusion of the rites of consecration. Hereby it was signified, first, that by this solemn service they were now brought into a relation of peculiarly intimate fellowship with Jehovah, as the ministers of His house, to offer His offerings, and to be fed at His table. It was further signified, that strength for the duties of this office should be supplied to them by Him whom they were to serve, in that they were to be fed of His altar."

Another dimension of the ordination is evident in Exodus 29:1, where Yahweh tells Moses to "sanctify" (קדש) Aaron and his sons לכהן לי. In many passages, the language of holiness is used not of Yahweh but of objects, persons, places, and times.[35] In these contexts, holiness was first an objective condition, accompanied by the demand that consecrated things, places, and persons be used or act in ways consistent with their status (Berman 1995: 10). A holy place was one claimed by Yahweh in a theophany (Exod. 3:5; 29:43), and only the chosen and sanctified were permitted to draw near and then only by observing strictly prescribed modes of approach. Holy things were relative to holy places, comprising the furniture of Yahweh's house and the tools of household service. So too, claimed by Yahweh, holy persons were stationed in the holy place, permitted to draw near, and required to "be holy." Israel became a holy nation after Yahweh delivered her in the Exodus, cut the Sinai covenant, and took up residence in her midst (Exod. 19:6). Within Israel, the priests were particularly holy with nearer access to Yahweh's enthroned glory, and greater freedom of movement and action in His palace. To "sanctify" was to position a person or thing in a holy geography; by "consecrating" Aaron and his sons, ordination granted permission to stand to serve in the holy house.[36]

---

[35]See Berman (1995: 1-19); Jenson (1992: *passim);* Poythress (1991: 33); David Wright (1992: 237-249); Gammie (1989: 9-44); Beet (1889).

[36]Anointing was the peculiarly sanctifying rite. As High Priest, Aaron alone was anointed on the head, thereby becoming the first משח in the canonical Old Testament. Exodus 30:30, however, speaks of all priests as anointed, and this seems to refer to the anointing with oil and blood that took place later in the rite (Exod. 29:21). Aaron's anointing highlighted his connection with the tabernacle. Oil was first sprinkled on the tent, its furniture, and the altar before being poured

"Consecration" also brings out a further sense in which Aaron's hands were "filled" by ordination. Under the Old Covenant, certain things were contagiously holy, so that, for example, anyone who touched most holy food was sanctified (Lev. 6:27), and thus brought under the stricter regulations governing consecrated persons. Ordination sanctified Aaron and his sons, however, so that their holiness matched that of the furnishings of the tabernacle. With hands consecrated by filling, they could safely lift up holy flesh to the altar, carry holy vessels, touch holy furniture.

Consecration was also in view when, toward the end of the sequence of sacrifices, Moses smeared blood from the ordination ram on the right ear lobe, the right thumb, and the right big toe of Aaron and his sons (Exod. 29:19-20; Lev. 8:22-24). According to Gorman, since these extremities "represent the whole person," *pars pro toto*, and "form the outer bounds of the person," coating them with blood enabled the whole person to pass safely across the dangerous boundaries of sacred space (1990: 105, 131-135; cf. Sabourin 1973: 140). This may be true as far as it goes but does not adequately explain the specifics of the rite: If one wanted to consecrate "extremities," why not smear blood on the forehead rather than the ear lobe? After citing parallels with Ancient Near Eastern rites and between the daubing of blood on the priests and the atonement of the altar in Ezekiel 43:20, 26, Milgrom concludes: "the function of the

---

upon Aaron's head to קדשׁ him (Lev. 8:10-12), so that he could serve in the house and at the altar, which were also קדשׁ. Priesthood and holy place came into being simultaneously, and each was sanctified by oil to the same degree (Gorman 1990: 118; Haran 1978: 177).

79

blood-daubing of the priests is for *kippûr,* and . . . the nature of this *kippûr* is purgative and apotropaic" (1991: 528-529). "Apotropaic," accompanied by citations from texts where daubing protects against demonic invasion, is surprising in light of Milgrom's earlier insistence that Israelite religion shows "no traces of demonic impurity" and that for the "priestly theology" only man acts demonically (1991: 259-260). Acceptance of the idea that ear, thumb, and toe were "vulnerable extremities" is thus contingent on a persuasive answer to the question, vulnerable to *what?* Since, according to Milgrom, "P" lacks a conception of demonic threat, the priests must have been vulnerable to impurity. While it is true that impurity posed greater danger to priests than to others because they stood before Yahweh, it is not clear why these specific extremities were vulnerable. Milgrom's explanation thus also fails to account for the specifics of the rite.

Dillmann's homiletical explanation of the daubing has been popular: A priest's ear was consecrated to hear the word of Yahweh, his hands sanctified to be filled with the holy instruments and food of ministry, and his feet to walk on holy ground (1880: 465).[37] This is better than a vague appeal to consecration of "extremities," and analogies with other institutions of Israelite worship and society provide further illumination. Three issues are relevant: the disposal of the blood of the ordination ram, the structure of the altar, and the rite for making a permanent slave.

First, blood from the ram of ordination was daubed on Aaron and

---

[37]See Kellogg (1988: 218); Harrison (1980: 100); Kurtz (1980: 334); Keil (1980: 340); Poythress (1991: 53).

his sons, dashed on the altar, then taken from the altar and sprinkled on the priests' garments.[38] Forming a "blood relation" between Aaron and the altar (Noth 1962: 232), the rite purified and consecrated priest and altar to stand to serve in the holy place. Daubing reinforced the connection between priest, tent, and furniture made by the anointing (Lev. 8:10-12).

The daubing rite also bears comparison with the smearing of blood from the purification offering on the horns of the altar,[39] a connection hinted at by the verbs used to describe the disposal of blood from the ordination sacrifices:

Hebrew Verb (Qal)	English translation	Object
נתן, Exod. 29:12; Lev. 8:15	"put"	Horns of altar
זרק, Exod. 29:16; Lev. 8:19	"throw" or "dash"	Around the altar
נתן, Exod. 29:20; Lev.	"put"	Ear, thumb, toe

---

[38]Against Jenson (1991: 121), who, citing Leviticus 8:30, claims that the blood was from the חטאת, which is impossible. The fact that the blood daubing came after the blood of the ram had been thrown around on the altar suggests that the blood was taken from the ram of filling. More importantly, blood from the חטאת was never placed on the altar but only daubed on the horns and poured at the base. Thus the blood used for the daubing, which comes from the altar, must have been either the blood of the עלה or that of the ordination ram, and perhaps is best understood as a mixture of both.

[39]Milgrom (1991: 528-529) recognizes the links between smearing the horns of the altar and smearing the priests' ears, thumbs, and toes but does not draw the conclusions I have suggested. Cf. Jordan (1992).

8:22		
זרק, Exod. 29:20; Lev. 8:24	"throw" or "dash"	Around the altar
נזה, Exod. 29:21; Lev. 8:30	"sprinkle"	Aaron, sons, garments

Blood is "put" (נתן) on the horns of the altar and the appendages of the priests but "sprinkled" or "thrown" elsewhere. By daubing the "horns" of the candidates' bodies, ordination sanctified them as "human altars."[40] This again reinforces the conclusion that ordination installed the priest as an essential piece of sanctuary "furniture."

Exodus 21:5-7 also illumines the ordination. This passage stipulates that a man or woman was marked as a (voluntary) permanent household slave by having his or her ear bored with an awl. In this way, the slave's ear was "opened" to the voice of his master, and this rite is background for later imagery of the "circumcision" of the ear (Jer. 6:10; Acts 7:51; Jordan 1984). Similarly, a priest's ear is symbolically "circumcised" as a sign that he has become a permanent tabernacle servant with his ear opened to the voice of Yahweh, and the connection with circumcision can be extended to the daubing of the thumb and toe. Priests had their hand "circumcised" to be filled with the materials for Yahweh's service and

---

[40]These analogies form the background for Ezekiel's description of the expiation of the altar. Drawing on the rite of ordination, he wrote that the altar was "decontaminated and purged," and that the altar had its "hands filled" (Ezek. 43:20; cf. Exod. 29:36; Milgrom 1991: 529). Condescending dismissal from modern scholars notwithstanding, Ezekiel displayed an penetrating grasp of the reverberating symbolisms of the tabernacle system, for the priest was a human altar and the altar a bronze priest. Milgrom (1991: 541) also defends Ezekiel's use of מלא יד, without explicit recognition of the analogies of priest and altar.

their foot circumcised to walk in His holy house.[41] Unlike the altar, priests were not "circumcised" in four "horns" because they had already been circumcised on the penis. All Israelite males were circumcised in one dimension; those who received this further threefold circumcision -- that is, those circumcised "globally" in four dimensions -- were consecrated to minister to Yahweh within the house. Ordination was thus a specification of circumcision, and, significantly, both were rites of the "eighth day" (Gen. 17:12; Lev. 9:1).

Conclusion

As noted at the beginning of this chapter, the duties of Israel's priests fell into two broad categories: cultic and sociological. My equation, p = ha, is obviously compatible with the cultic role of priests, but does it produce the whole set {a, b, c . . .}? Have I made good on my promise to provide a functional umbrella? I believe I have, but a bit more reflection on the nature of Yahweh's house is required to see the full value of "h."[42]

---

[41]Circumcision of the ear, thumb, and big toe was also a symbolic dismemberment and mutilation (cf. Judg. 1:6-7): By ordination, Aaron and his sons were made living sacrifices (Knight 1976: 178). See Revelation 7:14-17, where the saints are qualified to participate into the heavenly liturgy by martyrdom, and Hebrews 2:10, where Jesus is said to be "perfected" as High Priest by his sufferings.

[42]My concern here is with the theological significance of the house. On the question of historicity, scholars of the past several decades, building in part on improved archeological evidence, have challenged the extreme skepticism of Wellhausen, who called the tabernacle a "pious fraud." See Davies (1962: 502-506); Rothkoff (1972: 684-685); Cross (1947: 45-68); Friedman (1992: 292-295); Sarna (1986: 196-199); Rabe (1966: 132-134); Hyatt (1971: 259-262); Childs (1974: 531-534). For discussions of the architecture of the tabernacle and the physical

When Moses finished building the tabernacle, the glory of Yahweh, which had been burning atop Mount Sinai, took up residence in the Most Holy Place (Exod. 40:34-38), so that the tent became a "portable Sinai" (Fretheim 1991: 274). The structure of the tabernacle confirms this connection. During Israel's encampment, Sinai was divided into three zones: Israel stood at the foot of the mountain but might not touch it (Exod. 19:13); Aaron and his sons, with the elders, ascended halfway to feast in Yahweh's presence, but were separated from Him by a firmament pavement (Exod. 24:9-11); Moses alone pierced the firmament into the cloud on top of the mountain. Corresponding to this, all Israelites might enter the courtyard, the priests alone were admitted to the Holy Place, and only the High Priest, a permanent Moses, passed through the firmament veil into the Most Holy Place, where Yahweh was enthroned in the cloud. In keeping with this, the tables of the law, delivered to Moses on the mountaintop, were placed within the ark of the covenant in the inner sanctuary, and Yahweh promised to continue the mountain conversation by speaking to Moses from above the cherubim (Exod. 25:21-22). From this perspective, priests served in an architectural Sinai, and their standing at the altar and in the tent was an "ascent" to the mountain of Yahweh's presence.[43]

---

appearance of its furnishings, see, in addition to the above, Haran (1985: 150-158, 198-204); Strong (1987: 15-112); Kennedy (1902: 656-666).

[43]See Rodríguez (1986: 127-145); Childs (1974: 540); Sarna (1986: 203-204); Berman (1995: 35-56); Cassuto (1967: 319). Poythress suggests that an ascent is indicated by the metals at the bases and bands of the pillars and boards. The boards (or frames) of the tabernacle proper were overlaid with gold and set in silver bases, while the pillars that held up the curtain of the courtyard had bases of bronze with bands and hooks of silver at the top. This suggests that, in idea, the

One further act of analogous imagination is required: The architectural house of Yahweh paralleled not only the mountain but the human "house" of Israel (Poythress 1991: 31-32, 36; Sarna 1986: 204, 207). Yahweh fulfilled His promise to Abraham when He descended from Sinai to live among the *people*. Accordingly, the triple structure of the tent matched the socio-religious stratification of Israel, the graded holiness of layman, priest, and High Priest. Arrangement of the camp of Israel around the tabernacle in Numbers 2-3 also suggests connections between tent and people.

Aaron's High Priestly vestments underline this point. As a preface to its description of the garments, Exodus 28 twice says that they were given to Aaron "that he may priest to Me" (vv. 3, 4; את־בגדי אהרן לקדשו לכהנו לי עשו). Specifically, he wore the breastplate over his heart when he ministered in the house (Exod. 28:29); he donned the robe of the ephod, with its border of alternating bells and pomegranates, so that he might enter the tent without dying (Exod. 28:35); and both he and his sons wore linen breeches to ascend the altar without exposing their nakedness (Exod. 28:42; cf. 20:26). As Haran says, the priestly vestments are like another piece of tabernacle furniture (1985: 165-166); dressed in them, the priests also were welcomed in the tent. Just as the garments indicate that the High Priest was a servant of *Yahweh's* royal house, so they show that he was a servant of the house of *Israel*. Aaron bore the names of the tribes

---

tent is "on top" of the court, its silver bases fitting into the silver bands at the top of the courtyard pillars (Poythress 1991: 26-27). Though Blenkinsopp is correct that the tabernacle could not reproduce the three-story structure of the creation/ark (1976: 286), the tabernacle was symbolically a multi-story tent.

on his heart and shoulders whenever he ministered in his priestly vestments (Exod. 28:9-12, 29); Urim and Thummim were placed in the pouch of the breastplate, though they had no use in the sacrificial cult (Exod. 28:30; Lev. 8:8); and the ציץ or "flower" of gold on the front of Aaron's turban was for "bearing the iniquity of the holy things" consecrated by Israel (Exod. 28:36-39). Vested as priest, Aaron stood to serve in Yahweh's twin house.

Ministry to Yahweh in the sanctuary was ministry for and among Israel, and ministry among the people was also ministry in Yahweh's "house." Priests guarded boundaries of holiness as much by teaching Torah as by serving as custodians of the sanctuary gates, cleansed as much by leading sinners to repentance as by sprinkling blood, performed Yahweh's table service as much by conducting worship as by turning flesh and grain to smoke. Even when the priests moved out of the holy precincts to stand and serve among the people, they were attending to Yahweh by "housekeeping."

CHAPTER THREE

Baptism to Priesthood: Apostolic Conjugations of the Ordination Rite

For nearly two millennia, theologians and liturgies have viewed Christian initiation as a typological "conjugation" of priestly ordination, but the New Testament poses two basic problems for the tradition. First, no New Testament text states that "baptism corresponds to ordination," as Peter says of the flood (1 Pet. 3:18-22). Second, though most later texts associate priesthood with separate rites of anointing or investiture joined to water baptism,[1] no New Testament evidence for such rites exists. The Spirit anointed Jesus at His baptism (Acts 10:38) and Christians are anointed (1 John 2:20, 27), but John administered no *rite* of anointing (Matt. 3:13-17; Mark 1:9-11; Luke 3:21-23) and apostolic baptism used water alone (cf. Acts 8:26-40). Though Paul describes baptism under the metaphor of clothing (Gal. 3:27), no rite of investiture is evident in the New Testament. Laying on of hands may have accompanied baptism in water (Acts 8:16-17; 19:5-6; Heb. 6:2) but even here the evidence is too scanty to be altogether persuasive and, in any case, laying on of hands had no part in the ordination of Israel's priests. Does the church then have biblical justification for her belief that baptism forms priests?

---

[1]Tertullian wrote, "We come up from the washing and are anointed with the blessed unction, following that ancient practice by which, ever since Aaron was anointed by Moses, there was a custom of anointing them for priesthood with oil out of a horn" (*Exinde, egressi de lavacro, perungimur benedicta unctione de pristina disciplina qua ungui oleo de cornu in sacerdotium solebant, ex quo Aaron a Moyse unctus est. unde christus dicitur a chrismate quod est unctio, quae [et] domino nomen accommodavit, facta spiritalis, quia spiritu unctus est a deo patre* [*De baptismo*, 7; Evans 1964: 16-17; PL 1, 1206C-1207A]). See also below, chapter 4.

This chapter will seek to demonstrate that the answer is Yes. First, I summarize several *prima facie* Christological, ecclesiological, and liturgical arguments in favor of the typology. In my judgment, these establish that baptism initiates into the Christian priesthood, but they fall short of showing that New Testament texts *on baptism* draw on ordination symbolism. Attempting the latter demonstration is important for two reasons. First, it strengthens the claim that the New Testament writers were operating within a hermeneutical universe that included this typology. If I am to have a firm foundation for my effort to construct a theology of baptism from materials provided by the ordination texts, I must not only substantiate the loose formula that "baptism initiates to priesthood" but also defend the more rigorous proposition that "baptism fulfills the Aaronic ordination." Second, examining baptismal texts that allude to priestly ordination will reveal the full scope of the typology, moving toward a biblical reading of history.

In this chapter, I examine five passages: Hebrews 10:19-22, Galatians 3:27, 1 Corinthians 6:11, Luke 3:21-23, and 2 Corinthians 1:21-22, several of which patristic and medieval writers interpreted as evidence of the priestly typology (see below, fns. 28, 38, 53). Throughout, I operate on the foundational assumption that the New Testament is an "innerbiblical" rereading of the Old Testament and I assume the conclusions concerning priesthood and ordination from chapter 2. Otherwise, my treatment of these five texts is uneven, both in the space devoted to each and in the strategy of reading involved. For the first three passages, I use a tightly grammatical and historical method to address two issues: Does the text refer to water baptism? and, Does it allude to the ordination rite? From

88

these passages, I conclude that the New Testament writers taught or assumed that baptism fulfills the ordination rite. Discussion of these texts is comparatively brief, but I shall probe Hebrews 10 and Galatians 3 again in chapter 5 for their ecclesiological and cultural ramifications.

Having established that the first three texts refer to Christian baptism, my argument will proceed according to the following logic: Let O = the ordination rite; X = any person; P = priest; TP = priestly tasks and privileges; and B = baptism. Under the Old Testament, O applied to X produced a P who had TP. New Testament writers might indicate that B fulfills O in several ways. First, one might explicitly assert that B has replaced O, but we have no such proposition in the New Testament -- hence the difficulty. Second, a text might state that B produces Ps, but again we lack such an explicit proposition. Third, if a text states that B confers TP on X, it follows that X has become a P and that B has the same function in the church as O had in Israel, that is, producing Ps. Therefore, B fulfills and replaces O. Hebrews 10:19-22 states precisely that B confers TP, and I interpret 1 Corinthians 6:11 along the same lines.[2]

Galatians 3:27 falls into a final category, where the evidence is inherently less probative. We saw in chapter 2 that O consists of a series of ritual actions. If a text describes B in terms of one of the actions of O, an allusion to O is possible, and if B is described with imagery drawn from several actions of O, the possibility of an allusion becomes probable. Two problems arise here, however. First, proving that the imagery applied to B comes from O, rather than from another image-pool, is virtually

---

[2] I do not mean that O is the only rite that B fulfills and replaces. B also fulfills circumcision and the other washings of the Levitical system.

impossible to prove beyond doubt. I have narrowed the possible sources with my Augustinian assumption that the New Testament writers were "conjugating" Old Testament texts, rites, and institutions, but this often leaves several possibilities open. I shall consider an allusion to O plausible if I can show 1) that the text on B employs imagery more strongly associated with O and O-texts than with other Old Testament texts or rites, and 2) that a priestly reference makes sense in context. Second, even if a New Testament text explicitly declared it was describing B in terms of O, the status of the allusion would remain ambiguous. B-texts may borrow imagery from O without necessarily implying that B fulfills and replaces O. Yet, the imagery is relevant. It is of the nature of metaphor to refer to one thing in terms suggestive of another. If we can plausibly establish that a text describes B in terms suggesting O, then a metaphorical relationship is set up between the fields associated with B and O respectively, and we can survey the O-field to illuminate B.

I devote more space to the final two texts, which will support the typology in the same kind of general way as the *prima facie* arguments. Here, my reading will take on a more freewheeling literary character. Some features of Luke's account of Jesus' baptism allude to priesthood, but much of my discussion will show that the surrounding chapters are saturated with priestly concerns, so that the reader arrives at Jordan's banks expecting to meet a priestly Messiah. Likewise, though I cannot prove beyond doubt that the anointing of 2 Corinthians 1:21 alludes to ordination, Paul's metaphorical twists and turns in 2 Corinthians retrace the interpenetrating symbolisms of the tabernacle and ordination texts; these texts thus provide a map of Paul's argument, without which he seems to be meandering aimlessly through a forest of symbols. Though trying to establish textual warrant for my conclusions so as not to "put words in God's mouth," I confess that I go beyond a strictly "apostolic view," elaborating connections with the *sensus plenior* of the Old Testament and within the New Testament that may not have been apparent to the human authors. My aim is to tease out a theological rather than a historical understanding of baptism.

Union With the Totus Christus

First, the *prima facie* arguments: Augustine (and many others) developed the typology on a Christological basis. For Augustine, Christology is an explication of the "chrism" by virtue of which Jesus is the Christ: *Christus a chrismate dictus est, id est, ab unctione*. Christ, however, is not Christ except as He is *totus Christus*, Head and body (cf. Mersch 1936: 2.84-138). All included in the Anointed One are anointed; all in Christ, all who are Christ's, are christs. In a typical passage, Augustine writes, "Certainly we can properly apply the name 'anointed' to all who have been anointed with his chrism; and yet it is the whole body, with its head, which is the one Christ" (*De civitate Dei* 17.4; 1984: 724).[3] Participation in His chrism is conferred by the unction of Christian initiation, an external sign that the *donum gratiae* that overshadowed Jesus at His baptism as a dove anoints the entire body.[4]

---

[3] *Omnes quippe unctos ejus chrismate, recte christos possumus dicere: quod tamen totum cum suo capite corpus unus est Christus* (PL 41, 532).

[4] *Non utique oleo visibili, sed dono gratiae, quod visibili significatur unguento quo baptizatos*

Augustine expounds Christ's "chrism" typologically. Jesus was anointed as Davidic King to defeat Satan on the cross and as Priest to offer Himself as sacrifice and intercede before His Father.[5] Sharing His chrism thus means sharing His offices and ministries. Commenting on Revelation 20:6, Augustine reasons, "just as we call them all 'Christians' because of the mystical chrism so we call them all 'priests' because they are members of the one Priest" (*De civitate Dei* 20.10; 1984: 919).[6] In a sermon fragment preserved by John the Deacon, Augustine moves more directly from Old Testament priesthood to the anointed church: "Then one priest was anointed, but now all Christians are anointed."[7] Old Testament "christs" therefore prefigured the royal priesthood of the *church.*[8]

---

ungit Ecclesia. Nec sane tunc unctus est Christus Spiritu sancto, quando super eum baptizatum velut columba discendit (Matth. III, 16): tunc enim corpus suum, id est, Ecclesiam suam praefigurare dignatus est, in qua praecipue baptizati accipiunt Spiritum sanctum (PL 42, 1093).

[5]*Christus a chrismate dictus est, id est, ab unctione. Reges autem ungebantur (1 Reg. x,1; et xvi,13) et sacerdotes (Exod. xxx,30): ille vero unctus est et Rex et Sacerdos. Rex pugnavit pro nobis, sacerdos obtulit se pro nobis. Quando pro nobis pugnavit, quasi victus est; vere autem vicit. Crucifixus est enim, et de cruce sua, in qua erat fixus, diabolum occidit: et inde Rex noster. Unde autem Sacerdos? Quia se pro nobis obtulit* (*Ennaratio* on Psalm 149; PL 37, 1952-3).

[6]*Non utique de solis episcopis et presbyteris dictum est, qui proprie jam vocantur in Ecclesia sacerdotes: sed sicut omnes Christianos dicimus propter mysticum chrisma, sic omnes sacerdotes, quoniam membra sunt unius sacerdotis* (PL 41, 676).

[7] *Tunc enim unus sacerdos ungebatur, modo Christiani omnes unguntur* (*De calendis Januarius contra paganos*; PL 39, 1734-35).

[8]*Jam etiam unctus erat unctione venerabili, qua regale sacerdotium praefigurabatur Ecclesiae* (*Sermo* 351.5.12; PL 39, 1548-1549). A similar Christological argument underlies

Ecclesiological considerations ground the typology, though these are not, of course, sharply distinct from Augustine's Christological rendition. Since the church is the royal priesthood (1 Pet. 2:9-10; Rev. 1:6; 5:10; 20:6) and since through baptism the Spirit incorporates members into that community (1 Cor. 12:12-13), it follows that baptism inducts into Christian priesthood. This comes to clearest expression in 1 Peter,[9] and the argument is all the stronger if, as some commentators have suggested, a baptismal currents flow under the surface of that letter.[10] Alternatively, since the church is the new temple of the Spirit (1 Cor. 6:19), and since baptism inducts into ministry in the body (1 Cor. 12:12-31), baptism ordains "housekeepers."

Thomas's theory regarding sacramental character (*ST* 3a, 63, 3).

[9] 1 Peter 2:9-10 was employed in baptismal liturgies at least as early as the *Apostolic Constitutions*, a composite work of fourth-century Syria (Bradshaw 1992: 93-95; Finn 1992a: 55) based on the *Didascalia* and the *Didache*: "in the laying on of hands the bishop shall anoint her head only as the priests and kings were formerly anointed, not because those who are now being baptized are being ordained priests, but as being Christians, or anointed, from Christ the Anointed, *a royal priesthood and an holy nation* [1 Pet. 2.10], *the Church of God, the pillar and ground* [1 Tim. 3.15] of the marriage chamber, *who in time past were not a people* [1 Pet. 2.10], but now are beloved and chosen" (3.15; quoted in Whitaker 1960: 27; μόνον ἐν τῇ χειροθεσία τὴν κεφαλὴν αὐτῆς χρίσει ὁ ἐπίσκοπος, ὅ τρόπον οἱ ἱερεῖς καὶ οἱ βασιλεῖς τὸ Πρότερον ἐξπίοντο· οὐχ ὅτι καὶ οἱ νῦν βαπτιζόμενοι, ἱερεῖς χειροτονοῦνται, ἀλλ' ὡς ἀπὸ τοῦ Χριστοῦ Χριστιανοί, Βασίλειον ἱεράτευμα, καὶ ἔθνος ἅγιον, Ἐκκλησία θεοῦ. στύλος καὶ ἑδραίωμα τοῦ νυμφῶνος. οἱ ποτὲ οὐ λαός, νῦν δὲ ἠγαπημένοι καὶ ἐκλεκτόι 97A]).

[10] Wilhelm Pesch points out that the background to 1 Peter 2:9-10 describes the members of the church as "born again" (1:3, 23) and "newborn" (2:2), and refers to their having "put aside" evil (2:1) -- all of which may be connected with death and resurrection with Christ in baptism (Pesch 1970: 307 fn. 12). Some commentators have seen the "illumination" imagery of 2:9 as a baptismal reference (Elliott 1966: 44, 207-208; Spicq 1966: 90-94).

Liturgical and ritual evaluations of baptism also suggest a link with ordination. Two features are relevant: like the baptism of John, Christian baptism is 1) an unrepeatable initiatory rite; and 2) administered, that is, the baptized does not wash himself but is washed by someone else -- hence, Ἰωάννης ὁ βαπτιστής (Matt. 3:1, 13-15; 11:11-2; 16:14; Mark 1:4; Luke 3:21; Acts 8:38; 9:18; 19:5). These characteristics have made it difficult to identify baptism's historical source. Some suggest John borrowed the rite from Jewish proselyte baptism, but it is not certain that proselyte baptism predated John, and even if it did, proselytes baptized themselves (Gavin 1928: 35).[11] Others contend for parallels with the ablutions of the Qumran community, but their rites were repeated self-washings, and therefore closer to the cleansing rites of Leviticus 12-15 than to Christian baptism.[12]

The assumption that John, Jesus, and the apostles were composing variations on the themes of the Old Testament leads to a different

---

[11]Jeremias (1960: 24-40; 1963: 27-28) argues for infant baptism from analogy with proselyte baptism, which he claims originated in the second century B.C. at the latest. Kraeling (1951: 99-105) too argues that proselyte baptism was practiced sufficiently early to be a source of John's baptism, though he ultimately denies this was the actual source. Scobie (1964: 97-102) cites T.F. Torrance as a prominent exponent of the view that Christian baptism grew out of Jewish proselyte baptism, but he and Smith (1982: 13-32) deny that proselyte baptism pre-dated John's ministry. See also Beasley-Murray (1973: 18-31); Flemington (1948: 4-11); Barth (1951: 14-16, 102-104).

[12]Pace Thiering (1980: 266-77; 1981: 615-31) and Beasley-Murray (1973: 11-18); cf. Lathrop (1994: 509-514). Scobie (1964: 103-116) argues that the Qumran community did practice an initiatory baptism. I am inclined to agree with Dahl that the similarities of Johannine and Qumran washings arise from their common background in the Old Testament (Dahl 1955: 44).

conclusion. Contemporary Jewish and Greco-Roman practices may have been within the horizon of New Testament baptismal teaching and practice, and John's baptism, especially his baptism of Jesus, also formed a substantial background. Yet, for the New Testament actors and writers as for Augustine, the sacraments of the New are typological conjugations of the events, rites, and institutions of the Old. According to the apostles, baptism is crossing the Red Sea (1 Cor. 10:1-2), recapitulates the flood (1 Pet. 3:18-22), fulfills circumcision (Col. 2:11-12). These are not grafts on a non-typological trunk; the trunk is typology. Thus, the Old Testament is the primary context for answering the question, Why did Johannine and Christian baptism take *this* form?

Like Christian baptism, the washing at the beginning of the ordination rite was an administered initiation, and in these respects the ordination bath was unique in the Levitical system. While most Old Testament ablutions were self-washings, Moses washed Aaron and his sons (Exod. 29:4; Lev. 8:6; cf. Lev. 14:8; 15:16-18, 27); while most cleansing rites were repeated as often as one became unclean, the ordination washing was once-for-all. Though priests washed their hands and feet before approaching the altar or entering the tent (Exod. 30:20), this self-washing was not a repetition of the ordination bath since it was partial and not administered. Similarly, when the Levites were set apart to help the priests in tabernacle service, Moses sprinkled them with water, then they shaved themselves and washed their clothes before being installed through a sacrificial rite and the laying on of hands (Num. 8:5-15). The ordination bath and the closely related sprinkling of the Levites were the *only administered initiatory water "baptisms" in the Levitical system.*

95

Tracing the form of Johannine and Christian baptism to priestly ordination and Levitical consecration is thus more plausible than the rival explanations.[13] Baptism was described under other typologies, but its form points to a connection with ordination. Like the Qumran community and the Pharisees, John was preparing a holy, priestly community for the coming of the Lord (cf. Wright 1996: 434).

These arguments prove Aidan Kavanagh's claim that "the Church baptizes into priesthood" (1995: 268; 1991: 187-188). To support the stricter thesis that baptism fulfills and replaces ordination, we turn to specific texts.

Bodies Washed to Draw Near, Hebrews 10:19-22

In 10:22, the writer to the Hebrews encourages his readers to "draw near" confidently having "our hearts sprinkled from an evil conscience and our bodies washed with pure water" (ῥεραντισμένοι τὰς καρδίας ἀπὸ συνειδήσεως πονηρᾶς καὶ λελουσμένοι τὸ σῶμα ὕδατι καθαρῷ). My first concern here is to decide whether this is a baptismal text. Most commentators believe it is.[14] A prominent exception to this consensus is

---

[13]Lathrop (1994: 515) points out that the priestly washing was virtually unique in being administered by another. Dahl contends that the later Christian initiation rite "corresponds to the pattern of the Old Testament initiation of priests -- much closer than to rites for Jewish proselytes" (1955: 46).

[14]Dahl (1951: 407); cf. Bruce (1964: 250-251); Moffatt (1924: 145); Brown (1961: 461-464); Best (1960: 281); Lane (1991: 287); Arrington (1977: 85); Attridge (1989: 289); Hughes (1977: 412); Lehne (1990: 114); Pelser (1974: 50); Flemington (1948: 98); Pursiful (1993: 129); Thusing (1965: 9). Nauck (1960: 204) finds a reference to a baptismal confession in v. 23.

Markus Barth (1951: 473-479),[15] who presents two arguments that ultimately become one. On Barth's reading, Hebrews 7-10 does not encourage establishment of a new cult or priesthood but announces that the death of Christ fulfilled the whole Old Testament system. Anything added to this unique act casts doubt on its sufficiency. Barth, secondly, distinguishes "objective" and "subjective" dimensions of the Old Testament system; the first refers to sacrifices as means of expiation, and the second to rites of sprinkling and washing that applied expiation to individuals. Hebrews 10:22 can be a baptismal text only if these dimensions of the Levitical system are separated, such that Jesus' death fulfills the "objective" aspect while the rites and ceremonies of the church fulfill the "subjective." Hebrews, Barth argues, teaches instead that the cross fulfills and terminates both the objective and subjective.[16] Thus, Barth interprets "washing" as the power of the cross erupting into the church's life, and "body" as the "whole man."

Barth's very Barthian arguments prove too much, undermining a reference to a rite of baptism not only in Hebrews 10 but virtually anywhere in the New Testament. For, on Barth's premises, baptism as an act of repentance seems to cast as much doubt on the sufficiency of the cross as baptism understood as a sacramental application of redemption.[17]

---

[15]Other dissenters are Lang (1951: 167), who argues, woodenly, that if "sprinkling of the heart" is figurative, then "washing of the body" must also be; and Scholer (1991: 130, fns. 1, 4), who makes substantially the same argument as Barth.

[16]"Er bleibt nichts, aber auch gar nichts mehr aus dem alttestamentlichen Kult zu erfüllen oder fortzusetzen. In Christi Tod ist alles, alles ein -für allemal erfüllt" (1951: 477).

[17]Cf. Wedderburn (1987: 65-66), who reckons that an extreme cruxomonism

Contrary to Barth, Hebrews does envision an ecclesiological fulfillment of Old Testament rites and institutions: Sacrifice, specifically, is offered in the church's praise and good works (Heb. 12:28-13:17). Augustine is thus closer to the spirit of Hebrews when he insists that the charity, signs, and rites of the *totus Christus* as much as the historical work of Jesus fulfills the Old Testament. Exegetically, Barth fails to do justice to the language of the text. Hebrews speaks of "pure water," but Barth prefers the more abstract "Waschung" or "Reinigung." For Barth, when the writer says "bodies washed with pure water," he means that what are not really bodies are not really washed by what is not really water.

Though not following Barth, Attridge (1989: 288-289; 1986: 9) muses on what he sees as an abrupt turn in the argument of Hebrews. He describes the transition from first to second covenants as a shift from external and physical to internal and spiritual realities but finds this trajectory surprisingly disrupted by the writer's insistence that the bodily death of Jesus inaugurates the spiritual covenant. Baptism in 10:22 poses similar perplexities: How can a physical and external rite be part of an internal and spiritual covenant? Attridge's surprise, however, arises only because he has imposed categories alien to Hebrews. First and second covenants differ as "flesh" and "conscience," but it is a mistake to transpose this into internal/external, as if the two dualisms were equivalent. The first covenant was not flawed because it depended on bodies but because its cleansing agent was the blood of bulls and goats

---

renders baptism "superfluous as such" and requires one to "de-sacramentalize" or spiritualize the passages that speak of baptism as a saving event.

rather than the blood of a sinless man. As much as the first, the second covenant is concerned with bodies -- with Jesus' bodily self-offering and with the bodily consecration and living sacrifice of His people. Physical and corporate aspects of the Christian life are evident in the following verses (10:24-25), which warn against alienation from the public assembly of worship and good works. Neither Barth nor Attridge, therefore, convincingly undermines the majority opinion that baptism is the ritual that qualifies a people to draw near.

If the washing is baptism, two further questions arise. First, what is the relationship between the baptismal "washing of bodies" and the "sprinkling of the heart and conscience"? Dahl suggests that baptism is "the application of the work of Jesus to the individual" and thus the sprinkling of the heart identifies the "inner significance" of which baptism is the outer rite (1951: 407, fn. 27). Hughes, along similar lines, points to parallels with 1 Peter 3 to show that baptism is more than outward cleansing (Hughes 1977: 412). These responses will suffice until I take up the relation of "inner" and "outer" more theoretically in the chapter 4. Second, the sanctuary Christians enter is a "heavenly" sanctuary (9:24; 10:19), but how can baptism qualify for entry into heaven? Hebrews envisions the church also as the "house" of God (3:6; 10:21), and the contrast of heaven/earth in Hebrews is not so much spatial (up/down) as temporal (Old/New) (Luck 1963: 192-215). Thus, the writer assures his readers that they "have come" to the heavenly Jerusalem in their entry into the New Covenant people (Heb. 12:22).

Finally, what is the source of the imagery? Flemington represents the majority view: "The background of this language is to be found in the Old

Testament passages describing the consecration of priests. They needed to be purified from 'uncleanness' by being sprinkled with sacrificial blood (cf. Exod. 29.20-21; Lev. 8.23, 24, 30), and also to be washed with water" (1948: 98).[18] Details of the text support this conclusion. Christ's blood is definitely the agent for cleansing the heart and conscience. Most of the other uses of ῥαντίζω in Hebrews refer to sprinkling blood (9:19, 21-22; 12:24), and even the reference to the water containing the ashes of the red heifer (9:13) is not an exception, since the heifer's blood was burned and mixed with the water (Num. 19:5). Throughout the letter, the blood of Christ is alone sufficient to purify the συνείδησις (9:9, 14; 10:2). To draw near, one must come under blood and water – a comparatively rare combination in Levitical law but found in the ordination rite (Exod. 29:4, 21; Lev. 8:6, 30).[19] Thus, Hebrews 10:22 describes B with imagery borrowed from O.

This text also proves that "B replaces O." Sprinkled and washed, believers enter through the veil (10:20; διὰ τοῦ καταπετάσματος), a reference to the veil separating the Holy Place from the Most Holy Place (cf. 6:19; 9:3). Some commentators conclude that the Old Testament background is the High Priest's entry to the Most Holy Place on the Day of Atonement (Dunn 1970: 213). Atonement is prominent in the context

---

[18]Bruce (1964: 250, fn 105); Attridge (1989: 288); Dahl (1951: 406); Hughes (1977: 410-411); Pursiful (1993: 84); Scholer (1991: 129); Best (1960: 281); Floor (1971: 77); Moffatt (1924: 144).

[19]Two other rites combine blood and water as cleansing agents: cleansing from skin disease and from corpse defilement (Lev. 14:6-7; Num. 19:5, 9, 17-19). On the connections of the former with ordination, see chapter 4 below.

(e.g., 9:24) and the writer contrasts the restricted access under the Old system to the confident approach of the New. Yet, the Day of Atonement is not the immediate reference in 10:19-22. The High Priest washed before entering the Holy of Holies (Lev. 16:4; cf. Exod. 30:20), but he was sprinkled with blood only at his ordination. Lane suggests (1991: 287) that 10:22 refers to the blood and water of the Sinai covenant (cf. 9:18-22). Though undoubtedly included in the text's allusive web, the Sinai covenant does not strictly fit the bill. Constituted a "royal priesthood" by the sprinkling of blood (Exod. 19:6; 24:1-8), even then Israel was not permitted to touch the mountain, or, later, to enter the tent or approach the veil. One might rescue Lane's interpretation by observing that the writer conflates the Sinai covenant with the priestly covenant (see above, p. 65). This "confusion" underwrites what 10:19-22 implies, that the dual first covenant – priestly and national – no longer exists. All those baptized and sprinkled with the blood of Christ have privileges of access beyond those of Israel's High Priests.[20] Baptism to priesthood is thus a sign of the dissolution of boundaries between priest and people, a point I shall elaborate at length in chapter 5.

For the moment, we conclude that since B is the rite that confers the privilege of access through the veil (one of the set of TP), and since O conferred the same privilege under the Old Testament system by making Ps, then B is now the rite that produces Ps. B plays the same role in the

---

[20]Attridge (1989: 288) and Moffatt (1924: 144) deny that the writer intends to teach the priesthood of believers, but it is difficult to know how he could have made the point more clearly. For the contrary opinion, see Arrington (1977: 84); Dahl (1951: 407); Pursiful (1993: 128, 132-133); Floor (1971: 77); Best (1960: 273-299); Scholer (1991: *passim*); Swetnam (1966: 103).

church that O played in Israel. It follows that baptism fulfills and replaces ordination.

Investiture with Christ, Galatians 3:27

It seems that a reference to the baptismal rite in this passage, which employs the verb βαπτίζω, would be beyond dispute, and most commentators simply assume so. James D.G. Dunn, however, claims that "baptism" is a metaphor for the experience of conversion and incorporation into Christ, which may happen at baptism but is distinct from it.[21] Several of Dunn's arguments for this remarkable conclusion require attention. First, he argues the text is "disrupted" if "clothing with Christ" is metaphorical but "baptism into Christ" refers to a ritual. Whether authors and texts operate at either a literal or figurative level with this kind of rigidity is disputable; even when "baptism into Christ" refers to a ritual, the phrase is crowned with a metaphorical halo, for no one is actually, physically sprinkled with or dipped in or plunged into Christ. Dunn is, in any case, inconsistent, for he argues that the "washing" of Hebrews 10:22 is baptismal, though the same passage mentions an apparently metaphorical sprinkling of the heart (1970: 211-212). Second, Dunn avers that Galatians contrasts the Old Covenant, in which an outward rite established a relation with God, with the New Covenant, where sonship is by faith and the Spirit. Nevertheless, the contrast is not

---

[21]Dunn (1970: 109-113; 1993: 203-204). Bruce (1982: 185) and Fung (1988: 173, fn. 26) dispute Dunn's conclusion.

between "external" and "internal" as such, for the Galatians received the Spirit by hearing and believing the externally preached word (3:2). Dunn's contention that Paul would not have substituted another external rite for circumcision begs the question, for one might argue that this is precisely what Paul did.

For most commentators, the key issues are the source and significance of the clothing imagery (ἐνδύω). Scholars propose several sources, either alone or in combination. A few commentators suggest that it arose from the ancient initiation rite, when the candidate put on a white garment after being baptized naked, but most admit it is unlikely that investiture was part of apostolic initiation.[22] A few link Paul's imagery to the Roman custom of robing a young man at his majority.[23] Betz draws attention to parallels in the mysteries and other ancient religions,[24] but a resort to paganism seems unnecessary given the use of clothing symbolism in the Old Testament and Jewish tradition.[25] Paul himself employed this

---

[22]Longenecker (1990: 156); Beasley-Murray (1973: 148-149); tentatively, Dunn (1993: 204); George (1994: 276, 280).

[23]Dunn (1993: 204) calls this an "older" view, and Bligh (1969: 325) dismisses it. Lenski alludes to the custom but warns against immersion in details (Lenski 1961: 188).

[24]Betz (1979: 187-189, fns. 60-63). Beasley-Murray (1973: 148) concludes that influence from the mysteries is "not impossible," and Bruce (1982: 186) suggests that Paul's readers, though not Paul himself, may have read his imagery in the light of their experience with the mysteries. Bligh (1969: 325); Fung (1988: 172); Grail (1951: 508, fn. 2); and Flemington (1948: 57-58) dismiss the possibility. On the relation of Paul with the mysteries generally, see Wedderburn (1987).

[25]Old Testament writers used clothing as a metaphor for various virtues or states -- righteousness, salvation, shame -- and the passages where the Holy Spirit is said to "clothe" judges and kings (Judg. 6:34; 1 Chr. 12:18; 2 Chr. 6:41, Pss. 35:26;

imagery with some frequency, though normally as an imperative rather than, as in Galatians 3:27, an indicative.[26] In explaining the significance of the clothing image, commentators offer various suggestions: Christ envelops the baptized so they become identified with Him (Ridderbos 1956:148; Fung 1988: 172); or, like actors, Christians take on Christ's appearance (Dunn 1993: 204-205; Beasley-Murray 1973: 147); or being clothed with the Son confers a standing as sons (Burton 1921: 203); or Christ is like a dye that makes all the baptized the same color (Bligh 1969: 234); or baptismal clothing gives a new identity and admits to the life of the new age (Schlier 1962: 173). Behind this putting off/putting on imagery is the Old/New Adam scheme, so that "putting on a new man" implies "new creation."[27]

Assuming that Paul's baptismal theology grows from typological interpretation of the Old Testament, there are several reasons for suspecting the priestly ordination is part of his image-pool.[28] First, the

---

109:29; 132:18; Prov. 31:25; Isa. 61:10; Zech. 3:3-5; Luke 24:49). See Longenecker (1990: 156); Dunn (1993: 204); Mußner (1974: 263); Fung (1988: 172); Bruce (1982: 186); Burton (1921: 204); Betz (1979: 188); Flemington (1948: 57-58); Beasley-Murray (1973: 148); Grail (1951: 508).

[26]Longenecker (1990: 156); Burton (1921: 204); Betz (1979: 189); Grail (1951: 507). Bligh (1969: 325-326) points to the connection of "putting off" and circumcision in Colossians 2:11.

[27]Brinsmead (1982: 147-153); Jervell (1960: 231-232); Beasley-Murray (1973: 148-149), the latter in connection with Colossians 3:9-10. Early Syrian writers envisioned redemptive history as a series of costume changes (Brock 1982: 11-38).

[28]A priestly interpretation of the clothing image is not original. See Prosper of Acquitaine (PL 51, 668B); Cassiodore (PL 70, 950C, 952D); and Peter Lombard (PL 191, 1180C).

High Priest's garments were by far the most important clothes in the Old Testament. Two chapters of Exodus (28; 39) are devoted to them, and no other set of clothes receives anything close to the same attention. Likewise, Israel's main clothing rite occurred at ordination. Anointing was the leading rite for installing kings (e.g., 1 Kgs. 1:39) but investiture made the High Priest (Exod. 28:3-4; 29:5-9; 35:19; 40:12-13; Num. 20:25-28). Several Old Testament texts cited in commentary on Galatians 3:27, furthermore, refer to the priests' garments (2 Chr. 6:41; Pss. 132:9, 16; Zech. 3:1-5; prp. Isa. 61:10). Faced with the crossword puzzle clue, "official with special religious vestments," the first-century Jew would have immediately answered, "the High Priest."

An allusion to priestly investiture fits the context. Paul is discussing the relative status of Jew and Gentile in the church. To say that all wear the same clothes is to say that all have the same religious status -- that all can "stand" in the same place, and this is a notion within the zone of priestly concerns. Sartorial customs of lay Israelites are also relevant. Just as his vestments differentiated the High Priest from other priests and laymen, so every Israelite was distinguished from non-Israelites by the tassel at the corner of his garment (Num. 15:37-41). Hebrew tassels had a blue cord in them, and since ancient dyes worked only on wool, the blue thread was a woolen addition to what would have been a linen garment. Normally, such mixtures were forbidden because of their holiness (Lev. 19:19), so the mixed cloth worked into the common dress of Israel communicated Israel's holy status (Milgrom 1991: 548-549). Paul's statement that Jews and Gentiles now wear the same baptismal garment implies that all the baptized have been incorporated into the holy, priestly

105

people (cf. Wenham 1981: 132-133).

Sonship, inheritance, and the Spirit, among the leading concepts in this section of Galatians, are also connected to priestly concerns.[29] Romans 8 unravels this same knot of issues. In particular, κληρονόμοι θεοῦ in Romans 8:17 is explicated in Galatians 3-4 as inheritance of the Abrahamic promise of the Spirit (Gal. 3:14, 29; 4:5-6). Behind the notion that Christians are "heirs of God" is not only the Old Testament promise of land, but more specifically, promises to the tribe of Levi. Priests and Levites had no portion in the land, but Yahweh promised to be their inheritance (Num. 18:20; Deut. 18:2; Josh. 13:14). Priests were installed as members of Yahweh's house, and the Levites were reckoned "sons," since Yahweh adopted them in place of the firstborn sons redeemed at Passover (Num. 3:40-51; 8:14-19; cf. Exod. 13:11-16). When Paul calls the baptized "sons" who inherit the promised Spirit, he employs language associated with the priestly tribe. As the Levites became "heirs of Yahweh" through a rite that began with an aspersion and included a clothing change (Num. 8:7), so the Galatians became heirs of the Spirit through baptismal investiture. "Heir of God the Spirit" is the Christian conjugation of "priest" and "Levite."

Finally, ancient priests frequently wore the insignia and even the clothing of the gods they served, and Wedderburn suggests that this may provide background to Paul's imagery of "putting on" Christ (1987: 337-339). Consistent with this, Meredith Kline claims that the garments of

---

[29]As background, we can recall here our finding in chapter 2 that priests were installed as members of the house, so that ordination tended toward "adoption."

Israelite priests were sartorial replicas of the glory theophany of Yahweh; the garments of "glory and beauty" were "badges" identifying the King in whose service priests were enlisted (1986: 42-47; Exod. 28:2; see below on 2 Cor. 1:21-22). To be "clothed in Christ" is to be covered with the One who is glory in human flesh (John 1:14; Heb. 1:1-3).[30] "Clothed with Christ" conjugates "robed with garments of glory." Dressed in the glorious vestments of their God, the baptized are prepared to stand to serve in His house.

The last two paragraphs push toward the conclusion that Galatians 3:27 implies that B fulfills and replaces O. Since, under the Old Covenant, "heir of God" was a distinctive privilege of the priestly tribe (one of the set of TP), and since active membership in that tribe came through O and the O-like Levitical cleansing ceremony, then Paul's statement that B makes one an "heir of God" implies that B now does in the church what O did in Israel, that is, it confers TP. Likewise, if being robed in glory is one of the set of TP conferred on the High Priest by O, and if now B robes in *the* Glory, then B has replaced and fulfilled O. Yet, the explicit Old Testament background is the promise to Abraham, so any conclusions about priesthood are inferred rather than explicitly stated.

---

[30]Paul says that baptism clothes with "Christ," the "Anointed One," and Paul was quite aware of the etymological connection of "Christ" and "chrism," as 2 Corinthians 1:21-22 shows (see below). Being clothed with "Christ" thus links with sharing His "chrism," and since the "chrism" was the Holy Spirit, this fits Paul's argument that the baptized are heirs of the Abrahamic promise of the Spirit. Both priests and kings were Old Testament "Christs," yet the combination of "clothing" and "anointing" takes us to the ordination. In Galatians 3:27, clothing and christening imagery attaches to baptism, a water rite. Thus, Galatians 3:27 alludes to the three initial ritual acts of the ordination rite – washing (baptism), anointing (Christ) and investiture (clothing).

Thus, I cannot draw as decisive a conclusion from Galatians 3 as from Hebrews 10. Yet, the clothing imagery used to describe baptism is, in my judgment, more likely drawn from ordination than from any other Old Testament texts or rites. Thus, Galatians 3 sheds light on the New Testament "change of priesthood" (see below, chapter 5).

The Sanctifying Wash, 1 Corinthians 6:11

Beasley-Murray claims that scholars unanimously hold that this text is baptismal, and cites as evidence the parallel with Acts 22:16; the aorist tense of ἀπελούσασθε, ἡγιάσθητε, and ἐδικαιώθητε, which may denote a decisive event at a particular past moment of time; the reference to the "name" of Christ; and the mention of the Spirit, often associated with baptism.[31] Dunn, again, dissents (1970: 120-123). From the catalogue of sins in verses 9-10 he draws the conclusion that the washing must relate to "a cleansing of the heart and conscience." But the sins listed are as much "social" as "spiritual," so a transfer into a community with purified practices, habits, and goals is inseparable from the cleansing of the heart. Dunn also notes that the phrase "name of Jesus" is used with exorcisms and healings, but these are irrelevant since 1 Corinthians 6:11 refers to a *washing* in the "name." It is difficult to avoid the sense that this text refers to baptism.

---

[31]Beasley-Murray (1973: 162-163). See Flemington (1948: 55-56); Robertson and Plummer (1914: 119-120); Moffatt (1938: 66); Grosheide (1953: 141-142); Schrage (1991: 1.433-434); Conzelmann (1975: 107); tentatively, Barrett (1968: 141-143); Meyer (1892-1894: 1.173-174).

Some conclude from verse 11 that baptism "purifies" or "cleanses,"[32] but the text uses ἁγιάζω, and Paul was a sufficiently well-trained Pharisee to know the difference between cleanliness and holiness.[33] Under the Levitical system, one needed no special position or ritual to be "clean" but from this median status, one could move in either of two directions: By a consecrating rite or through contact with a contagious holy object, one became "holy"; alternatively, through sin or contact with contagious unclean persons or things, one became "unclean." To become "holy" was to become Yahweh's property; in a word, to be holy means "you are not your own" (1 Cor. 6:19). In 6:11, it seems best to understand the three verbs not as different moments in the process of salvation but as dimensions of a single event of washing in the name of the Lord Jesus Christ.[34] Baptism thus sets apart the baptized as divine property, as a ἅγιος.[35]

---

[32]Conzelmann (1975: 107); Beasley-Murray (1973: 164); Schrage (1991: 433).

[33]On the distinction of clean or pure (טהר) and holy (קדש), see Nelson (1993: 17-31). Gerstenberger is quite wrong to say that "holy" and "pure" are "synonymous" terms (1996: 129).

[34]Several details support this. First, the three verbs are introduced by the strong adversative ἀλλά; in contrast to the preceding list of sins, they provide a three-dimensional portrait of what the formerly dissolute Corinthians have become. Second, if the verbs are arranged in temporal sequence, we are left with the anomaly of unjustified saints. Third, "sanctify" and "justify" are framed by ἀπολούω and ἐν τῷ ὀνόματι τοῦ κυρίου Ἰησοῦ Χριστοῦ. If the washing is a reference to baptism, then one would expect "name" to follow immediately -- "washed in the name." That the other verbs intervene suggests the following sense: "You received the sanctifying and justifying washing in the name of the Lord Jesus Christ."

[35]A number of commentators recognize this specific sense of "sanctify," and

Few sanctifying rites existed in the Old Testament system and even fewer sanctifying ablutions. Most washings rendered the unclean clean (טהר; Lev. 11:40; 13:6; 14:9; 15:6-7, 10-11, 13, 16-18), but ordination included a bath that was part of a "consecration." Dahl is correct that "even ordinary men in Israel used to 'sanctify' themselves [by washing] before entering into contact with the divine sphere," but this does not undermine a priestly connection (1955: 38, 48, fn. 17). In the texts Dahl cites, lay Israelites consecrated themselves, sometimes with a bath, because the Lord was drawing near to cut covenant, to judge, or to receive sacrifice, that is, because they were going to stand, in quasi-priestly fashion, in the presence of God (Exod. 19:10, 14, 22; Josh. 3:5; 7:13; 1 Sam. 16:5).[36] A sanctifying washing thus sanctifies for standing before God. It may be significant also that Paul uses the aorist, referring to a definitive sanctification, for only the priestly bath was part of a once-for-all consecration. Verses 19-20 also support a priestly reference: The

---

connect it to being enlisted among the "saints." See Barrett (1968: 142); Robertson and Plummer (1914: 120); Moffatt (1938: 66); Grosheide (1953: 141). Fee (1987: 246) says that "sanctify" means being "set apart for holy living." Meyer (1892-1894: 174) rejects the "theocratic" notion that links "sanctification" with membership among the "saints," but holiness in the biblical sense is *defined* theocratically.

[36]Brian Rosner (1996: 250-253) has suggested that Exodus 18 and Deuteronomy 1 lie behind 1 Corinthians 6. In both passages, Moses appoints judges over Israel, just as Paul, a new Moses, suggests in the opening verses of this chapter. Also like Moses, Paul issues ten prohibitions (vv. 9-10; cf. Exod. 20:1-17). If Rosner is correct, a reference to Israel's preparations for Yahweh's coming to Sinai would make sense (v. 11; cf. Exod. 19:10, 14, 22). Just as Israel sanctified themselves by washing their clothes in preparation for the covenant-cutting at Sinai, so Paul reminds his Corinthian readers that they received a sanctifying wash, by which they have been consecrated as a priestly people and temple of the Spirit.

Corinthians are a holy temple of the Spirit, and all who stand to serve the Lord in this temple must be sanctified with the baptismal washing.

The connection between the sanctifying wash (6:11) and the temple of the Spirit (6:19) points to a conclusion developed in later chapters: The sanctified priesthood is now identical, without remainder, to the temple of the Spirit. Yahweh now dwells in His people, invalidating Old Testament distinctions of people and house. This transformation will, of course, have important implications for the meaning of New Testament "housekeeping."

For now, we conclude that 1 Corinthians 6:11 supports the typology of baptismal ordination. The ordination bath, with other actions, "sanctified" Aaron and his sons, consecrating them to stand to serve in the holy place. On my exegesis, Paul claims that baptism sanctifies; since B now accomplishes what O once accomplished, B fulfills O.

Levi's Homage to Adam, Luke 3:21-23

I suggested above that John's baptism derived its form as an initiatory washing administered by a "baptizer" from the Aaronic ordination. My purpose in the following pages, however, is not primarily historical. Instead, I examine how Luke, writing as a member of the church, theologized on the historical event of Jesus' baptism. It is a commonplace of post-World War II discussions that the New Testament understanding of baptism grows out of the baptism of Jesus.[37] Assuming

---

[37]Flemington (1948: 25-32); Cullmann (1950: 9-22); Barth (1951: 56-132); Dunn (1970: 23-37); Beasley-Murray (1973: 45-67); Wainwright (1977: 67-86).

111

this to be the case, if Jesus' baptism inaugurated His priestly ministry, it follows that Christian baptism is also initiation to priesthood.[38]

Priestly Messiah

Several features of Luke's gospel set up an expectation of a priestly protagonist.[39] First, the temple is prominent in the gospel and particularly in the opening chapters (cf. the statistics in Chance 1988: 1-2). Beginning with Gabriel's announcement to Zacharias at the incense altar (1:9), the "infancy narratives" close with Jesus in the temple at twelve (cf. 1:5, 2:1 and 3:1; cf. Chance 1988: 48). While the geographic trajectory of John's history is from temple to wilderness, Jesus begins in the despised province of Galilee and moves toward the temple. Mary conceives Jesus through the "overshadowing" Spirit (1:35), an image borrowed from the descent of the glory upon the Mosaic tabernacle (Exod. 40:34-35; Goulder and Sanderson 1957: 20). Concern with the temple is not confined to the early chapters. Jesus' progression from Galilee to Jerusalem as a child foreshadows His solemn procession to the holy city (cf. Luke 9-19); the boy who astonished the teachers reappears in the temple, clears it, occupies it as teacher, and again all marvel at His authority (19:45-48; Nolland 1989: 40). Ending where it began, the gospel closes with the

---

[38]Ancient Syrian writers claim that John transferred the priesthood to Jesus at His baptism (Brock 1978: 329; 1977: 181; Murray 1975: 179-180).

[39]On these chapters, see Burrows (1940: 1-58); Brown (1993: 235-495); Davis (1982: 215-229); Fuller (1978: 37-52); Goulder and Sanderson (1957: 12-30); Nolland (1989: 17-173); Ruddick (1970: 343-348); Laurentin (1957).

disciples of the Risen and Ascended Lord rejoicing in the Lord's house (24:53).[40]

John's preaching likewise centers on the temple. He urges repentance with the warning that the "axe is already laid at the root of the trees" (Luke 3:9), alluding to Isaiah 10, where Yahweh wielded the axe of Assyria against the barren forest and unfruitful garden Israel had become (Isa. 10:15-19). Harmonizing with this are echoes of Psalm 74:4-7, where the cedar-paneled temple is a forest hammered and smashed by the enemies of Zion. Jesus makes it clear that the tree is the temple (21:6) and that the axe is Rome (21:20-24; cf. 13:34-35; 19:43-44; cf. Wright 1996). On his way to the cross, Jesus employs John's tree imagery to warn the daughters of Jerusalem of woes to come (23:28-31). John also warns that the Messiah will clear the threshing floor by separating wheat and chaff (3:17), and, significantly, Solomon built the temple upon the site of a threshing floor (2 Sam. 24:18-25; 2 Chr. 3:1). Jesus therefore clears the "threshing floor" by "cleansing" the temple.

If the temple is dominant, so is priesthood. Alone among the gospels, Luke informs us of John's descent from a son and daughter of Aaron.[41] Gabriel's prophecy that John will "turn back many of the sons

---

[40]Allusions to Daniel in the annunciation scenes of Luke 1 also highlight the sanctuary. Gabriel appeared to Daniel to deliver the prophecy of the "seventy weeks," which included the threat that the "people of the prince who is to come will destroy the city and the sanctuary" (Dan. 9:24-27). When Gabriel appears to Zecharias, it is to announce the fulfillment of the "seventy weeks of years" (see Laurentin 1957: 43-63; Nolland 1989: 29).

[41]This has led Laurentin to suggest that John is being presented as the "priestly Messiah" mentioned in Qumran literature and the Testament of Levi. For rebuttals to this view, see Wink (1968: 72-79) and Oliver (1964: 220-221). On the priestly messiah theme, see also Böhlemann (1997: 216-222, 228-230).

of Israel to the Lord their God" (1:16-17) quotes from Malachi, where, condemning the priests for their failure to instruct the people, the prophet said that Levi "turned many back from iniquity" through the instruction of his mouth (2:6-7). The ministry of the "messenger" of Malachi 3:1 is also modeled on Levi's, and the Elijah figure of Malachi 4:5-6 (Heb. 3:23-24) also teaches to turn hearts. John is the new Levi as well as the new Elijah who prepares the way for the Lord's fiery purification of the temple (Laurentin 1957:56-57; Wink 1968: 75-76).[42]

That Luke presents Jesus as John's younger twin is underlined by similarities between the announcement scenes to Zacharias and Mary (1:5-38), their "songs" (1:46-55; 67-79), the parallel stories of circumcision and naming (1:59-63; 2:21), and the application of "growth in wisdom and stature" to both boys (1:80; 2:40, 52). When John protests that he merely prepares for One greater than he, these parallels are percolating in the background. To be sure, the comparison is within the sphere of prophetic ministry: John is the "voice" and new Elijah, and Jesus is the prophet like Elisha and Moses (Luke 4:25-27; but cf. Wink 1968: 42-44). In Luke, however, John's priesthood has been so unrelentingly presented that any

---

[42]In a fascinating 1957 article, M.D. Goulder and M.L. Sanderson observe that Luke 1-2 is working not only from Malachi but also Zechariah. In the LXX of Zechariah 3:8, Yahweh tells Joshua the High Priest He is going to bring His servant the ἀνατολή, apparently a reference to a Davidic king. John's father Zecharias applies the same title to another "Joshua" (Luke 1:78), hinting that Jesus is both the Davidic Branch and the new High Priest. Significantly, the earlier Joshua is given a crown in Zechariah 6:11, and this is followed by a prophecy of a "branch" who will build the temple and take a seat as a "priest on His throne" (6:13). Luke's allusions to Zechariah thus point to Jesus' role as Melchizedekan priest-king.

comparison of John and Jesus must also be in respect of priesthood. Luke's allusions to Malachi 2-3 belong to the same set of concerns, for Jesus like John is a teacher of Israel (Luke 2:41-51; 19:47-48; 21:37-38). By his preaching and at the baptism, John, a priest of the order of Aaron and Zadok, pays homage to Jesus, as Levi did to Melchizedek (Luke 3:16; cf. Heb. 7:4-10).[43]

Interlaced with these parallels are numerous borrowings from the early life of Samuel (Burrows 1940: 1-34). Zacharias, like Elkanah in 1 Samuel, is a childless priest (cf. 1 Chr. 6:16-30) given a son in old age. Mary's and Zacharias's prophetic poems draw heavily on Hannah's Old Testament "Magnificat" (1 Sam. 2:1-10; Luke 1:46-55, 67-79). "Grew in wisdom and strength" (Luke 1:80; 2:40, 52) is drawn from 1 Samuel 2:26 and 3:19, and the appearance of young Jesus in the temple recalls Samuel's early life in service to Eli. God's purpose in Samuel was to cut the corrupt line of Eli, Hophni, and Phinehas, and raise up "a faithful priest who will do according to what is in My heart and in My soul" (1 Sam. 2:35). As Samuel catalyzed the transfer of priestly privilege, so the appearance of John and Jesus signals a climatic change of priesthood accomplished by One greater than Samuel.

Baptized to Priesthood

These considerations illuminate several details of Luke's account of

---

[43]It is neither necessary nor desirable to resort, as Laurentin (1957: 112-116) does (following patristic commentators), to speculations about Mary's Levitical lineage to establish that Luke presents Jesus as a priestly figure. See Wink (1968: 79) and Oliver (1964: 220-221).

Jesus' baptism. First, why did Jesus accept a baptism "of repentance for the forgiveness of sins" (Luke 3:3)? Theologians have often answered, correctly it seems, by saying that Jesus' baptism identified Him with Israel as her sin-bearing Substitute; Jesus was baptized "when all the people were being baptized" (3:21). This fits snugly with a priestly interpretation, for the High Priest was the Old Covenant sin-bearer. Aaron wore a crown on his turban to bear the iniquity of Israel (Exod. 28:36-38), and on the Day of Atonement Aaron transferred the sins and uncleanness of Israel to the scapegoat (Lev. 16; cf. Kiuchi 1987). Like Aaron, Jesus was "baptized" into substitutionary ministry, not only to offer but to be a sacrifice, His baptism at Jordan climaxing in His baptism in blood at Calvary (Luke 12:50).[44]

Second, after His baptism Jesus "began" His ministry, being "about thirty years of age" (Luke 3:23; but cf. Ogg 1959: 291-293). Levites, and perhaps priests, entered ministry at the same age (Num. 4:3, 23, 30, 35, 39, 43). Joseph and David were also raised to high political "standing" at thirty (Gen. 41:46; 2 Sam. 5:4), and Luke may allude to the royal typology, for Jesus is David's Son, endowed, like David, with the Spirit (cf. 1 Sam. 16:13). Immediately after the baptism, however, Luke provides a genealogy (Luke 3:23-38), and unlike the genealogy of Matthew 1, Luke's

---

[44]Luke, unlike Matthew and Mark, places his account of the baptism immediately after John's arrest and imprisonment (3:20). This is not, as G.O. Williams (1944: 34) suggests, an effort to diminish John's importance by putting him out of the way before Jesus' ministry begins; rather, given the parallels of John and Jesus, it hints that Jesus faces a similar future. By His baptism, He embarks on a pilgrimage that, like John's, ends in arrest and martyrdom. Cf. Stegner (1985: 36-46), who examines links between the baptism and the "sacrifice" of Isaac in Genesis 22.

does not trace Jesus' descent through Solomon and other Davidic kings, but through the collateral line of Nathan (v. 31). David's sons, perhaps including Nathan, were "priests" (2 Sam. 8:18), and "Nathan's" son Zabud served Solomon as "priest" (1 Kgs. 4:5), though one cannot be certain that the "Nathan" in these texts was David's son. If it is not a royal genealogy, what is it doing here? Generally, we can observe that genealogies were particularly important for priestly houses. To qualify for service, Israel's priests had to prove descent from Aaron, and later from Zadok (Ezra 2:61-63).[45] Luke's genealogy contains tantalizing hints that it establishes Jesus' priestly credentials.[46] Contrary to expectation, Jesus is *not* a descendant of Levi but of Judah. Like Hebrews, Luke shows that this faithful Priest is from an order older than that of Aaron, yet Luke

---

[45]The genealogies of the Pentateuch end with the genealogy of Aaron (Exod. 6:14-27). Thus, the genealogy of the Pentateuch runs from Adam to Aaron, while Luke's runs (chiastically) from the Melchizedekan priest, Jesus, back to Adam. I owe this observation to James B. Jordan, but I have unfortunately lost the reference. A number of scholars observe that genealogies were particularly important among priestly families: Fitzmyer (1981-1985: 1.490); Bovon (1991: 181); Goulder (1989: 1.289); cf. Hood (1961: 1-16).

[46]Goulder (1989: 1.287) and Wink (1968: 76-77) point out the number of names in the genealogy associated with priesthood: Eli, Levi, Melchi (Goulder suggests a link with Melchizedek), Matthathias. Burrows (1940: 27 fn.1) claims that the church fathers saw Luke's genealogy through Nathan as an indication of the sacerdotal ministry of Jesus, though he provides no citations. Johnson (1988: 240-252) argues from a Jewish tradition identifying David's son Nathan with the prophet Nathan that Luke intends to highlight Jesus' prophetic role. The evidence he assembles is intriguing, and is supported biblically by the fact that the relation of prophet and apprentice is sometimes described as father-son (2 Kgs. 2:9, 12; cf. 2:3, 7; 4:1, 38). Yet, prophetic office was not literally passed from father to son, and therefore genealogical connection to a prophet would be irrelevant.

presses the case even further: Jesus is Priest after the order of Adam (Luke 3:38).

To attack from another angle: I am arguing that "Son of God," applied both to Adam and Jesus in Luke 3, is a priestly title. In some texts, "son" is royal (see 2 Sam. 7:14; Ps. 2:6-7), and, given the emphasis on Jesus' Davidic ancestry in Luke 1-2, it surely carries that resonance here. Yet the Bible links priest and son as well. According to some Jewish literature, Adam was a priest because he was "first born of the world" (Scroggs 1966: 43-44). As noted above, the Levites, who served in semi-priestly capacity, replaced the redeemed firstborn sons of Israel (Num. 3:40-51). In chapter 2, I argued that by ordination Aaron and his sons became members of Yahweh's household, adopted "sons." Hebrews 4:14 identifies the new High Priest as "Jesus the Son of God," and Hebrews 5:5 reads Psalm 2:7 ("Thou art my Son"), alluded to by the voice from heaven (Luke 3:22), as a prophecy of Jesus' glorification as High Priest. So, "Son of God" possibly has a priestly timbre.

Examination of the theme of Jesus' sonship in Luke 2:41-51 strengthens the plausibility of this interpretation. When Mary and Joseph find Jesus after a three-day search, Mary claims parental high ground, "Your *father* and I have been anxiously looking for You" (2:48). Jesus' surprised answer reminds them of His transcendent Sonship that relativizes even the closest familial loyalties: "Did you not know that I had to be ἐν τοῖς τοῦ πατρός μου" (2:49). Whether one fills the ellipsis of this enigmatic question with "in my Father's house" or "about my Father's things," Jesus' unique Sonship is associated with teaching in the house of God. Structurally, Jesus' appearance in the temple at twelve is paired with

118

the "presentation" (παραστῆσαι) scene in Luke 2:22-38. This passage is full of difficulties: Under Levitical law, Mary alone was unclean, yet Luke speaks of "*their* purification" (v. 22); the law requires redemption of the firstborn son *from* service rather than presentation *for* service (Exod. 13:11-13); and verse 23 differs from Exodus 13:2, 12, commonly cited as its source. Without resolving all the problems, Burrows argues that the "presentation" fulfills Numbers 8:14-19, where Yahweh appoints the Levites to assist Aaron in tabernacle ministry. Not being a Levite, Jesus was in actual ritual fact "redeemed," but Luke interprets this "redemption" theologically and typologically as the fulfillment of Levitical consecration to household service. In the very next scene, Jesus is found teaching in the house of His Father (Burrows 1940: 17-19; Laurentin 1957: 114-117). Jesus is thus dedicated as "firstborn son" and "Levite." When the Father announces that He is the "Son," these Levitical overtones of the title are still heavy in the air.

Parallels between the transfiguration and the baptism are also relevant. In both, Jesus is declared the "Son," and the voice at the transfiguration urges the disciples to "hear Him" (9:35): Jesus is the *teaching* Son. Other details of the transfiguration have priestly connotations: The event occurs on the "eighth day," which was the beginning of Aaron's ministry (Lev. 9:1; Luke 9:28); Jesus' clothing is transformed into garments of flashing glory like those worn by the High Priest (Luke 9:29); glory surrounds Jesus (Luke 9:31, 32); Peter wants to build "tabernacles" (Luke 9:33); and Moses and Elijah disappear after a cloud overshadows the mountain (Luke 9:34; cf. Exod. 40:34-38). Shortly after, Jesus begins His march to Jerusalem, where He will cleanse the

119

temple, begin to teach, and eventually offer His once-for-all sacrifice (Luke 9:51; cf. v. 31). The transfiguration publishes the truth of the baptism: Jesus has been, and will be, glorified as High Priest over the house.

Luke mentions John's baptism for the last time in 20:1-8. Challenging Jesus, the priests demand, "Tell us by what authority You are doing these things, or who is the one who gave you this authority?" (20:2). Ταῦτα are Jesus' recent activities in the temple, so that the question contests His ἐξουσία in the house of the Lord; the conflict is about rival claims to priesthood. Typically, Jesus answers by asking the scribes and priests to pass judgment on John's baptism. Some have interpreted this response as a "divine red herring," but it perfectly suits the situation, *if* we see that Jesus' baptism, with the gift of the Spirit and authorization by the heavenly voice, conferred authority to do precisely ταῦτα. John's baptism endowed Jesus the Son with ἐξουσία to inspect and cleanse, and to sit in the seat of the teaching priest.

Christian baptism, formed on the model of Jesus', similarly inducts the baptized into household service. This does not mean that the baptisms of the Head and of the body have precisely the same significance; only Jesus could call on John's baptism as testimony to His supreme authority in the temple. With the other passages we have examined, however, Luke shows that the typology of baptismal induction to priesthood was a living paradigm in the imagination of the early church.

Christs Christened Into Christ, 2 Corinthians 1:21-22

Between Paul's first and second letters to the Corinthians, his apostolic standing had come under attack from "false apostles" who, though disguised as angels of light, were in reality "servants of Satan" (2 Cor. 11:13-15). Paul, a faithful Adamic guardian, intervened to protect the betrothed bride from Satanic attack (11:1-4), and this involved a defense of his own status as an apostle, for if Paul's apostleship was in doubt, so was his gospel. His opponents charged that he operated according to the flesh rather than the Spirit (1:12, 17; 10:2), and put into evidence his apparent vacillation concerning travel plans, which they interpreted as a sign of fundamental unreliability (1:15-16). Underlying this charge was the assumption that life and message must be consistent: If Paul's Yes in travel plans was not Yes, could anyone trust his gospel? Far from dismissing the charge as trivial, Paul accepted the criterion by which they were judging him: Hence, "our word to you is not Yes and No" (1:18) refers both to his travel plans and to the gospel he preached at Corinth.

In the letter, Paul's defense comes in several stages. First, he insists that his message is an unequivocal Yes because the content is Christ, in whom God affirms all His promises (1:19-20). In 1:21-22 he reminds the Corinthians that his stability is not a personal achievement but ensured by God (Hughes 1962: 39). Paul's use of "us" and "you" in these verses is significant. Throughout the first chapter, he contrasts the experience of the apostles to that of the Corinthians (1:6-7, 10-11, 12), but in 1:21-22 he mentions a common establishment in Christ through "anointing,"

"sealing," and the "gift of the Spirit" (χρίσας, σφραγισάμενος, δούς). [47]
By associating himself with the Corinthians, he is saying, "I have received
the gift of the Spirit as surely and in the same way as you."[48] Finally, Paul
tells the Corinthians he decided to change plans not out of fleshly self-
interest but out of compassion, to avoid another painful visit (v. 23; 2:1).
His "No," as much as his "Yes," affirms his pastoral concern for the
Corinthian church (Hafemann 1989: 332).

Unlike Paul, New Testament scholars equivocate when asked if this
is a baptismal passage, and I shall do the same.[49] Several details support a
Yes. The participles are in the aorist; εἰς Χριστόν may refer to baptismal

---

[47]Against Martin (1986: 28), who suggests that the primary reference is to Paul's
apostolic charisma, Thrall (1994: 1.154) argues that ἡμᾶς σὺν ὑμῖν must be read
not only with βεβαιῶν but also with the following participles. If Paul is speaking
of a specifically apostolic anointing, he must also be referring to a specifically
apostolic reception of the ἀρραβῶνα of the Spirit, which is highly unlikely.
Hafemann recognizes that the Corinthians are all sealed with the Spirit, but
interprets verses 21-22 as part of Paul's defense of his apostolic role as mediator
of the Spirit (1995: 96-97, 149). See also Bultmann (1985: 42) and Plummer
(1915: 39).

[48]There is also an *ad hominem* element here, for by giving his reliability and that of
the Corinthians the same basis, he turns their charges back on them (Thrall 1994:
1.152).

[49]Many scholars who do not see a direct baptismal reference admit that there may
be an allusion to it. For more negative evaluations, see Webb (1993: 109); Martin
(1986: 27-28; though cf. 1988: 119); Furnish (1984: 148); Barrett (1973: 148);
Delling (1963/4: 107); Fee (1994: 295, 862); Dunn (1970: 131-134). Positive
answers come from Allo (1956: 29-30), who follows Lietzmann in interpreting the
"unction" as baptism and the "sealing with the Spirit" as confirmation, and
Dinkler (1962: 173-191), who speaks of an anointing with water, as well as de la
Potterie (1959: 112-29); Flemington (1948: 67); Lampe (1951: 3-7); Beasley-
Murray (1973: 171-177).

incorporation into Christ; both Βεβαιόω and ἀρραβών concern guarantees in commercial transactions and sales of property, and thus are appropriate terms to describe the baptismal transfer to ownership by the Lord Jesus; the giving of the Spirit is frequently (though not invariably) linked with baptism (Matt. 3:13-17; Acts 2:38; 1 Cor. 12:12-13); and σφραγίζω ("seal") referred to circumcision both in rabbinic writings and the New Testament (Rom. 4:11) and to baptism in postapostolic literature.[50] None of these arguments is absolutely compelling; unlike the passages discussed above, this one does not refer to washing or water. Even if baptism is not immediately in view, however, it is legitimate to integrate this passage into a biblical theology of initiation. Its reference to sharing the chrism of Christ assumes the reality of union with Christ, established by baptism (Rom. 6). Though Paul may not have called baptism an "anointing" or "sealing," baptism (at least) symbolizes the union of which anointing and sealing are aspects. Thus, these verses give us warrant to elaborate baptismal theology in the light of these metaphors. Is this a baptismal passage? I assume neither Yes nor No; but, in very unPauline fashion, Yes *and* No.

Anointed Priests

Rites of anointing were not part of apostolic initiation (Furnish 1984: 137), so χρίσας does not reflect the *lex orandi*. Normally commentators interpret the anointing in the light of Acts 10:38, which describes Jesus'

---

[50]For Jewish evidence, see Thrall (1.157). For patristic citations, see Flemington (1948: 66-67); Lampe (1951: *passim*); Bultmann (1985: 42).

reception of the Holy Spirit as an unction. On this interpretation, the Corinthians are anointed because, like Jesus and with Him, they have been "christened" by the Spirit.[51] Yet this does not explain why Paul should describe the gift of the Spirit as an "anointing." Here, I am interested less in the *referent* of χρίσας than in the typological horizon of the metaphor. In the LXX, χρίω is used most often with reference to royal anointing, which was *the* rite of installation of kings and which sometimes involved reception of the Spirit (1 Sam. 10:1, 10; 16:13; 1 Kgs. 1:39). To say that Christians are anointed, then, means that by the Spirit they share in the rule of David's greater Son.[52]

Several considerations raise the possibility that Paul may also be alluding to priestly anointing.[53] Jewish messianic speculation included

---

[51]Thrall (1994: 1.154); Hafemann (1995: 96-97); Webb (1993: 109); Martin (1986: 28); Furnish (1984: 137).

[52]Margaret E. Thrall provides a typologically sensitive interpretation that denies direct reference to baptism but does justice to the quasi-baptismal terminology. In the Old Testament, anointing was consecration to high office, whether prophet, priest, or king. Thrall rejects as overloaded Chrysostom's interpretation of the anointing as consecration of prophets, priests and kings, but she admits that the verb may refer to incorporation into the community over which the Anointed One is King, and that the anointing promises a share in His eschatological reign. Though she denies that "χρίσας is merely a symbol for baptism," she claims that "the moment of this 'anointing' to (future) royal privileges will of course be baptism, since it is at this point that their attachment to the messianic community begins." Likewise, Paul does not here call baptism a "seal," yet baptism is the occasion of sealing (1994: 1.154-156).

[53]Chrysostom and Eusebius both connect the Christian anointing with induction to prophetic, priestly, and royal status (cited in Hughes 1962: 40; Thrall 1994: 1.154). Ancient Syrian tradition saw the Spirit as the witness of Jesus' priesthood (Murray 1975: 179). Plummer cites Neander's comment on the passage: "Es ist dies die Weihe des allgemeinen Priesterthums" (1915: 39).

predictions of a priestly as well as a royal Messiah (cf. Ps. 110).[54] At
Qumran, the messianic community was a community of priests. Thus, in
the first century setting "Christ" could bring into play either priestly or
royal connotations or both. After the Babylonian exile, however, the
responsibilities of both prophet and king devolved on Israel's priests.
High Priests were civil leaders, and John reflects the belief that they also
had prophetic powers (John 11:51). To be sure, Jews of the first century
expected a Davidic Messiah, but the most immediately available
"Anointed One" was the High Priest. Finally, Davidic anointing was
reserved for the king alone, but Paul refers to a communal anointing, and
all priests were anointed (Exod. 28:41). Paul's pun on Χρίστος / χρίω
may pick up the symbolism of Psalm 133, where unity among brothers
comes by sharing in the chrism of Aaron.[55]

An examination of links with other sections of 2 Corinthians suggests
a Levitical background to Paul's discussion. 1:22 is the first reference to
the Holy Spirit in an epistle that very much highlights His role in the New
Covenant (Belleville 1996: 281-304). The Spirit is the ἀρραβών, used in
commercial Greek for a "down payment" and in the LXX for a "pledge"
(cf. Gen. 38:17). Crystallizing the already-not yet of New Testament
eschatology, the word emphasizes both the present bestowal of a gift and

---

[54]See Böhlemann (1997: 216-222, 228-230); Wink (1968: 72-79).

[55]The only other New Testament passage that describes a Christian anointing, 1
John 2:20, 27, uses the word χρίσμα, which is never used in royal texts in the
LXX, but several times of the anointing of priests, the tabernacle, and its utensils
(cf. Exod. 29:7; 30:25; 40:9, 15). Though Paul does not use this word, he is
evidently referring to the reality described in 1 John 2, and the two passages can
be brought together.

that the gift is a pledge of an eschatological inheritance.[56]   Ἀρραβών
recurs in 5:5, where the Spirit is the first installment of an inheritance that
Paul calls, with marvelous mixture of metaphors, a heavenly building that
clothes the believer.[57]

Debate on 2 Corinthians 5:1-10 has revolved around determining the
referent of Paul's metaphors: Is the heavenly house the resurrection body
or does it refer to the "intermediate state" between death and the general
resurrection? Reconstructions of the development of Paul's eschatology
also rely heavily on this passage.[58]   Questions such as these are not
theologically uninteresting, but I do not wish to extract the referent from
"below" or "behind" the text but to luxuriate in the space created by the
dizzying interplay among texts. Whatever it is, I want to know why Paul
calls it a "tent" or "house," and how Paul arrived at the idea that a house
might "clothe" believers? Exploring this question would, I think, meet
with Paul's approval. Paul did not develop his eschatology in "abstract"
systematic terms, and then seek out decorative imagery. Instead, Paul's
thought moves forward by types, and he often seems to throw a handful
of metaphors onto the page to see what chemical reactions occur. Yet
Paul's method is not arbitrary, since the symbolic perichoresis is
circulating already in the Old Testament Scriptures that were Paul's

---

[56]See Belleville (1996: 285-287); Fee (1994: 293); Kerr (1988: 92-97); Lillie (1977: 64-65).

[57]Belleville (1996: 283-287) and Webb (1993: 108) discuss the links between these two passages.

[58]Cassidy (1971: 210-217); Ellis (1960: 211-224); Harris (1971: 32-57); Hettlinger (1957: 174-194); Lincoln (1981: 59-71); Lillie (1977: 59-70).

primary locus of theological reflection. For Paul, metaphors of tent, building, and clothing are not husks that enclose the literal and important theological kernel but are themselves theologically significant. At least, the imagery provides clues to the Old Testament realities that Paul is conjugating.

Old Testament texts concerning the tabernacle, High Priestly vestments, and ordination form part of the "text pool" into which Paul dives. "Clothed with a house" is perfectly coherent Levitical imagery, for the High Priest was virtually clothed in tabernacle curtains (Kline 1986: 35-47). Thus, one clothed in a tent is both a priest and a human tabernacle (cf. John 1:14). Paul's desire for a solid and eternal building-house to replace his present tent-house recalls the historical transition recorded in 1-2 Samuel, which begins with the ruin of the Shiloh tabernacle (1 Sam. 1-4) and ends with David's purchase of the threshing floor on which Solomon would build the temple (2 Sam. 24; 2 Chr. 3:1; cf. Jordan 1988: 221-237).[59] Paul hopes to wear an οἰκοδομή, a permanent temple garment rather than continuing in the earthen vessel of a tabernacle existence.[60]

---

[59]That the "building" for which Paul groans is a temple is suggested by its contrast with σκηνή, which alludes to the Mosaic tabernacle, and by the term ἀχειροποίητον, used elsewhere to describe the new temple Jesus builds (Mark 14:58; cf. Heb. 9:11).

[60]On my interpretation of the passage, σκηκή does not describe mortal life in a generic way, but the pre-eschatological existence of the believer. Mortal life as such, the Adamic existence of those who are not clothed in the chrism of Christ, is not "tent" but "nakedness." William Lillie suggests that the "clothing" metaphor in 2 Corinthians 5 is baptismal, analogous to Galatians 3:27. Thus, Paul is describing Christian existence as a "series of changes of garments, beginning with the putting on of Christ at baptism, occurring as a condition of each step in

Following Paul's thought from 2 Corinthians 4 to 5 makes clear that the heavenly house for which Paul yearns is equivalent to the glory into which believers are transformed. Paul believes the affliction he endures in apostolic ministry will produce an αἰώνιον βάρος δόξης (4:17), which is one of the unseen things on which Paul concentrates his affections (4:18). Immediately he expresses his hope for a building that, like the "weight of glory," is "eternal" and, being in the heavens, presently "unseen" (5:1). Affliction is producing the glorious temple-clothing that Paul desires; the δόξα is weighty because it is an οἰκία. Thus, to the lively stew of tent, house, and clothing is added a dash of "glory." Again, Old Testament texts on tabernacle and priesthood provide Paul's recipe, for the sanctuary and priestly vestments were architectural and sartorial replications of the glory theophany at Sinai (Kline 1986: 35-47; cf. Jordan 1988: 41-51) -- hence "garments of glory and beauty" (Exod. 28:2). Though now endowed as a priest with a tent-like glory, through suffering ministry Paul will be progressively transformed into a house-like glory.[61]

We are now able to assess the linkage of 1:21-22 and 5:1-5, and the implications for "anointing." By incorporation into Christ, believers are chrismated by the ἀρραβών of the Spirit, and 5:1-5 specifies that the Spirit

moral and spiritual progress. . . , and culminating in God's provision of the heavenly body" (1977: 68). Thus, if there is a baptismal reference here, it links specifically to the clothing with a σκηνή, for the investiture with the οἰκοδομή is a matter of longing rather than present possession (v. 2).

[61]Pate (1991: *passim*) has argued that the deep background of 2 Corinthians 5 is found in Paul's Adamic Christology. I would add that Paul's language indicates that the Adamic glory being restored is the glory of Adamic priesthood, anticipated in Aaron.

is an ἀρραβών of the heavenly house-garment, which, as σκηνή, now clothes the believer with an initial gift of glory. If 1:21-22 is a baptismal text, it suggests that the gift of the Spirit in baptism is an initial investiture with priestly tent-garments, and places the baptized on the pathway of suffering transfiguration that leads to full investiture with eschatological house-glory. Even if 1:21-22 is not a baptismal text, baptism signifies the anointing of the Spirit, and thus points to investiture with the priestly tent and promises a future house.

Removing the Veil

Paul's longing for the heavenly house is also linked to his discussion of the New Covenant in 2 Corinthians 3.[62] As Scot Hafemann (1995) has argued, this chapter continues Paul's defense of his apostolic ministry. Paul's question ρὸς ταῦτα τίς ἱκανός (2:16) alludes to Moses' words in the LXX of Exodus 4:10, and Paul's answer is that, by grace, he is sufficient (3:5; Hafemann 1995: 43). Chapter 3 expands the parallels of Paul and Moses, but a marked contrast emerges in relation to glory and Spirit, revolving around the image of the "veil" (κάλυμμα). Because of their hardness of heart, the Israelites were unable to gaze intently on Yahweh's glory in the face of Moses, and he therefore had to veil his face (3:14). Since it resulted from hardness of heart, Moses' veil was, symbolically, "on the heart" (v. 15). As minister of the New Covenant, however, Paul mediates the Spirit who, fulfilling the promises of Jeremiah

---

[62]On this chapter, see especially Hafemann (1995) and Stockhausen (1989). Webb (1993: 109) links 1:21-22 with chapter 3.

31 and Ezekiel 36, exchanges stony hearts for hearts of flesh (Hafemann 1995: 372, 380). With hearts made new by the Spirit and the veil removed, believers can gaze with unveiled faces upon the glory and be transfigured progressively into its image (3:18). Structurally and theologically, the veil of Moses' face parallels the veil separating the Holy Place from the Most Holy Place (though different words for "veil" are used both in Hebrew and in the LXX). In both cases, the veil separates Israel from glory; in both cases, the separation is due to sin; in both cases, there is a promising exception, with Moses ascending into the cloud and the High Priest entering annually before the Lord. If the Spirit of the New Covenant removes the veil that separated the hardhearted from the glory of Moses' face, He also, in the same movement, removes the veil that separated the people from the glorious throne room of Yahweh's house.

Again, 1:22 reaches forward to chapter 3. The Spirit who anoints the church as ἀρραβών removes the veil from the heart and enables an unveiled *visio gloriae* that transfigures from glorious tent to glorious house. If 1:21-22 is baptismal, it suggests, like Hebrews 10:19-22, that the baptized are priests and beyond priests, welcomed into the inner chambers where only High Priests once dared enter. Exposure to glory is no longer limited to office-bearers: ἡμεῖς πάντες gaze intently at the glory (3:18). Even if the text is not baptismal, baptism symbolizes the removal of the veil and thus the destruction of Israel's holiness system.

In 2 Corinthians, anointing with the Spirit (possibly in connection with baptism) links, through a theology of glory, to a theology of priesthood. "Theology of glory" has a naively triumphalist sense, however, has nothing to do with Paul, for his most elaborate development

130

of a theology of glory occurs in the same letter as his most detailed inventory of apostolic affliction. Faced with this tension, one is tempted to privatize the glory, and Paul seems to do this with his references to treasure in earthen vessels and the inner/outer man language of 4:16. Overall, however, Paul's theology is more paradoxical, for through his preaching -- his public, visible, external proclamation in the midst of affliction -- the Spirit removes the veil and shines the light of the glorious gospel on those who believe (4:1-6). Paul bears the death of Jesus within his body, but the life of Jesus, which is inseparable from glory, is manifest in his mortal flesh (cf. 4:7, 10-11). As for John, so for Paul: The cross is the glorification of the Son of Man and of all who serve Him. Union with the Anointed One that confers the ἀρραβών of priestly glory simultaneously consecrates the Christian as a living sacrifice who is swallowed up in glory precisely as he is delivered up to daily death for Jesus' sake. For Paul, the glory that shimmers from behind the veil, the glory into whose glowing image the believer is translated, is thoroughly cruciform.

Conclusion

Both the weaker and stronger formulation of the typology are warranted by the New Testament. From Hebrews 10:19-22 and 1 Corinthians 6:11, I argued that since B now does what O did in Israel, B fulfills and replaces O. The other texts support the weaker thesis that B is described in terms reminiscent of O. Overall, the combination of evidence is sufficient to establish that the New Testament practice and

131

theology of baptism were founded, *inter alia*, on priestly ordination. Moreover, some wider implications of this typology have emerged. This brings us to the threshold of seeing how baptism is the "beginning of the gospel." Before we step through that door, however, we will spend the next chapter wandering through adjoining rooms cluttered with the dusty scholastic questions of baptismal liturgy and theology. Perhaps we can discover something to hold our interest.

CHAPTER FOUR

Baptismal Ordination as Ritual Poesis

Sacramental theology has always proceeded by analogy, by reflection on how the sacraments are "like" and "unlike" a philosophical concept, a cultural institution, a natural phenomenon, or some combination of these. For Thomas, sacraments are "instrumental causes," so that God's relationship to them is like that of a carpenter to his tools. Thomas takes this to be a sufficiently close analogy to draw substantive theological conclusions. An instrumental cause, he argues, does not act *per virtutem suae formae* but *per motum quo movetur a principali agenti*, yet instrumental causes act in a way proper to their form. Though cutting is proper to a saw, therefore, a bed does not resemble the saw used in its construction but the pattern in the mind of the principal agent, the carpenter. Water, similarly, by its *propriam virtutem* cleanses the body, but baptism washes the soul as an *instrumentum virtutis divinae* (*ST* 3a, 62, 1).

Illuminating as Thomas's comments are, his choice of analogies implicitly separates technical *quaestiones* from the typological *lectio*, a method that, by my argument, betrays "semi-Marcionite" assumptions (above, chapter 1). In this chapter, I argue that baptism is more similar to priestly ordination than to a hammer. Working from this sensible premise, I hope to show that biblical typologies are rich and elastic enough to address, sometimes in unexpectedly contemporary ways, even the most esoteric of scholastic *quaestiones*. There is no need to supplement a sacramental typology with a sacramental ontology, for under intense interrogation the typology will divulge an implicit ontology.

What I attempt is scarcely original. Theologians have frequently answered questions in sacramental liturgy and theology through Augustinian "conjugations" of Old Testament rites and events. Thus, from the Pauline analogy of circumcision and baptism (Col. 2:11-12), they have inferred that infants should be baptized, that baptism is a "seal" (Rom. 4:11), that it signifies the fulfillment of the promises to Abraham, and that it incorporates into the new Israel. Discontinuities also emerge: The Council of Carthage (254) determined that the church need not baptize infants on the eighth day (cf. Cyprian 1964: 216-219), and no one to my knowledge has suggested limiting baptism to males. Similarly, Eucharistic theology and liturgy have drawn inspiration from Old Testament sacrifices and meals. Remnants of semi-Marcionite sacramental theology, however, have often created dissonance; thus, as we saw in chapter 1, paedobaptists "spiritualize" the promises sealed by circumcision to bring them into accord with the supposedly "spiritual" ordinance of baptism (above, pp. 21-22). Renouncing Marcion and all his pomp and all his ways, I hope my polyphonic composition on the themes of priesthood and baptism has a more harmonious sound.

This chapter has two sections. First, I address the liturgical implications of what, for the sake of convenience, I shall affectionately call "our typology." Second, and at greater length, I construct some components of baptismal theology from the materials provided by the ordination and related texts and rites. Questions of baptismal efficacy and causality take priority, and I argue that this typology implies a form of baptismal regeneration and a "poetic" conception of causality. Chapter 5 examines the ecclesiological, and therefore social and political implications of baptism as induction to priesthood, but since liturgical, theological, and sociological perspectives are connected, at various points I anticipate issues more fully developed later.

To prove the elasticity of the priestly typology requires that I stretch, push, and pull a bit – a risky venture since the concepts can snap back painfully against my fingers or expand past their breaking point. As far as I can see, this chapter ends with no one injured, nothing broken.

Making Priests: The Liturgy of Initiation

The Aaronic ordination rite is perhaps *the* key to understanding the patristic and medieval enhancements of the initiation liturgy; if it does not open every door, it opens many.[1] Two rites especially highlight the connection: the baptismal anointing(s) and the investiture of the baptized with white linen. Anointing rites varied in number, the type of oil used, parts of the body anointed, and their placement in the sequence of the baptismal liturgy. Liturgists interpreted these rites under marital and martial metaphors, as effecting union with Christ, as imprinting a seal (σφράγις), as perfuming with the fragrance of Christ, as exorcizing, as

---

[1]For patristic texts, see Finn (1992a; 1992b). One of the most convenient collections, which includes medieval and Eastern material, is Dabin (1950). Dabin, however, is so intent on proving a moral unanimity concerning participation in the threefold office of Christ that he gives little attention to significant differences in formulation among theologians. His stated thesis is that the Fathers and theologians "reconnaît dans les baptisés ou les confirmés l'existence d'un certain sacerdoce, d'un certain prophétisme, d'une certaine royauté" (1950: 52), but the doctrine has a very different texture depending on whether priesthood is conferred by baptism or confirmation and depending on whether "confirmation" is part of the complex initiation or a separate rite of strengthening at adolescence.

offering the oil of paradise, as conferring the gift of the Spirit or the name "Christian."[2] According to Georg Kretschmar, however, the baptismal anointings result from "a conscious resort to principles of Old Testament ritual: Baptism is the hallowing of kings and priests" (Kretschmar 1995: 27). Evidence from church orders and liturgies shows that even if the anointing did not derive from Old Testament custom, it early took on this significance. Concerning the prebaptismal anointing, the *Didascalia Apostolorum*, a North Syrian composition of the early third century (Bradshaw 1992: 88), states: "As of old the priests and kings were anointed in Israel, do thou in like manner, with the imposition of hand, anoint the head of those who receive baptism, whether of men or of women" (3.12; Connolly 1929: 146).[3] As we have seen, the *Apostolic Constitutions* refers to 1 Peter 2 to describe anointing as an induction into the royal priesthood (chapter 3, fn. 9). Later liturgical texts also link anointing with Christ's triple office,[4] and this typology appears in

---

[2]For details, see Mitchell (1977); Bradshaw (1992: 161-184); Lampe (1950); Winkler (1995a: 58-81; 1995b: 202-218); Levesque (1995: 159-201); Quinn (1995: 219-237); Fisher (1965); Riley (1974: 104-107, 189-211, 358-396).

[3]Written originally in Greek, the only complete extant text of the *Didascalia* is in Syriac. Latin fragments also exist, and some Greek portions are found in the *Apostolic Constitutions* (Connolly 1929: xi).

[4]The *Gelasian Sacramentary* notes that the washing-anointing pattern of initiation is found also in Moses' ordination of Aaron: *Quod in novissimis temporibus anifestis est effectibus declaratum, cum baptismatis aquis omnium criminum commissa delentibus, haec olei unctio vultus nostros jucundos efficiat ac serenos. Inde etiam Moysi famulo tuo mandata dedisti, ut Aaron fratrem suum, prius aqua lotum, per infusionem hujus unguenti constituerit sacerdotem* (*Sacramentum Gelasianum*, 1.40; PL 74, 1101A-B). See also *De liturgica Gallicana*, 3.37 (PL 72, 277C); *Liber sacramentorum* (PL 78, 83B, 85A); *Monumenta liturgica, benedictio olei* (PL 138, 1065B). For discussion, see Winkler (1995b: 202-

contemporary Roman Catholic, Orthodox, and Anglican baptismal rites.[5]

Since the candidate for baptism was naked during the water rite, postbaptismal investiture had obvious practical value, but the rites were extended beyond necessity and given mystagogical interpretations. Besides a full clothing with a white robe, we find such festive accouterments as veils, linen bands, caps and crowns. White clothing signified putting on Christ, resurrection, bridal adornment, replacement for the skins of Adam, sharing Christ's glorious radiance, or a spotless covering for the judgment.[6] As with anointing, priestly interpretations were common, especially among medieval liturgists. According to a letter of the sixth-century figure John the Deacon, chrism inducts into priesthood and royalty, and the linen head covering represents the headgear of priests.[7] Similarly, Rabanus Maurus (780-856) explains that

---

218); Levesque (1995: 159-201); Mitchell (1977: 104-130).

[5]For Roman Catholicism, see the *Rite of Christian Initiation of Adults* (1986: 205-206, 248, 283); for Orthodox, Schmemann (1974: 86-103); for Anglican, *Proposed Book of Common Prayer* (1977: 307-308); for Lutheran, Pfatteicher (1990: 54-55).

[6]For details, see Riley (1974: 413-451); Levesque (1995: 173-15, 190); Fisher (1965: 26, 33, 39, 48, 59-61, 65, 71, 84-85, 95, 98, 174; 1970: 51-52); Danielou (1960: 49-53); Finn (1992a: 16-17, 57, 60, 87-88, 157, 233; 1992b: 71-72, 96, 109, 126-127, 168-169); Mitchell (1977: 41, 75, 98, 127, 129); Brock (1982: 11-38); Mingana (1933: 47); Bradshaw (1992: 171).

[7]*Sumptis dehinc albis vestibus, caput ejus sacri chrismatis unctione perungitur; ut intelligat baptizatus regnum in se ac sacerdotale convenisse mysterium. Christmatis enim oleo sacerdotes et principes ungebantur, ut illi offerendo sacrificia, illi populis imperarent. Ad imaginem quippe sacerdotii plenius exprimendam, renascentis caput lintei decore componitur. Nam sacerdotes illius temporis quodam mystico velamine caput semper ornabant (Epistola ad Senarium virum illustrem 6; PL 59, 403B).*

the linen placed on the head after postbaptismal anointing signifies the diadem of kings and the dignity of priests, sharing with John the mistaken belief that Israel's priests veiled themselves with a *mysticum velamen*.[8] Rupert of Deutz (*c.* 1075-1129) calls attention to the washing-investiture sequence in the ordination of Aaron and deduces that initiation makes the candidate a member of the royal priesthood.[9] Honorius of Autun (*c.* 1080/90-*c.* 1156) likewise describes the baptismal garments as priestly.[10]

These ornamentations of initiation are consistent with biblical typology, and therefore preferable to the migration of priestly symbolism to confirmation and ordination that distorted later medieval liturgical theology (see chapter 6). This does not, however, necessarily imply that the rites are suitable. The Reformers charged that chrism and linen garments, as well as spittings and breathings, exorcisms, gifts of tabers and other rites polluted the water of New Testament baptism.[11] In their

---

[8]*Tegitur enim post sacram unctionem caput ejus mystico velamine, ut intelligat se diadematis regni, et sacerdotalis dignitatis portitorem . . . . Nam sacerdotes in Veteri Testamento quodam mystico velamine caput semper ornabant (De clericorum institutione (c.* 819), 1.29; PL 107, 313D).

[9]*Sed et illud non praetereundum quod non prius nisi loti aqua ex praecepto Domini vestiuntur sacerdotali gloria, ut videlicet per hoc significetur quod non nisi per baptismum efficimur "regale sacerdotium et gens sancta" (De Trinitate et operibus ejus,* on Leviticus 8; PL 167, 787D).

[10]*Baptizati autem ideo vestes albas portant, quia amissam innocentiam se recepisse insinuant. Illorum* **mitra** *regni coronam,* **alba** *vero sacerdotii praefert stolam. Jam enim facti sunt reges et sacerdotes et Christi regis et sacerdotis cohaeredes (Gemma animae,* 1.243; PL 172, 616B).

[11]Zwingli (1953: 153); Calvin (1960: 1319-1320; *Institutes* 4.15.19); cf. the comments of Bucer in Fisher (1970: 99-100; cf. 35-37); Old (1992: *passim*). Luther was slow to reject traditional forms. His 1523 *Taufbüchlein* includes a prebaptismal anointing, multiple exorcisms, and endowment with a cap, but in the epilogue attached to the liturgy he admitted that such "external things" as insufflation,

interpretation of the New Testament rite, the Reformers were undoubtedly correct. If baptizing three thousand converts on Pentecost strained the logistical capacity of the church (Acts 2:41), it is incredible that the apostles could assemble sufficient supplies of oil and linen to anoint and invest the baptized. Philip baptized the Ethiopian eunuch along a highway out of Jerusalem, so he was hardly able to chrismate and invest the eunuch as well (Acts 8:26-40). Laying on of hands may have accompanied baptism in the apostolic period, but even its status is uncertain. On the evidence of the New Testament, initiation was originally a simple affusion or aspersion of water. Water was charged with the whole significance of the Aaronic rite.[12]

---

consignation, salt, spittle and clay on eyes, anointings, chrisms, and the gift of a taber are the least important acts of initiation. He avoided radical changes for strategic and pastoral reasons, to head off complaints that he was introducing a "new baptism" and to avoid causing worry that "adorned" baptism was invalid (Fisher 1970: 7-8, 13-16). Luther's 1526 baptismal liturgy dispenses with anointing but retains a prebaptismal consignation and a postbaptismal robe (Fisher 1970: 23, 25).

[12]Nor is there incontrovertible evidence of baptismal anointings during the immediate postapostolic period. Though several second-century writers refer to anointing, it cannot be determined whether they describe a rite. In his *Libri tres ad Autolycum*, Theophilus responds to pagan mockery of the name "Christian," derived from χρίσμα, by pointing out that both athletes and ships must be "anointed" to be serviceable (PG 6, 1041). Mitchell suggests that the anointing in this case seems to be actual but concedes that it may be metaphorical (Mitchell 1977: 13). In a discussion of the types of Christ in the Old Testament, Justin refers to Jacob's anointing of the rock at Bethel (Gen. 28:18), and this leads into a discussion of other anointings, which all point to Jesus the Anointed One (Καὶ γὰρ οἱ βασιλεῖς πάντες καὶ οἱ χριστοὶ ἀπὸ τούτου μετέσχον καὶ βασιλεῖς καλεῖσθαι καὶ χριστοί· ὃν τρόπον καὶ αὐτὸς ἀπὸ τοῦ Πατρὸς ἔλαβε τὸ βασιλεὺς, καὶ Χριστὸς, καὶ ἱερεὺς, καὶ ἄγγελος, καὶ ὅσα ἄλλα τοιαῦτα ἔχει ἢ ἔσχε [*Dialogue with Trypho* 86; PG 6, 682].) Yet Justin nowhere in this passage says that Christians are anointed, and it is striking that his description of the baptismal

For Protestant liturgists, the fact that medieval "manmade" rites lacked Scriptural warrant was sufficient to call them into question. Christ, they argued, governs His church through the word, and departure from His instructions is defiance of His Headship. Adornments of initiation, they believed, distorted the rite and obscured its significance. Augustinians that they were, they had no doubt that Catholic baptisms encrusted with extraneous ceremony were valid, but they recognized that ripples from a distorted *lex orandi* could grow to engulf remote islands in the doctrine and practice of the church and thus did not see their opposition to secondary rites as "overkill" (cf. Spinks 1995: 315). Efforts to mix oil and water, they feared, could only end with the oil rising to the top.

The Reformers' Scriptural opposition was not a "formal" concern but went to the evangelical heart of the Reformation, a point brought out with clarity in Calvin's *Inventory of Relics* (1958). No doubt, Calvin's mockery of relic veneration combines an almost Voltairean rationalist ingredient with a dash of spiritualist distrust of material means of communication with God, but centrally Calvin's concern is pastoral: He encourages sinners to seek the gracious God where He has promised to make Himself known. As He promised, God dwells among the people marked out by the preaching of the word, baptism, the Eucharist, and ordered fellowship. Word and sacrament are inseparable for Calvin not

---

rite in the first *Apology* (1.61-65) does not mention any unction. On the origin of anointings, see Winkler (1976: 317-324); Mitchell (1977: 15-20); Dudley and Rowell (1993: 59-83); Jones, et. al. (1992: 112-119); Lampe (1951: 64-82).

because the word magically invigorates the inanimate sign but because it identifies the Lord's saving "address" in this world. Since there is no authorization in the word for baptismal anointing or investiture, either by explicit command or by example, there can be no expectation that these rites mediate the presence of Christ, however subjectively meaningful they may be. Seeking contact with God through a lock of the Virgin's hair, John the Baptist's foreskin, a vial of St. Stephen's blood, or through the oil and linen of initiation is doomed to frustration.

Consideration of the multivalent biblical symbolism of water supports the Reformers' position. Baptism fulfills the flood (1 Pet. 3:18-22) and Israel's crossing of the Red Sea (1 Cor. 10:1-2), types that indicate that the peril of entering the waters is within the symbolic reach of baptism (cf. Lundberg 1942); the font is a tomb as well as a womb. Water was a common cleansing agent in Levitical law; likewise, baptism purifies. At least since Tertullian, baptism has been taken to represent the waters of Genesis 1:2, from which the brooding Spirit gave birth to the ordered cosmos. Since man is of dust (Gen. 2:7), water poured on human beings gives promise of fruitfulness. Genesis 1:6-7 distinguishes the waters above the firmament from the waters below, so that water falling upon the baptized symbolizes the descent of the heavenly Spirit (cf. Poythress 1997b: 151). Rain falls from clouds, so baptismal aspersion is associated with Yahweh's appearance in a cloud of glory. Keeping the ritual focus on water thus maintains the complex typology of Christian initiation. Oil, for all its symbolic potential, does not have the same density; here, water is thicker than oil.

Though I agree with the Reformers that chrisms and investitures are

141

unnecessary and can discordantly interrupt the symbolic resonances of baptism, our investigation encourages inserting references to priesthood in the prayers and performatives of the initiation liturgy, alongside more common allusions to Noah's flood, the Red Sea crossing, Pentecost, and the baptism of Jesus.[13] Protestant liturgies might, for example, transfer the language of the *Rite of Christian Initiation of Adults* from chrismation to the water rite. Thus, one is baptized "so that, united with his people, you may remain forever a member of Christ who is Priest, Prophet, and King" (Roman Catholic Church 1986: 205-206). The 1977 American Episcopal *Proposed Book of Common Prayer* includes a moment of reception for the newly baptized that encourages him or her to confess the faith, proclaim the resurrection, and "share with us in [Christ's] eternal priesthood" (1977: 308).

Holy Food for the Holy Ones

In one respect, our typology carries more substantive implications for

---

[13]In my examination of Fisher (1970), Jagger (1970), and Old (1992), I have found no hint of a priestly interpretation of initiation in the liturgies of any Reformation church, including the Anglican, from the Reformation until this century, and in many churches this typology still has virtually no place. Even early Lutheran liturgies that retain anointings and some form of investiture are silent on priesthood. In Luther's 1523 *Taufbüchlein*, the oil is called the "oil of salvation" and the investiture is a symbol of innocence in the judgment (Fisher 1970: 13-16). This is a curious silence because Luther, while harshly criticizing the subordination of baptismal water to the oil of chrism, insists that believers are initiated by baptism into a share of Christ's priesthood and kingship: Having been born of God and of His Bride, Christians "have become true clerics in Christendom in a hereditary manner" (Luther 1971: 187; cf. 1959: 112-113).

liturgical practice. For several decades, many have recognized that Orthodox "full initiation," which enacts water baptism, confirmation or chrismation, and first Eucharist as a single ritual sequence, is an ancient pattern.[14] The consensus is not exactly in favor of "full initiation," since some churches confirm at adolescence, when the confirmand has long since been admitted to the Eucharist (Müller-Fahrenholz 1982: 70-81; Holeton 1981: 27-31).[15] Nonetheless, there is increasing ecumenical agreement that baptism and Eucharist are liturgically inseparable, so that baptism, without any additional experience or rite, is the ticket to the Eucharistic banquet.

Reasoning from our typology, we can make several points in defense of this conclusion. As we saw in chapter 2, the phrase "filling the hand"

---

[14]Recent work that casts doubt upon the idea of a single "norm" of initiation in the early church (see Bradshaw 1992:161-184 and Kretschmar 1995:11-34), yet there is a consensus that early Christian initiation, whatever rites it involved, led to the Eucharist (e.g., Finn 1992b: 39-40).

[15]Persuasive early evidence of a separate rite of confirmation, however construed, is lacking. Some twentieth-century formulations transfer to confirmation what the New Testament attributes to baptism. In his well-known pamphlet on confirmation, Gregory Dix (1946) asserts that consignation with oil, rather than baptism, is the sacrament of the Spirit, and Louis Bouyer goes so far as to say that without confirmation "water baptism is so imperfect that the person who is merely baptized is not qualified to participate in the Eucharist" (quoted in Wainwright 1969: 34). Lampe (1951) is a persuasive response to this view, but the Dix-inspired dispute had the salutary effect of forcing clarification regarding the effect of baptism (United Reformed Church 1988: 16). The significance of "confirmation" remains a matter of debate, especially in the wake of Kavanagh's 1984 article arguing that the rites that eventually developed into confirmation originally formed the episcopal *missa* of the baptismal rite, dismissing the newly baptized into the Eucharistic community. Johnson (1995) includes Kavanagh's as well as other recent articles on the subject.

means in part that Yahweh filled the priests' hands with portions of sacrificial food. Ordination began with washing in water and ended with a meal in the holy place, exhibiting the same form as other covenant-cutting rites (cf. Exod. 19:17-24:1-11). Aaron and his sons entered covenant with Yahweh by exchanging gifts of food and sharing a meal. Once installed, priests might eat holy portions of the sacrifices. Lay worshipers ate only the peace offering, the least holy of the animal sacrifices (Lev. 7:11-18). Priests, however, received not only specified portions of peace offerings (Lev. 7:28-34), but also the flesh of some purification[16] and trespass offerings, and the greater part of every tribute (grain) offering (Lev. 6:14-7:10). As personal attendants in Yahweh's house, priests served at His table to offer "the bread of God" (Lev. 21:21-22), and it was fitting that they share Yahweh's bread. The food rite conferred food rights.

Distribution of sacrificial food and access to holy places thus traced out Israel's hierarchal holiness system. We can summarize information from Leviticus 6-7, 21-22 [17] and Deuteronomy 14-16 as follows:

---

[16]Flesh of a חטאת whose blood was taken into the Holy Place was burned outside the camp, but priests received the flesh of animals whose blood was applied to the bronze altar (Lev. 4).

[17]Disposition of priestly food is at the center of the concentric structure of Leviticus 21-22, the main text detailing regulations for priests. The passage is structured as five speeches from Yahweh, the first four of which Moses is to pass on to Aaron:
A. Profanation of priesthood forbidden, 21:1-15
 B. Defective priests, 21:16-24
  C. Disposition of holy food, 22:1-16
 B. Defective sacrifices, 22:17-25
A. Age and timing of sacrifice, 22:26-33

Sanctuary Environment	Personnel	Food
Most Holy	High Priest	Shewbread and sacrifices
Holy	Priests	Shewbread and sacrifices
Courtyard	Priestly households	Priestly portions of peace offering; tithes
	Israelite	Feasts; lay portions of peace offering
Land of Israel	Sojourner	Feasts other than Passover; clean food
Gentile Lands	Gentiles	All meats

Priests ate the food of sons, not the comparatively meager fare of זרים, "strangers" to the house.

Though the rationale for these distributions was bound up with the contagious holiness of the Old Covenant, the typological parallel with baptism and Eucharist is evident. Jesus is the "bread of God" (John 6:33) not only in the sense that He feeds His people but also in the sense of Leviticus 21: His flesh, sacrificed on the altar of the cross, ascends in a cloud to satisfy the Father, who then pours out the libation of the Spirit. After Jesus fed the five thousand, the leftovers were more abundant than the original food; likewise after the Father has "eaten His fill," the heavenly bread is not consumed but multiplied. Crumbs fall from His table, and baptized priests who continually offer the bread of praise through the Priest may eat the "most holy" food reserved from His sacrifice. As Aaron began at the laver and moved to the altar, so the Christian, washed in the font, enters the house and approaches the table. If B fulfills and replaces O, then it makes no sense to baptize without filling hands with holy food; for baptism, on our typology, *is* the church's rite of hand-filling. To baptize and refuse admission to the table is, absurdly, to treat the baptized as זרים.

The Kingdom Belongs to Such as These

Most churches recognize that baptism admits to the Eucharist when the subject is an adult, but from the Middle Ages until recent decades only the Eastern churches have admitted baptized infants and young children to the meal. Yet, the consensus described above involves a growing sense that baptized children belong at the Lord's table.[18] Our typology implies as much: If infants are consecrated in baptism, they should receive holy food. But is the priestly typology consistent with infant baptism? In what sense can infants be "priests" or even, more loosely, "members of the Christian priesthood"? Does priestly service not require conscious

---

[18]See Müller-Fahrenholz (1982); Young (1983); United Reformed Church (1988); Holeton (1981). Also Eastman (Anglican, 1991: 25-27); Hovda (Roman Catholic, 1976: 162); Hamilton (Church of Scotland, 1990: 102-103); Keidel (evangelical Presbyterian, 1975: 301-341); Leithart (evangelical Presbyterian, 1992). Geoffrey Wainwright, who ultimately urges believer's baptism as the best ecumenical option, argues that if infant baptism is justifiable there is little warrant for excluding infants from communion (1969: 28-30, 40).

participation? And therefore, does not the notion that the church baptizes to priesthood undermine infant baptism?[19]

Historically, many churches, both Eastern and Western, have claimed that baptism initiates infants as well as adults to priesthood, and several typological considerations vindicate the wisdom of the tradition. As evident from the chart above, members of a priest's household -- including slaves, unmarried children, and divorced or widowed daughters -- shared certain kinds of priestly food (Lev. 22:11-13; cf. 6:16-18, 29; 7:6). Infants were included, since the holy gifts were a prime food source for priestly families, who had no landed inheritance. Lay Israelites, sojourners, or hired men who were not permanent members of the household were forbidden to "approach" holy things or eat sacred flesh, on pain of being "cut off" from the covenant people (Lev. 22:2, 10). If an Israelite layman inadvertently ate holy food, he had to make restitution, adding one-fifth of the value as penalty and presumably offering a trespass offering for his "sacrilege" (Lev. 22:14; cf. 5:14-16). Though only the priest was "baptized" into priesthood, his entire household received food denied to laymen. By virtue of the priest's consecration, the entire household was holy (cf. 1 Cor. 7:14). Transposing this into a New Covenant mode, all the sacred meals of the Old Covenant are now conjugated by the Eucharist, and thus every member of a "priestly" family

---

[19]Infant baptism has come under persistent attack in the past half century. Among the most powerful treatises are those of Barth (1948: 34-54; 1969: 164-194); Jewett (1978); and Beasley-Murray (1973: 306-395). For exegetical and theological defenses of the practice, see Cullmann (1950); Murray (1980: 45-82); Flinn (1982: 111-151); Pannenberg (1996: 77-88); Poythress (1997a: 13-29; 1997b: 143-158); Mark Searle (1995: 365-409); Bromiley (1979).

should be admitted to the holy meal, regardless of age. Nearly every Christian tradition, however, insists that baptism is the threshold of the Eucharistic community.[20] Thus, children of Christian priests who are admitted to the Lord's table must first be baptized.[21]

Infant boys were, moreover, initiated into a kind of priesthood even in the Old Testament. Though there were degrees of holiness and ranks of priesthood, all Israel was a holy priesthood (Exod. 19:6). Infant boys circumcised on the eighth day were therefore admitted to a priestly people, and there is no reason why the priesthood of the new Israel should be less inclusive. Proof of the priestly status of lay Israelites is found in the rite for cleansing skin disease (Lev. 14). The overall trajectory of the rite is the same as that of ordination. Lepers were cut off from the liturgical assembly of Israel, and the rite reintroduced them to tabernacle, just as priests in the ordination rite moved from the outskirts into the house. In several details, the cleansing rite duplicates the rite of filling:

1. Both rites began with washings, Lev. 14:8-9; 8:6.
2. Both followed a 7 + 1 day structure, 14:9-10; 8:33 and 9:1.
3. In both, blood was smeared on the right ear lobe, thumb, and toe, 14:14; 8:23-24.

---

[20]With the renewal of the practice of admitting children to the Lord's Table, this order has become problematic in some churches (Müller-Fahrenholz 1982: 11-12; United Reformed Church 1988: 11-12; cf. 22-23, 27).

[21]This inverts the usual argument, which reasons from paedobaptism to paedocommunion. A similar inversion can be employed with Jesus' statement concerning infants in His kingdom. If the kingdom belongs to "such as these" (Matt. 19:14), and if the kingdom is, as Jesus constantly says, the eschatological feast proleptically offered in the Eucharist (e.g., Matt. 8:11), then the feast belongs to "such as these." And if infants are admitted to the feast of the kingdom, they must first be baptized. Children know they should wash up before dinner.

4. Both High Priest and leper were anointed on the head, 14:18; 8:12.[22]

These parallels suggest that the rites are mutually interpreting. Ordination cleansed Aaron and his sons from defiling affliction, and the cleansing rite inducted the leper into a kind of priestly ministry. Cleansed lepers were not, however, made priests for the first time, for that would have positively encouraged proliferation of skin disease as a means of ascending Israel's liturgico-social hierarchy. The cleansing rite *restored* lepers to a priestly standing from which their uncleanness separated them. When did the leper first receive this priestly standing? A clue to the answer is found in the temporal structure of the cleansing ritual: The main rite took place on the eighth day after the priest pronounced the leper clean (Lev. 14:10), and this recalls the eighth-day rite of circumcision (Gen. 17:12). Cleansing a leper, then, renewed his circumcision, as the priestly ordination was an extension of circumcision to the four corners of the priest's body. Since in a number of details the "re-circumcision" of the leper took the form of an ordination to priesthood, it follows that circumcision inducted to the general priesthood of Israel (cf. Leithart 1995). Though Israelite males were circumcised, women evidently shared some degree of priestly status, for women with skin disease would have

---

[22]There were also significant differences. Though the leper washed his clothes before the rite, there was no investiture; intriguingly, the leper, though not the priest, was anointed with *oil* on the right ear, thumb, and big toe; the leper offered a guilt offering, which was not part of the ordination rite, and the blood placed on the leper was taken from this guilt offering; there was no "filling the hands" in the cleansing rite, nor any meal, though a cleansed leper probably offered a peace offering for thanksgiving to celebrate the end of his separation from Yahweh's house.

been cleansed according to the same quasi-priestly rite as men.

Similar assumptions undergird the rite for deconsecrating a Nazir (Num. 6:1-21). Any lay Israelite could take a Nazirite vow, and this put him or her in a state of intensified holiness for a specified time. During the vow, the Nazir refrained from all grape products,[23] let his or her hair grow, and avoided all contact with the dead. When the time of consecration ended, he or she returned to normal lay status by a rite including features that resembled ordination:

1. Both included three sacrifices in the same order: purification, ascension (whole burnt), and a form of peace offering (Num. 6:16-17; Lev. 8:14, 18, 22).
2. During the deconsecration rite, the priest placed portions of the peace offering and meal offerings on the palms of the Nazir (Num. 6:19; Lev. 8:25-27).[24]

As with the leper, deconsecration restored the Nazir to pre-vow status as a lay Israelite, ritually imagined as a priestly standing. Again, women taking Nazirite vows would have been restored to the priestly people through this quasi-ordination.

Thus, the priestly typology is consistent with the practice of infant

---

[23]The prohibition of wine is highlighted (Num. 6:3, 20), which parallels the requirement that priests not drink wine when they enter the Holy Place (Lev. 10:9). Evidently, for the Nazirite the entire world was consecrated as holy space.

[24]During the ordination rite, "fat" and inner organs were placed on the palms of the prospective priest, along with the right thigh and unleavened bread, but during the rite of deconsecration, the Nazir received only the shoulder of the ram and the bread, not the fat. Though their hands were filled as they returned to their normal status, Nazirites might not approach the altar, where fat was turned to smoke for Yahweh.

baptism. Yet our discussion begins to highlight a difference between Israel and the church that I develop more fully in chapter 5. For the moment, we can characterize the difference as a remodeling of the house, the locus of priestly ministry. Under the Old system, Yahweh's house had, architecturally and ritually, three thresholds: The circumcised crossed the first into the courtyard,[25] but only priests circumcised in four dimensions went through the curtain into the Holy Place, and only the High Priest went through the veil into the Most Holy Place. In the remodeled house, the dividing curtains are rent and the wall of separation broken, so a single baptismal doorway opens into an undivided house (cf. Heb. 9). Whereas priestly "baptism" once marked out an inner ring within the community of circumcision, ordination and circumcision are now enfolded into Christian baptism. B fulfills and replaces not only O but also circumcision, and this radically reconfigures the people of God. We are beginning to see the grammar of the Christian conjugation of priesthood.

The typology implies a further refinement of paedobaptism. Reflections on infant baptism frequently highlight the benefits infants receive as members of the body of Christ. Augustine (1872) stressed that baptism cleanses the stain of original sin, and Protestants commonly

---

[25]Numbers 15:14 indicates that sojourners in the land, who were not necessarily circumcised, might sacrifice in the tabernacle courtyard. Circumcision was, however, required for participation in Passover (Exod. 12:43-51).

emphasize the catechetical pedagogy that follows baptism. Infants are objects of the church's care, "passive" members of the congregation. If baptism initiates to priesthood, however, it initiates to ministry, and this must also be true of infants.

To show how infants serve as personal attendants in God's new house, we must develop further some implications of our discussion of 1 Corinthians 6:11. As N.T. Wright has pointed out, the Old Testament records of Israel's restoration from Babylonian captivity nowhere indicate that Yahweh descended in glory upon the second temple in the public, visible way that He had with previous sanctuaries (1996: 621). Christ, as new Moses and new Cyrus, definitively leads Israel from exile, and fulfills the promises to Ezekiel and Zechariah, who saw Yahweh's return in vision. The One in whom glory dwells bodily fulfills Israel's hopes (John 1:14). Further, the Pentecostal descent of the Spirit parallels the coming of the glory-cloud on the tabernacle and temple (Acts 2; Exod. 40:34-38; 1 Kgs. 8:10-11), but here the glory Spirit falls upon the gathered disciples, consecrating the church as the new holy house; and, unlike the priests of Old, the apostles, burning with altar fire, stand to serve in the presence of the Spirit. Thus, the Old gap between temple and people, between house and house is filled, for the assembly of saints is identical to the dwelling place of the Spirit. There is even a kind of circumincession, since each member of the house is individually sanctified as a temple. As 1 Peter 2:4-10 makes clear, the priesthood *is* the house. Baptism inducts into the service of the body of the Priest, whose body is the temple. In this house, priestly service is reimagined – significantly, with an architectural metaphor – as οἰκοδομή of the body (1 Cor. 14:3, 12). Housekeeping is conjugated as bodybuilding.

Baptized into the priesthood that is the house, therefore, infants contribute positively to the edification of the church. The late Mark Searle wrote,

> a newborn infant alters the configuration of family relationships from the day of its birth, if not sooner, having a major impact on the lives of its parents and siblings. . . . Children will test the sacrificial self-commitment, the self-delusions, and the spurious faith of those with whom they come in contact for any length of time. They summon parents particularly to a deeper understanding of the mystery of grace and of the limitations of human abilities. . . . All this is merely to suggest that in their own way children in fact play an extremely active, even prophetic, role in the household of faith. The obstacle lies not in the child but in the faithlessness of the adult believers (Searle 1995: 400-401; cf. Poythress 1997a: 26).

Evidently, this is part of what Herder means when he argues that man is "*born* for society." Though Herder is making the point that human life is an altogether social life, in context he implies infants forge and strengthen social bonds. The radical vulnerability of infants, and the long period necessary for their development to maturity, fosters sympathy, inhibits dispersal, and encourages a common sense of responsibility (Herder 1969: 269-70). So also the society of the church is bound together by common concern for her children's Christian nurture, a concern manifested in baptismal liturgies that require a promise from all members, as well as parents or godparents, to contribute to the infant's training. Because they are utterly incapable of sustaining their own growth toward maturity, infants help coagulate the community; precisely because infants are entirely passive, their presence is powerfully active and activating.[26]

Infant baptism thus implies the question of who is considered a productive member of the Christian priesthood. Physically and mentally disabled persons, social outcasts and refugees, orphans and widows are as much at issue as infants (cf. Hauerwas 1981: 187-194).[27] Paedobaptism enacts Paul's revolutionary assertion about the Body of Christ: "the members of the body which seem to be weaker are necessary; and those members of the body, which we deem less honorable, on these we bestow more abundant honor, and our unseemly members come to have more abundant seemliness" (1 Cor. 12:22-23). Jesus forms a priestly people from the blind, the lame, the blemished, the weak -- precisely those excluded from Old Covenant housekeeping and from the Old Covenant table (Lev. 21:16-24).

Sacramenta Causant Quod Significant

---

[26]In pursuing this line of thought, I am opposing the view of, for example, Geoffrey Wainwright, who says that paedobaptism implies that the church has two different kinds of membership: "it seems to me impossible that 'Church membership' should be an internally undifferentiated category in substance or in practice" (1969: 38). Of course the body is differentiated; such is the nature of bodies, as Paul is at pains to point out. The ear lobe is a different body member from the hand, but is it any less a member?

[27]Virtually my last act as a pastor was to baptize a premature Downs baby. Her mere presence in the church called out expressions of love and practical aid to the parents, and drew the members of the congregation into closer fellowship. She was, however unconsciously, a "minister in God's house," edifying the body. She continues to edify me, for no book or article on baptism has been such a powerful source of stimulation.

Thus far, my pushing and stretching have been somewhat modest. My next task, however, is to suggest how the priestly typology sheds light on questions of baptismal efficacy (does baptism *do* anything, and, if so, what?) and causality (*how* does it do what it does?). Especially here I push the typology – not, I hope, producing grotesque distortions but squeezing old questions into more serviceable shape. For the moment, I work from John Skorupski's notion of an "operative ceremony," a sequence of actions that sets up or cancels a set of rules to govern the person who is the subject of the ceremony (1976: 93-115). I shall eventually agree with Skorupski that sacraments are something more than operative ceremonies, and our paths will diverge; but I hope to show that we can go quite a long way with "operative ceremony" and "priestly baptism" as coordinates.

We can begin with the obvious: The ordination texts imply an emphatically objective notion of ritual efficacy. At the beginning of the rite, Aaron and his sons were not allowed to approach the altar or enter the tent, but when it ended Aaron was ministering at Yahweh's table and in the house. Details of the ritual underscore this transition. In the ordination, Aaron and his sons offered a bull as a חטאת (Lev. 8:14), the proper sacrificial animal for priests (Lev. 4:3). Yet there is a discrepancy in the blood rite. According to Leviticus 4:5-7, the blood of a purification for priests was sprinkled in the Holy Place and smeared on the horns of the *golden* altar of incense. Moses, however, smeared blood from the ordination חטאת on the horns of the *bronze* altar and did not take it into the house at all (Lev. 8:14-17). If Aaron had offered a purification on the day after the ordination, he would have taken the blood into the Holy Place (cf. Gorman 1990: 122). During the rite, the ordinands did not offer the

המלאת for priests; after the rite, they did. Before the rite they were not priests; after the rite they were.

As Milgrom has pointed out, the disposal of the flesh of the "ram of filling" also reflects Aaron's ambiguous status during the ordination week (Milgrom 1991: 534-535; Exod. 29:31-34). On the one hand, its meat had to be eaten in a holy place, and this corresponded to the requirements for most holy offerings (Lev. 6:16-17, 26; 7:6). On the other hand, the breast given to Moses as officiant links the ordination ram to the peace offering (cf. Lev. 7:30, 34), the least holy of the sacrifices, whose flesh was distributed among the priest, his family, and the lay worshiper and might be eaten anywhere (Lev. 7:11-18, 28-34). Thus, the ordination ram was poised in liminal space between holiness categories. After the ordination, however, priests offered no more sacrifices of this type, but only most holy ascension (whole burnt), tribute (grain), purification, and trespass offerings and holy peace offerings. Ambiguous ordination sacrifices were not offered until the next priest was ready to cross the threshold into the house.[28]

In this way, the ordination texts suppress traditional sacramental uses

---

[28]If then. It is not clear in Exodus 29 or Leviticus 8 whether the ordination rite was purely a founding rite, instituting the priesthood, or if it was repeated with each new generation of priests. Numbers 20:23-29 suggests that High Priestly office was passed to the succeeding generation by a simple *traditio* of the garments. Lest we make too much of that text, however, it should be remembered that Eleazar had already undergone the rite of "filling" before receiving the High Priesthood. Various turns of phrase suggest the rite was repeated. Leviticus 21:10 speaks of the High Priest "on whose head the anointing oil has been poured," referring not only to Aaron but all subsequent High Priests. If all High Priests were anointed, the rest of the ordination rite must have been performed as well.

of *signum-res*. Some commentators have attempted to explain the rites of Leviticus in categories drawn from Christian sacramental theology. For Keil (1980: 2.335-336), the washing of Aaron and his sons signified the spiritual cleansing requisite for approaching Yahweh, the garments of glory and beauty represented the "character required for the discharge of [his]duties" since "the official costume [was] the outward sign of installation in the office which he was to fill," and the anointing symbolized the Spirit who equipped the priests for their tasks. There is doubtless some truth in Keil's interpretation. One can well imagine an Israelite priest reflecting on the tropological implications of the rite and robes of his office. In several senses, one may even say that "faith," understood as a trustful and obedient response to Yahweh and His word, is presumed. Faith preceded the rite, first, because Aaron submitted to ordination as a response to Yahweh's choice and favor (cf. Num. 16:5). Had Aaron not trusted Yahweh's promise to accept him as priest, he would not have dared draw near the danger zone of His house. Second, Yahweh revealed the ordination rite on the mountain, and Moses performed it in trustful obedience to the vision and voice. Persevering faith was also required after the rite, for maintaining priestly standing depended on hearing, believing, and obeying the word of Yahweh. Nadab and Abihu became watchwords, warning that unfaithfulness in priestly ministry was deadly (Lev. 10:1-5).

Nonetheless, such considerations, crucial as they are, should not obscure the objective efficacy of the ordination *per se*. Keil, with much of the tradition, confuses different senses of "symbol," explaining the actions of the ordination service by the Augustinian definition of a symbol as "something that brings another thing to mind." In the ordination texts, symbols or, better, "ritual acts," were primarily "pragmatic" or "performative" rather than cognitive. Contrary to Keil, the symbols did not simply point to invisible graces required for priestly ministry but *accomplished* the ordination. Aaron was not made a priest because his heart was right, or because he experienced or possessed what the ritual symbolized. As far as qualification for priestly standing was concerned, the inner state of his heart *was* indifferent. He was made a priest *by means of* the prescribed sequence of ritual acts, because the ritual event became a moment in his life story.

As an operative ceremony, the ordination imposed new tasks, regulations, and responsibilities and conferred new privileges. Priests had their "hands filled" with sacrificial flesh to offer on the Lord's table and were appointed over the house. The intensified holiness of priestly standing also came with strict regulations, for as one drew near to Yahweh, he had to exercise greater care to avoid defilement. Leviticus 21-22 enumerates priestly regulations concerning mourning customs, marriage, physical defects and treatment of the body, and the punishment of a wayward daughter. Regarding privileges, we have already seen that the priest stood in Yahweh's house and shared His food.

If ordination can be construed as an operative ceremony, so, by our typology, can baptism. Faith, again, is necessary. An adult comes to the font in response to the Lord's electing call through the gospel; he draws near because he trusts Christ to accept him among His people and lead him to the Father. Parents bring infants to the font because they believe Jesus welcomes their children into His family and gives them a ministry in

His house. Both adult converts and baptized infants must persevere as disciples of the One whose name they bear. Finally, Christ prescribes the baptismal washing as the initiation rite of the church, so the church expresses her faith that the Lord accepts the baptized into His fellowship whenever she performs it. Yet, baptism makes priests regardless of the faith of the baptized or of the minister of baptism. Rightly done, baptism inducts, *ex opere operato*, into the priesthood of the Christian church.[29] One may offer strange fire in the Lord's house immediately following his baptism (Lev. 10:1); but he offers it, and will be judged, as a member of the priesthood.

Like ordination, baptism places the baptized under a stricter rule, imposes new obligations, confers new privileges. Fleshly forms of life and relation common elsewhere – strife, ambition, rivalry – are not tolerated

---

[29]Reformed theology has generally rejected *ex opere operato*, interpreting this phrase as implying that power is inherent in the sacramental rite or materials (Heppe 1950: 605; Beardslee 1965: 125). Yet, Reformed theologians accept that baptism functions *ex opere operato* to incorporate a person into the visible church, which is all, at this point, that I have argued for. Johannes Wollebius claims, for example, that sacraments are *signa exhibientia*, like the scepter by which a king is installed in office and the keys by which someone is granted access to a house (Beardslee 1965: 122). Traditional qualifications concerning the intention of the minister also arise. Reformed theology has, strangely enough, sometimes been more objective at this point than Roman Catholic theology. According to Wollebius and others, making baptism dependent on the minister's intention to "do what the church does" throws a slender shadow of doubt over the validity of baptism, and therefore threatens to undermine assurance. Validity rests upon Christ's institution and objectively proper performance, the application of water in the Name of the Trinity (Heppe 1950: 606; Beardslee 1965: 121). While I am sympathetic to this, intention must play a role, for one cannot accept as valid a formally proper baptism performed as a joke or in a theatrical production. Perhaps the problem is that "intention" has been construed as existing in an inaccessible internal realm, rather than being embodied in act, sign, and context.

within the new household, but are to be replaced with love, mutual encouragement, contentment, service, and edification. As Aquinas emphasizes, the seal of baptism is a "deputation" to participation in the liturgy that is the church's life and worship (*per ea deputamur ad cultum Dei secundum ritum Christianae religionis*; *ST* 3a, 63, 2). All the baptized contribute to house-keeping/body-building by cleansing the house of defilement, guarding it from sin, trimming the wicks so that its light burns brightly, continually offering the incense of prayer and the sacrificial bread of praise through the heavenly Priest. Finally, the baptized are privileged to enter the house and approach the table, to share in the sacrificial meal.

So far with "operative ceremony." To this point, we have affirmed without hesitation the traditional view that baptism "causes what it symbolizes." The truth of this claim depends, of course, on what baptism is understood to symbolize. Baptism, I have argued, fulfills and replaces ordination, and thus signifies the making of Christians, those who share in the chrism of the Anointed Priest. Baptism, like ordination, *does* what it symbolizes by symbolizing what it does, fills hands for household service by "filling hands" in ritual play, "manufactures" priests by acting out the manufacture of priests.

Baptismal Regeneration

The ordination texts invite us to stretch from operative ceremony to baptismal regeneration. To show how, we will inspect the structure of the tabernacle texts. Recent studies of the ordination have examined it, according to an anthropological taxonomy, as a *rite de passage* or *rite de*

160

marge.[30]   Of Mosaic rituals, the ordination most closely resembles the triple structure discovered by van Gennep and developed by Victor Turner.   After a day of initial rites, the priests remained in the sacred precincts for a week before taking up their duties at the altar and in the house; hence, the rite progressed from separation, through a liminal period, to reintegration.[31] Ordination was, moreover, literally liminal: It took place in the "doorway" of the tabernacle and the priests passed over the threshold. Van Gennep's picture of society as a house whose rooms correspond to social positions and whose thresholds correspond to rites of crossing (1960: 26) provides an important clue to the significance of priesthood and sanctuary in ancient Israel.

As Milgrom's discussion shows, however, not all the details of the ordination correspond to anthropological paradigms (1991: 566-569). During the ordination week, the priests were *not* subjected to ritual abuse, *not* stripped of their official robes, and *not* in a state of undifferentiated

---

[30]See Leach (1976: 85-92); Jenson (1992: 120); David Wright (1992: 247); and Milgrom (1991: 566-569).

[31]A somewhat van Gennepian pattern is evident in cleansing from corpse defilement (Num. 19:11-19), skin disease (Lev. 14:1-32), long-term genital flows (Lev. 15:13-15, 28-30), and childbirth (Lev. 12:1-8). Liminal states were completely absent in other rites of entry and transition in the Old Testament. Seminal emission caused uncleanness until the evening sacrifice and was cleansed by washing (Lev. 15:1-12, 16-18). Circumcision was performed on the eighth day, but the first seven days of life were scarcely a "liminal" period. Nothing is explicitly said about cleansing from menstruation, and, given the leniency of the Levitical regulations governing menstruation (Milgrom 1991: 948-953), the implication is that a woman did not have to perform an elaborate cleansing rite (Lev. 15:19-24). In these cases, the person was *not* in a liminal state but simply unclean until cleansed.

communitas, since Aaron remained visibly distinct by virtue of his High Priestly vestments.[32] The most serious danger in the Procrustean effort to cram biblical squares into anthropological circles is that such an approach ignores the shape of the texts themselves.[33] Old Testament passages prescribing longer-term cleansing rites, like the rites themselves, frequently have a seven- or eightfold arrangement that links to circumcision on the eighth day, which, in turn, recapitulates the creation week of Genesis 1. Rather than huddling every feature of ordination under the umbrella of boundary-crossing, the Bible places it under the rubric of creation.

From an investigation of occurrences of "completion formulae" (cf. Gen. 2:1-2; Exod. 39:32; 40:33) and "command-execution formulae" in "P," Joseph Blenkinsopp concludes that the construction of the tabernacle recapitulates creation. Links between the tabernacle and creation are also indicated by the prominence and placement of the Sabbath commands (Gen. 2:1-4; Exod. 31:12-17; 35:1-3), the intervention of the Spirit (Gen. 1:2; Exod. 31:3; 35:31), and the fact that the tabernacle was set up on New Year's Day (Exod. 40:2; cf. Gen. 8:13; Blenkinsopp 1976: 275-292). In a similar vein, Peter Kearney notes that the instructions for building the tabernacle are arranged in seven speeches, marked by the phrase "Yahweh spoke to Moses" (Exod. 25:1; 30:11, 17, 22, 34; 31:1, 12). Significantly,

---

[32]Despite these differences, Milgrom is so enamored of the "help" that anthropology provides that he describes the ordination as a rite of passage, sees the ordination week as a liminal period, and even asks whether the priests were subjected to a "ritual of verbal humiliation," though he admits the Bible provides no evidence for this (1991: 569).

[33]See chapter 1 above for discussion of the formalism of cultural anthropology.

the seventh speech commands Sabbath observance, and Kearney makes an effort, not always persuasive, to find correspondences between the previous speeches and the six days of creation (Kearney 1977: 375-387). James B. Jordan has gone beyond Kearney in suggesting that the lengthy first speech (Exod. 25:1-30:10) also has a heptamerous structure. In Jordan's analysis, Exodus 29, the passage prescribing the ordination rite, occupies the sixth-day slot, connecting it with the creation of man (Jordan 1992: 126; Gen. 1:24-31).[34] Besides textual allusions to creation, the form of the tabernacle bolsters the ancient view that the sanctuary was a microcosm.[35] Its three zones match heaven, earth, and sea (Gen. 1; cf. Exod. 20:4) and the three-story ark of Noah (Gen. 6:16).[36] Edenic cherubim adorned the tabernacle curtains and veils, and also the cover of the ark of the covenant (Gen. 3:24), suggesting that the tabernacle reconstituted the garden environment (Poythress 1991: 19, 35; Berman 1995: 21-34). These parallels lead to two related theological conclusions:

---

[34]Blum (1990: 306-312); Sarna (1986: 213-214); Berman (1995:14-15); and Fretheim (1991: 269-71) also note that the tabernacle sections sway to the rhythms of Genesis 1. This highlights the significance of the golden calf episode, which is, as Fretheim puts it, "Genesis 3 all over again" (Fretheim 1991: 281). Kearney notes the creation-fall-restoration pattern of Exodus 25-40 (1977: 383).

[35]Philo (1966: 493; *de Vita Mosis* 2.18.88) links the materials of the tabernacle to the four elements of earth, air, water, and fire, emphasizing the appropriateness of constructing a temple to the Creator from the elements of His creation, and Josephus (1967: 385; *Jewish Antiquities* 3.146) sees planetary symbolism in the lampstand. Though Keel's discussion focuses on the temple rather than the tabernacle, his explanations of cosmic symbolism apply equally to the tent (1978: 118-120; cf. Poythress 1991: 28). For brief reviews of the history of tabernacle interpretation, see Fretheim (1991: 265-268) and Childs (1974: 537-539, 547-550).

[36]Sarna (1986: 214); Fretheim (1991: 268-269); Jordan (1988: 167-178).

Though mediated through Moses' words and through human labor, the tabernacle, like the original creation, was ultimately the product of the word of Yahweh. Thus, second, the tabernacle is, in some sense, a "new creation."

Against this background, it is significant that Milgrom discovers a sevenfold structure in the ordination text in Leviticus 8, each section marked by a variation of the execution formula, "as Yahweh commanded Moses." We can diagram Milgrom's scheme as follows:

1. Assembling material, vv. 1-5
2. Washing priests, dressing Aaron, vv. 6-9
   A. Anointing the sanctuary, vv. 10-11[37]
3. Anointing Aaron, dressing sons, vv. 12-13
4. Purification offering, vv. 14-17
5. Burnt offering, vv. 18-21
6. "Ordination" offering, vv. 22-29
   A'. Anointing the vestments, v. 30
7. Seven days of probation, vv. 31-36 (Milgrom 1991: 542-544).

Without trying to correlate each of these seven sections with a day of creation week, some correspondences are striking. The "ram of ordination," which was the climax of Aaron's qualification as priest, fits into the "sixth-day slot," suggesting that Aaron's ordination made him a "new Adam" in the tabernacle "garden." The "seventh-day" slot, which

---

[37]The two "A" sections protrude from the structure, since neither is concluded by an execution formula. At these points, Leviticus 8 differs from the parallel text in Exodus 29 and both sections have to do with anointing. The prominence given to the anointing in Leviticus may be connected with its elaborate attention to the "golden plate" of the High Priest (v. 9; cf. Exod. 29:6), since the plate, similar in color to oil, was a permanent anointing (cf. Lev. 21:12: "consecration of the anointing oil" is נזר שמן משחת, and נזר is a name for the crown/plate).

stipulates the week-long probation and grants permission to eat in the holy place, has Sabbatical overtones.[38] Thus, the eighth day, when Aaron began his ministry (Lev. 9:1), was the first day of a new creation week, tragically marred by yet another "fall" (Lev. 10:1-7). Through the "operative ceremony" of ordination, Aaron did not merely acquire a new social status or religious office. He became a new man.[39]

You Must Be Born Again

Applied to baptism, then, our typology leads to a doctrine of "baptismal regeneration." Aaron and his sons received new tasks, a new title and name, new privileges and responsibilities, and baptism likewise forms new creatures. But here we meet a sharp objection from traditional sacramental theology, for I seem to have reduced "baptismal regeneration" to "operative ceremony." This typology produces a theology of baptism that seems purely "external," "merely legal," and

---

[38]Jordan has suggested that Leviticus 8 follows the account of Adam's creation in Genesis 2 more closely than the general creation account of Genesis 1, but also argues that Genesis 2 has a heptamerous structure that tracks Genesis 1 (Jordan 1989: 25-28). As he explains, "the contrast between Ex. 29 and Lev. 8 is the presence of the Garden/Tabernacle. In Exodus, the world is made first and then man, as in Genesis 1. In Lev. 8 both sanctuary and man are made simultaneously, as in Gen. 2. Exodus is cosmic; Leviticus is sanctuary (microcosmic)" (personal correspondence, January 10, 1998). Jordan may well be correct, but establishing a general creation reference is sufficient for my purposes.

[39]Exodus 39:1-31, which describes the making of the priestly garments, also has a heptamerous structure, indicated by the phrase "as Yahweh commanded Moses." Describing the "recreation" of Aaron by reference to Genesis 1 suggests that, like the tabernacle, the priest was something of a "microcosm."

"juridical," while baptism is something far "more profound and more inward," related to "an inner salvation-event to which the outward confession is only a precondition" (Schnackenburg 1964: 125-126, 145). This objection goes to the heart of the problematics of sacramental theology, for it poses the question of the relation between outward sign and inward grace. Semi-Marcionite sacramental theology arises here as well, for Schnackenburg's comments suggest that baptism has a more "inner" and "spiritual" significance than baptism.

Louis-Marie Chauvet raises similar objections in his warnings against sociological reductionism. Comparing the sacraments with speech acts, Chauvet cautions that grace is "*irreducible* to any explanations," and baptismal grace in particular cannot be reduced "*theologically* to the symbolic efficacy of a language act." This caution is necessary lest theology dissolve into anthropology and become "only a variant within the social sciences." Thus, "it is one thing to be proclaimed a son or daughter for God and brother or sister for others in Jesus Christ, to be recognized as such by the group, and to be authentically so on the *social* level; it is quite another to be so on the *theological* level of faith, hope, and charity" (Chauvet 1995: 439, 443). Distinctions of this sort are central to Chauvet's work, manifested in a pervasive contrast of Christian identity and salvation (e.g., 1995: 425). In Chauvet's terms, my account of baptism confuses the sociological with the theological, identity as priest with salvation. Perhaps it is time to cut my losses, abandon the ordination typology, and admit that Marcion's disciples were right after all. All this stretching and pulling may be even more dangerous than I feared.

Brief consideration of Chauvet's strictures will begin to lead us out of

166

this predicament. Despite its surface plausibility, his distinction between "sociological" and "theological" is erroneous at two levels. Ontologically, Chauvet assumes that "language acts" and, apparently, other social and cultural processes are secular realities, not already permeated with religious significance. Even membership in the church, thus, might, for Chauvet, be merely "social." Especially in the church, this is *never* the case. Chauvet's reminder that church members may be dissembling, though correct enough, is beside the point. A dissembling member is not a "social" Christian but a "false son" or "unfruitful branch," and this is a theological fact with eternal consequences. Based on this ontological assumption, Chauvet implies that social science can provide an adequate account of immanent social mechanisms, but theology must be trundled out to account for grace. But if social reality is not secular, if every immanent process has a transcendent dimension, then an a-theological sociology cannot give an adequate account of any social process. Moreover, if, as Milbank has powerfully put it (1990), sociology is an alternative theology, and if theology is *the* social science, then a theological account *is* sociological, and vice versa. If the social sciences are already theologically committed, then theology cannot supplement them but must revise, perhaps radically, sub-orthodox or heretical social scientific descriptions.

With much of the tradition, Chauvet assumes a conception of personal identity such that the interior self is ontologically fundamental. Since this self is untouchable by external social roles and rituals, no rite can effect truly "ontological" change but can only skim the surface of personality. For Chauvet, sacraments can affect "identity" or "social"

167

standing but not "theological" status or "salvation." The way round this obstacle is to abandon the ancient soul imprisoned in the body and its modern counterpart, the Cartesian ego (Kerr 1986), or, to put it differently, to challenge the effort to mark an absolute boundary between inner and outer.

A "narrative" conception of personal identity is helpful here.[40] At a social level, any particular baptism is, as MacIntyre implies, an event in the history of baptism, which is to say, a moment in the church's story (1989: 100; cf. Jones 1987: 53-69). Baptism immerses a person in that history. Identities are formed at the intersection of various narratives of which one is a part (of family, community, nation, and so on), so that when baptism embeds one's story in that of the church, his identity is objectively modified. To "I am an American, or Scot, or Chinese" is added "I am a member of the Christian priesthood"; one's "forefathers" now include not only Washington, Robert the Bruce, or Mao but Abraham, Isaac and Jacob; the story that once began, "my father sailed to the Cape from Amsterdam," now begins, "my father was a wandering Aramean." At an individual level, identity is bound up with the events of one's life and his (selective) memory of those events. Roles acquired and significant actions done become part of my "record," a story that marks my difference from others and traces the continuity of *my* life through time. Objectively, baptism makes me a priest, and this becomes an episode in the story of who I am. Subjectively, the baptismal narrative into which I am

---

[40]See the essays in Hauerwas and Jones (1989); Stroup (1981: 100-131); Kerby (1991).

submerged may break violently against the story that, before baptism, identified me, forcing what may be a painful revaluation of my past and producing a revised self-image (Stroup 1981: 95).

In this framework, one can rehabilitate the traditional notion that baptism imprints an "indelible character."[41] Baptism irreversibly plants my story in the story of the church, for even if I renounce her, my renunciation is part of her history. As a facet of individual identity, baptism is equally permanent, for one is never unbaptized (Pannenberg 1993: 268). A baptized man can renounce Christ, turn persecutor of the church, reject everything he once confessed, forget his baptism. Having once passed through the waters, however, his every action thereafter, including those that are wholly inconsistent with his baptismal identity, are actions of a baptized man. Forgetfulness of baptism is the culpable forgetfulness of the baptized. Even those who leave the Father's house are priests and sons, however prodigally they may squander their inheritance in riotous living.

Thus, what is ontologically fundamental is not the naked "I" laid bare by stripping away layers of accidental cultural clothing, any more than God is the "bare minimum" of deity that remains after we peel off His attributes, word, and works. Rather, the ontologically fundamental self, what makes me uniquely me, is a combination of the roles, stories, actions

---

[41]On sacramental character, see Haring (1948a: 109-146; 1948b: 217-219); Houssiau (1978: 138-165); D'Argenlieu (1929a: 219-233; 1929b: 289-302); Dittoe (1946: 469-514); Kiesling (1963: 385-412); McCormack (1944: 458-491); Nicolas (1974: 309-328); O'Neill (1963: 88-140); Thils (1938: 683-689); Walsh (1974: 557-583).

and events of my life; the individual and his world are not hermetically sealed from one another, but mutually defining. Thus, while it is true that *I* am a husband, it is equally important to see that I *am* a husband. "Husband" is not an accident inhering in an unmarried self but one of the roles that makes up my identity. Importantly, I am a husband because I have gone through the ceremony of marriage. Operative ceremonies, thus, by placing us in new roles, vesting us with new clothes, and imposing new sets of obligations and rules, effect an "ontological" transformation, a change in who we are, who we think we are, and who others think we are. Baptism clothes us as priests, and these clothes remake the man.

Having cleared some ground, we can return more explicitly to our typology to show that it implies a theological, not a reductively sociological, view of baptismal regeneration. Aaron received a new "standing" to serve Israel but the more specific result of ordination was that, as personal attendant and son of the house, he stood to serve Yahweh. Yahweh regarded Aaron differently after the rite, permitting him to enter the house, stand at the altar, offer and eat His bread. Baptism, analogously, effects a transition, as Rowan Williams puts it, not only in the regard of men but in the "gaze of God," and this makes us "new creations" in the deepest possible sense. Identity is enmeshed with relations in community, but our most fundamental belonging is to the community of Adam or of Christ, and therefore our basic identity is not constituted by social or cultural factors, but by the transcendent "regard of God upon us" (1996: 90-94; cf. Rom. 5-6). The baptized is no longer regarded as "stranger" but born again as a "son of the house." Chauvet notwithstanding, prying apart social and theological "levels" is simply impossible.

It is also helpful here to look more carefully at the blueprints of the remodeled house. In the New Covenant, the house in which the glory-Spirit dwells is the community of believers. Yet, no group's existence as group is either temporally or logically prior to its common practices. Thousands may be addicted to Tintin comic books, but these teeming multitudes do not form a Tintin fan club until they have declared the club exists, established membership fees and entry requirements, instituted procedures (including the secret handshake), and adopted club identities (e.g., Capt. Haddock, Bianca Castafiore, Prof. Calculus, Rastapopoulos, Snowy, etc.). The club as club exists only in and through these institutions and practices. Likewise, theoretically, any number of individuals may sincerely believe that Jesus is Lord without forming a church. The church as a recognizable human community exists only in her common confession of Christ, obedience to the word, liturgical practices, fellowship and mutual aid, and formal and informal procedures of correction and forgiveness. If the Spirit dwells in the church as church, He dwells in the people constituted by these practices. Baptism is one of the practices without which the church does not exist. Initiation is thus not so much a doorway through which one passes into the house as the first act of membership, and therefore the first contact with the Spirit who circulates through the body (cf. Acts 2:38; 1 Cor. 12:12-13). Baptism into the ecclesial priesthood that is the house therefore also confers the ἀρραβών of the Spirit.

Finally, we may consider the relation of baptism to salvation. Salvation is not an entity, substance, or power that floats free of persons in concrete situations. Rather, salvation is "adjectival": Persons, communities, and, in a sense, the nonhuman creation are or will be saved. A saved person is one who, redeemed in Christ from sin and death, lives as God created him to live, walking with God, submissive to His rule. A saved people consists of the redeemed whose communal life is conformed to the New Covenant under the Lord Christ. Salvation in its fullest sense is eschatological; only at the end will death be swallowed up in victory and "God's will be done on earth as it is in heaven." Yet because the church is on the path toward this eschatological consummation she anticipates, to the extent that she conforms to the will of Christ, the final peace of the kingdom. The church, as a concrete, historical community is thus not merely the means of salvation but the already partially realized goal (Milbank 1987: 204). More specifically, Adam was created to be priest and king, so a saved person is one restored, through Christ, to this Adamic status and task; the eschatological people is the kingdom of priests (Rev. 1:5-6; 5:9-10; 20:6). By baptism into the royal priesthood, one is incorporated into the race of the Last Adam. It is thus not correct that the Spirit first enlivens and then at some second stage equips for ministry. Living the life of salvation *is* ministering in God's house; as baptism authorizes and deputizes to such ministry, it grants a share in the life of salvation.

Bringing together the arguments of the two preceding paragraphs, and in the light of our discussion of Augustine's *Contra Faustum* 19 in chapter 1, we can also address the issue of the "necessity" of baptism, a question best answered in a corporate rather than individual frame of reference (cf. *ST* 3a, 61, 1). Within this context, baptism is not merely a

172

pointer to but a necessary part of the now of eschatological salvation. Without her practices, the church would not be the saved people of God because she would not exist at all as a recognizable human community. And that would mean that salvation is not a historical reality. Since it is one of the divinely authorized practices by which the church exists as church, baptism is necessary to her existence; and since the church is the site where salvation has occurred and is occurring, baptism is necessary for salvation.

What of baptism's relation to the eschatological "not yet"? Here I focus on baptism's effects on the individual. Baptism to priesthood does not guarantee an eternal standing among the people of God, for priests may be removed from the house and cut off from the table. Yet, baptism is not irrelevant to eternal salvation; though baptism "by itself" does not guarantee a standing, baptism never is "by itself" but always a step on a pathway. Perseverance to the end of the pathway, the mark of eschatologically saving faith, is, as Augustine insisted, a gift of grace, which, being grace, is gratuitously distributed as God pleases. God determines which priests stand or fall and brings this about through a variety of specific instruments. He can even use the same means to make one stand and another fall; frogs, pestilence, and hail hardened Pharaoh's heart but the same plagues prompted others to transfer their loyalty to Yahweh (Exod. 9:20). What we bring under the heading of "the grace of perseverance" are the concrete ways God holds close and brings nearer, baptism among them. Baptism holds us close by admitting us to His table, where we feed on Christ in the Spirit; by putting us within hearing of His life-giving word; by joining us to people who encourage, exhort, and comfort. Through continual baptismal *anamnesis*, we stir ourselves to faithfulness in housekeeping and to thankfulness for priestly privileges. In baptism, we are inducted into ministry in God's house, and continuing in that ministry is the way of salvation. Clothed in the tent, the baptized enters the path of suffering service and living sacrifice whose destination is a weighty and glorious house, the brightness of endless day.

Priestly baptism, therefore, implies not a thinly sociological view of "baptismal regeneration" but a thick theological one, which is equally cultural-linguistic. To say that baptism "regenerates" by conferring new tasks, a new role, and new privileges is not reductionist, for the task is service to the Lord in His house, the role is as His priest, the privileges include fellowship at His table. These are "merely social" facts only if one assumes that this house is not really God's house and this table not really His table; but that, of course, is simple unbelief.

How Can Water Do These Wonders?

A final question concerns the relation of divine and human action in baptism. Theologians have generally answered Luther's question, "How can water do such wonders?" by echoing Augustine's insistence that God is the principal actor who confers the blessings attributed to baptism. Yet the tradition faces the challenging fact that baptism is palpably a human action. No fire falls, no dove descends, the heavens are not rent, no voices thunder from above. It all seems so very mundane. Is there *really* a divine action occurring here? *How* is this God's act? And if it is, as it appears to be, a human act, how can it confer a spiritual grace? How can

174

washing the body cleanse the soul? (Leeming 1956: 284).

Again, our typology points beyond the impasse. The discussion of "operative ceremony" and "baptismal regeneration" has already profoundly disrupted the complacent semi-Marcionism that produces such questions. Our typology, as I have extrapolated it, challenges the basic conception that a sacrament is an "outward sign of inward grace" by insisting that the outward signs reach to the innermost parts and that God extends His grace to us in the outward form of concrete favors. Baptism is not, strictly, a "means of grace," a "bottle containing the medicine of grace" or a "channel" through which the fluid of grace flows. Rather, baptism *is* a gift of God's grace, since through it He adopts us as sons.[42] And the "sonship" conferred by baptism is not "external" to our basic identity but constitutive of it.

Underlying the dilemmas concerning sacramental causation is often a questionable theory of finite causality, for which Thomas Aquinas may serve as an example. According to John Milbank's account, Thomas taught that being is an effect of creation and cannot depend on any contribution from finite causes. Creative agency requires not just "having

---

[42]Meredith Kline defines the covenant as God's administration of a "law-order," and argues that baptism, like circumcision, effectively brings the candidate under the covenant sanctions, which may be for blessing or cursing. Thus, according to Kline, the rite does not prejudge the outcome either way and is not itself an act of grace (Kline 1968). Though superior to Kline's strictly legal notion of the covenant, P. Richard Flinn's alternative is also finally unsatisfactory. Using Austin's distinction between the illocution and perlocution of a speech act, Flinn argues that baptism should be defined by its illocutionary intent to offer grace, though its actual outcome may be to bring covenant curses (Flinn 1982: 111-151). Contrary to Flinn, the sacrament of entry into the church is not merely "intended to be a gracious act" but actually is so.

being" but "being as such," and thus, though finite causes give new shapes to things, only God creates. Though Thomas was seeking, rightly, to protect the uniqueness of God's existence *in se*, he wrongly confined "human transitive causation to the level of form/matter, rather than the level of *esse/essentia*" and thus reduced human making to "mere *bricolage*" (Milbank 1991-1992: 1.23-26, 28).

According to William J. Courtenay, scholastic sacramental speculations assume a sharp distinction of creation and causation, the former being reserved to God alone (1972: 189; van den Eynde 1951: [141]). The human enactment of baptism, then, cannot be creative in any strong sense. For much of the tradition, the answer to the question, "How can water cleanse the soul?" is, it cannot; therefore, the Spirit must intervene "directly" alongside the rite to make it effective. But this suggests that the "real" divine-human relationship has moved outside the economy of signs that constitutes human being in the world, and this carries the troubling implication that it is not fully within the compass of human experience. Thus, the scholastic distinction of causality and creation leads to what Peter Cramer identifies as the withdrawal of sacrament "from *poiesis* ['making'] into the intangible *mysterium* of metamorphosis -- into a secret mechanics no less mechanical for being secret" (Cramer 1993: 237).[43] A sounder sacramental theology must

---

[43]This was an aspect of a more general separation of sacraments from cultural processes more generally. Courtenay writes, "For Bernard, as for earlier generations, symbols *qua* symbols cause the effect of the action in which they were used. For Thomas, symbols *qua* symbols only declared or 'symbolized' an action or effect that was achieved through other means." Only a small number of symbols were actually effective (1972: 208-209).

rehabilitate poesis, and for that we turn again to Milbank, who has made this a centerpiece of his assault on secularism.

Milbank claims that a fundamental assumption of modernity is that what is humanly constructed (the "made" or *factum*) is secular or religiously neutral (Milbank 1990: 10-11).[44] With the Renaissance discovery that culture is wholly a human construction, historical "all the way down," the whole of culture came to be conceived as secular, and religion was pushed into a closet of inner piety. To challenge the identification of *factum* with the secular, Milbank taps into a "counter-modern" thread of philosophy and theology found in the work of Nicholas of Cusa and Giambattista Vico, and also in the later metacritical philosophies of Hamann and Herder. At the center of Vico's thought is the axiom that *verum et factum convertuntur* (Milbank 1991-1992: 1.5), and a key source of this Vichian motto is Cusa, who on Milbank's reading, makes creation rather than *esse* the principal philosophical concept (1991-1992: 1.22). This has an epistemological dimension, implying that knowledge proceeds by linguistic, scientific, and other cultural constructions, but for Vico the convertibility of *verum* and *factum* is absolute, finding its ultimate ontological ground in the interTrinitarian relations. Earlier, Cusa had speculated that the Second Person of the Trinity is the "Art" of God, so that without denying the Nicene Creed, he could speak of a kind of eternal "making" in the Father's begetting of the Son, which rendered "God's inner creativity definatory of the divine

---

[44]In addition to the works cited in the text, see Milbank (1990: 23, 56, 149-153, 218, 242, 355-356; 1997: 32, 73, 79, 123-30).

essence." Since the Word, "made" by the Father, contains all truth and wisdom, *verum* and *factum* are convertible in the Godhead. "Factum" therefore became one of the transcendentals, along with the good, true, beautiful. Creativity is the chief attribute of the Trinity; a "creation" *ab intra* grounds the *ad extra* (Milbank 1991-1992: 1.27-30, 82-84, 126-132).

Man, made in God's image, is *homo creator* and, just as the Father is never without His eternal "Art," so human artifacts are not pasted onto an a-cultural existence but "fully equiprimordial" with human being (Milbank 1991-1992: 1.31, 88, 101); Adam, we recall, first lived in a *garden*. Since human making reflects the eternal character and the continually creative work of God, it is not "secular" or "neutral," but a reaching for transcendence, an imitation of and participation in God's ongoing *creatio ex nihilo*. Reflecting the divine poetry, human construction even partakes of its *ex nihilo* character. Though the original creation is unique, the inner essence of created existence is ongoing origination, a continual bringing-into-being of new states of affairs. A table is not "merely rearranged lumber" but a new thing that simply did not exist before being built; Edison created an entire new *category* of thing with the invention of the light bulb. Thus Milbank, following Cusa and Vico, contests modernity *not* by rejecting the Renaissance discovery of the "fictional" character of cultural life, but by extending divine concursus to creative cultural activity; though culture is a thoroughly human product, God is the ultimate Author of cultural fictions.

The tabernacle and ordination texts lend support to a fully poetic conception of human being and culture. As we have seen, textual indicators show that the tabernacle was an architectural cosmos, so that when Moses built Yahweh's house, he was fashioning a "new creation." To be sure, the connection between the tabernacle texts and the creation account is an example, in Michael Fishbane's phrase, of "innerbiblical interpretation," evidence of nascent typology within the Old Testament. Yet, the analogy is not a mere trope, nor is it introduced simply to emphasize the tabernacle's cosmic symbolism. In an objective, historical sense, the erection of the sanctuary inaugurated a new religious and sociological universe. By building it, Moses remade the socio-religious structures not only of Israel but of the world, since the nations were, from Israel's vantage point, oriented to the sanctuary. Exodus 26:31-35, where the hanging of the veil formed the previously unknown division between Holy and Most Holy space, highlights this point.

Similarly, the heptamerous arrangement of Leviticus 8 suggests, as we have seen, that ordination produced new men. This is underlined by the ambiguity about how Aaron and his sons were "sanctified." Exodus 29:43 states that Yahweh Himself sanctified His house, altar, and priest with His glory, yet it is also said that Moses sanctified Aaron and his sons, the tabernacle, and its furnishings by anointing them (Exod. 29:21; Lev. 8:10-12). The text offers no harmonization, but one may infer that Yahweh sanctified Aaron and his sons through the actions of Moses. Ordination and consecration of priests was ritual poetry, a participation in Yahweh's construction of a new world and His consecration of new men. By our typology, baptism too is poetic, for through this human act Christ in the Spirit produces new creations.[45]

---

[45]For recent poetic treatments of sacramental theology, see Jones (1959) and

The ordination texts also hint at the sense in which we are to take ordination as a divine act. Moses' actions were poetically creative because they were authorized by the word of Yahweh and revealed on the mountain. Not every act of construction is so authorized. Vico's idea of "mis-making" comes to the fore here (Milbank 1991-1992: 2.5-6, 47-54), for the tabernacle texts are interrupted by the episode of the golden calf, presented in Exodus as a kind of "negative tabernacle" (Sarna 1986: 215-220). Though an artifact of human "poesis," more importantly the calf had an ultimately destructive effect. An unauthorized cultic "poem" ended in decreation (Exod. 32-34). Numbers 16 makes a similar point concerning priesthood: Korah's assertion of priestly privilege did not make him a personal attendant to Yahweh, and the result of his presumption in "making" himself a priest was catastrophic. Yahweh was determined to dwell only in the house constructed after the pattern on the mountain and maintained according to His Torah, and only a priest "manufactured" according to His word might approach His house with confidence that he would be accepted as a new man.

To this point, I have come close to the "covenantal" view associated with the *sine qua non* theory of sacramental causation (cf. Courtenay 1972: 185-209). On this theory, the causality of the sacraments is like that of cultural institutions and social customs, which depend on value ascribed

---

Rowan Williams (1987: 32-44). Verbally, at least, many writers link sacrament with *factum*. Tertullian states that *fiunt non nascuntur Christiani*, and it is through the postbaptismal rite of anointing that one is *facta spiritalis* (above, chapter 3, fn. 1). Rupert of Deutz comments that *non nisi per baptismum efficimur "regale sacerdotium et gens sancta"* and Honorius of Autun claims that the initiated are *facti . . . reges et sacerdotes* by baptismal union with the royal priest Jesus (cf. above, fns. 9-10).

by an authority within a contingent semiotic economy. Signs have creative power but of a more cultural than magical kind. Because this conception seeks sociological rather than natural/physical analogies for the sacraments, it protects, better than Thomas, the principle that *sacramenta causant significando*.[46] Covenantal causality locates the divine role more at the level of institution than at the moment of administration. Contrary to some criticisms, this does not imply that the sacraments lack ontological bulk, that baptism is "really" only water, any more than pound notes are "merely paper" or boundary stones are "mere rocks" (cf. John Searle 1995; Beardslee 1965: 121). Baptism is efficacious because Jesus assigned *this* rite value as the entry token for the feast, as the induction ceremony into His Spirit-filled house, as ordination into priesthood. Baptism works because, like the tabernacle and ordination, it conforms to the verbal תבנית revealed on another mountain (Matt. 28:18; Exod. 25:40).

A robust sacramental poetry demands a further stretch of our typology; fortunately, the ordination texts comply. The word of Yahweh is not merely a word of authorization but a heptamerous creative word. Moses' construction was not absolutely originary because it was a response to the Word who was in the beginning, yet it was originary, not only as *response* but as authorized *performance*. Because it was the *creative* word that was performed, the human performance was also creative, producing a new world and new men. Likewise, baptism is efficacious not

---

[46]Thomas, on the other hand, has a firmer grasp of why *these* objects or actions have been assigned particular meanings. A gift of flowers receives its meaning within a particular culture, but the natural properties of flowers make them appropriate for that purpose.

only because it is authorized, but because it enacts the word of the Incarnate Word by whom the world was made, through whom the world was renewed.[47] The word provides the score: If the church chooses a different arrangement, her music will be dissonant; but as the church sings the creative word, her song is taken up as harmony on the ineffable song of the Creator.

Conclusion

Through our typology, we have examined, perhaps with some fresh insight, significant issues of liturgy and theology: the relation of baptism and Eucharist, infant baptism, sacramental efficacy, baptismal regeneration, and sacramental causality. Stretching and pulling have somehow produced a surprisingly lyrical apparatus, for our expansions have ended in poetry and song. Yet the poetry extends further. In the next chapter, we will see that baptism not only makes new men; through it, the body of Christ shares with Christ in making a new cosmos.

---

[47]Thus, in several senses, we must locate the divine action also at the moment of administration. First, the Spirit as Lord of life concurrently enables all human acts, including baptism. Second, since baptism is incorporation into the Spirit-filled body, baptism is a "trysting place" of God and man (Beasley-Murray 1973: *passim*; cf. Trigg 1994), the Spirit's reaching out in a gesture of love. Third, Word and Spirit are inseparable, especially in creation; the Spirit is therefore creatively active in the baptismal enactment of the word.

CHAPTER FIVE

The Priesthood of the Plebs [1]

In the previous chapter, I developed a theology of initiation in which "baptismal regeneration" was construed as induction into the "cultural-linguistic" practice of the church (cf. Lindbeck 1984). This is not, as I have argued, an immanentization of transcendent faith, for the "cultural" practice of the church is above all a continual sacrificial liturgy before the face of God, her linguistic practice one of ceaseless prayer and praise. Far from being reductionist, this typology and the framework extrapolated from it permits a richer and stronger affirmation of the objectivity of baptismal grace than found in traditional sacramental theology, which has hesitated to affirm that baptism confers grace *ex opere operato* (Leeming 1956: 330). If grace is the favor of God manifested in the bestowal of favors, then baptism is and confers grace: the grace of a standing in the house of God, the grace of membership in the community of the reconciled, the grace of immersion in the history of the bride of Christ, the grace of God's favorable regard upon us. It would be churlish to complain that it does not also guarantee perseverance.

Objections may, however, arise from a different quarter. Thus far I have used "regeneration" in the traditional sense of individual transformation, but παλινγγενεσία (cf. Tit. 3:5), the Greek term

---

[1]"Plebs" is not, in general, used in a technical sense here. Strictly speaking, the plebeians were a free gentry order of ancient Rome that organized against the patricians, eventually winning, through a series of secessions from 494-287 BC, virtually equal political rights (cf. Sainte Croix 1981: 333-335; Alföldy 1985: 13-19). I am using the term here because of its more general connotation of a despised and rejected class, but I also wish to highlight that the social orders of the Greco-Roman world were religious orders.

underlying this doctrine, can have a broader significance. Stoic philosophy speculated about cosmic παλινγγενεσίαι following periodic ἐκπυρόσες (Dibelius and Conzelmann 1972: 148), and Matthew 19:28 shows the word could be used in a cosmological sense in first-century Judaism and the early church.[2] For some, this cosmic connotation undermines the use of Titus 3:5 as a baptismal text, for how can baptism be a washing that brings cosmic renewal? (cf. Barth 1951: 463-466).

Aided by the typology developed in previous chapters, I maintain that baptism signifies and extends a covenant renewal portrayed in the New Testament as a "cosmic" transformation; it is, in the widest sense, a "washing of regeneration." In chapter 4, I focused on the effect of the ordination rite on Aaron and his sons, and reasoned toward some conclusions concerning baptism's effects on individuals. Ordination, however, also structured Israelite religious society. When, at the end of the rite of filling, Aaron approached the altar and entered the tent, a spatial distance opened between priests and the congregation who assembled at the "doorway" (Lev. 8:3; cf. Gorman 1990: 115). Performing the word of Yahweh, Moses composed a new configuration of Israel. On page 123

---

[2]Büchsel (1964: 1.686-689) argues that Philo uses the term in a Judaized Stoic sense, and notes that Josephus applies the term to the return of Israel from exile. Burnett (1984: 468-470) disputes the evidence from Philo, and argues that in Philo "regeneration" invariably refers to the soul's "rebirth into incorporeal existence." Dibelius and Conzelmann (1972: 148-149) argue for a strong association of the New Testament usage with the Greek mysteries. Derrett (1984: 51-58) claims that the word means "resurrection" in Matthew 19:28, not "new world." Spicq's comment is apt: "Le choix même du mot palingénésie suggère qu'il faut lier étroitement la régénération individuelle du néophyte à la nouvelle ère du cosmos inaugurée par Jésus-Christ" (1969: 653).

above, I have sketched Israel's concentric order of "graded holiness" (Jenson 1992) radiating from the tent, its ranks marked out, among other things, by clothing, food, and access to or exclusion from holy environments. Two fundamental divisions existed -- between priests and people, and between Jews and Gentiles. Both were ritually constituted, by ordination and circumcision respectively, and both marked divisions regarding priestly standing. By comparison with "lay" Israelites, priests were attendants to Yahweh in His house, but in comparison with Gentiles, Israel could be called (with apologies to Adam Smith) a nation of housekeepers (Exod. 19:6; cf. Rom. 9:4). Thus, the order of the "first covenant" was a graded continuum of priesthood that encompassed not only Israel but the nations. By instituting this continuum, ordination, along with the construction of the tabernacle, formed Israel's antique order. The "eighth" day of Aaron's ordination was the first day of a new socio-religious cosmos.

If baptism is the Christian conjugation of ordination, if baptism does now what ordination did then, we have reason to suspect that it also reconstructs the religious landscape. To explain this, I return to two passages discussed in chapter 3, Hebrews 10:19-22 and Galatians 3:27, each of which intimates that, as a sign of the "second covenant," baptism relocates and redistributes priestly privilege and responsibility. Since the structure of the "first covenant" emerged from the construction of the house and the installation of Aaron and his sons as Yahweh's attendants, the baptismal formation of a new priestly community, historically extending the veil-rending work of Jesus' ministry, contests and remaps antique Israelite topography. I further argue that the structure of Greek

185

and Roman social life closely resembled Israel's system of graded holiness, so that the priestly community formed by baptism embodies a critique not only of antique Hebrew but also of antique Gentile order.

This chapter will thus develop the theme with which I began this thesis, that baptism is the "beginning of the gospel." Lay Israelites and especially Gentiles, long excluded from Yahweh's house and table, are, following Jesus' work, invited in, their hands filled in baptism. If we follow de Lubac's insistence (1950) that the gospel is an inherently social proclamation about the eschatological restoration of human community in Christ, then baptism, as the washing that effects a global "social regeneration," is the beginning of the gospel of the new creation. Like ordination, baptism is an "eighth day" rite, frequently administered in an octagonal baptistery or font (cf. J.G. Davies 1962: 16, 20-21).

To the Jew First

Though the identity and historical setting of the writer and original recipients of the letter to the Hebrews are subjects of considerable and unresolved debate,[3] the writer describes the theological situation under several metaphors. The first covenant is growing old and becoming obsolete (8:13). Metaphorically the church finds herself at Kadesh Barnea; having left Egypt behind, she must choose, like Israel, between entering to conquer and shrinking back (Heb. 3-4; cf Vanhoye 1968: 9-26). Some of

---

[3]For summaries of the issues of authorship, recipients, and setting, see Lane (1991: lvii-lxvi) and Attridge (1989: 1-13).

the book's descriptions are "apocalyptic." Earthquakes shake heaven and earth, toppling what can be shaken so that the unshakable kingdom alone remains (12:26-27). A new αἰών has come and is coming. The Son is rolling up and changing the "garments" of heaven and earth (1:10-12), for He is the One through whom God made the αἰῶνας (1:2; cf. Radcliffe 1987: 498). That these "garments" and "shakable things" refer to the institutions of the "first covenant" is evident from the first lines of the epistle, where the author contrasts the filial word with the Torah spoken through angels (1:1-2; 2:1-4; cf. Gal. 3:19).

The exhortation of 10:19-22 springs from this new situation. Several structural features and allusions suggest that this admonition concludes the entire discussion of priesthood, covenant, and sacrifice from the previous chapters. Quotations from Psalm 110 and Jeremiah 31 in Hebrews 10:12-17 form an *inclusio* with the quotations in 8:1, 8-12,[4] suggesting that 10:19-22 is based on the material of chapters 8:1-10:18. But the allusive web stretches more widely. 10:19-22 is similar to 4:14-16 (Nauck 1960: 203), and the combination of παρρησία and οἶκος reaches back to 3:6, which identifies Jesus as υἱός rather than ἱερέα over the house. The author's address to his readers as ἀδελφοί resonates with the ἅγιοι ἀδελφοί of 3:1, which concludes the discussion of the brothers of Jesus (2:11, 17). Thus, 10:19-22 draws implications from the entire discussion of 2:5-10:18.

---

[4]Attridge (1986: 1-5; 1989: 279) and Swetnam (1974: 335). Lane (1991: 279) points out that the change to direct address in 10:19 also marks a seam in the text. On the structure of Hebrews more generally, see Vanhoye (1963; 1989); Bligh (1964; 1966); Gourges (1977: 26-37).

How the pathway leads to this destination is not, however, self-evident. Indeed, the exhortation is surprising. The typological argument of the previous chapters seems to establish only *Christ's* entry into the heavenly sanctuary. It seems entirely reasonable to argue that Jesus, the greater Aaron, entered the heavenly sanctuary alone – to cleanse His people to be sure, but not to take His people in. Such a construction would avoid some glaring discontinuities between the Yom Kippur ritual and its fulfillment. Under the law, the High Priest was utterly alone in his approach to the Most Holy Place (Lev. 16:17) and, Calvin's hints notwithstanding (1853: 234), Israel was not even represented by the stones of the High Priest's breastplate (Exod. 28:15-30), for on the Day of Atonement he wore linen garments, not the mixed garments of his daily ministry (Lev. 16:4). If Jesus takes a multitude into the inner sanctuary, he shatters the whole rite. Truly to fulfill the law, Jesus must enter alone.[5] On this view, the second movement transposes the themes of the first to a higher key, but the melodic and harmonic structure remains entirely intact.

10:19-22, however, offers a more creative variation of the Levitical theme, apparently leaping from the argument concerning Christ's priesthood to the conclusion that not only Christ but all Christians may enter the ἅγια. Presumably, the author believed he laid the groundwork in the first ten chapters. Like most foundations, this one is all but invisible to superficial observation, though no less secure for that. Nonetheless, some digging is required.

---

[5] John Brown (1961: 455) suggests that 10:19 refers not to the entry of Jesus, not believers, into the heavenly sanctuary.

First, the epistle opens with four chapters in which the themes of priesthood, sanctuary, and sacrifice figure very little. Jesus is High Priest (2:17), but this title apparently bobs up from some deep current, and it is immediately submerged for two more chapters, only to resurface just as suddenly in 4:14. The focus of the opening chapters is the restoration in Christ of Adamic dominion over the creation. A careful reading of Hebrews 2, however, reveals that the priestly title of 2:17 has been prepared for by several terms that carry, *inter alia*, Levitical connotations. That crown in 2:9 seems to make Jesus a king, but Israelite High Priests too wore crowns (Exod. 28:36-38; Lev. 8:9) and Jesus' connection with the priest-king Melchizedek is a leitmotif throughout the letter. According to 2:10, Jesus "brings many sons to glory," which must, in Hebrews above all, refer to the glory enthroned above the cherubim. Jesus' purpose in tasting death was to bring His sons and brothers to the glory in the sanctuary, to crown them with priestly (and royal) honor. To accomplish this, He had to be "perfected" (τελειῶσαι, 2:10), a verb used in the LXX translation of the technical ordination phrase, "fill the hand."[6] 2:11

---

[6]In the LXX, τελειῶσαι is used absolutely of ordination only at Leviticus 21:10, leading many commentators to suggest that the word by itself did not connote "ordain" for first-century writers and readers. Moises Silva notes that Leviticus 21:10 indicates that the "head word" of the phrase might take on the meaning of the whole phrase, but cautions against reading the full phrase into every use of the word (1976/77: 61). David Peterson, who has done the most extensive study of perfection in Hebrews argues for a "vocational" sense, so that Jesus is perfected in that he is qualified to act as Redeemer. This qualification includes but is not limited to priesthood (1982: 26-30, 70-73). In response to Silva, one might suggest that in the presence of the semantic catalysts of sacrifice, priesthood, and sanctuary that are so abundant in Hebrews, we can expect the word to undergo an alchemical transformation. As for Peterson, it is not clear that he has grasped the richness of the Old Testament concept of "filling the hand," which, as we have seen, goes beyond simply "installation into office." Yet, I am happy to concede

189

further describes Jesus as the Sanctifier who shares a common origin (ἐξ ἑνός) with those He sanctifies, so that together Sanctifier and sanctified might form a holy fraternity (3:1), analogous to the Aaronic community of "holy ones" (cf. Exod. 29:1). Incarnation in this passage forges a quasi-familial connection between Jesus and the brothers consecrated to stand to serve with Him. Thus, giving him the title of "High Priest" is appropriate (2:17).

Underlying the argument of Hebrews 2-3, moreover, is the "Shiloh pattern," named for the events recorded in 1 Samuel 1-4 (see above, pp. 98, 108). The priestly family of Eli had become incurably corrupt, and Yahweh threatened to remove the "house" of Eli, to set up the "house" of another priest, and to desolate His own "house." At the same time, He promised a "faithful priest" who would minister in a purified sanctuary (1 Sam. 2:27-36; 3:10-14). Soon after, Eli and his sons died, and the Philistines took the ark into captivity. Under Solomon, Yahweh established a new set of houses -- the priestly house of Zadok presiding over the Jerusalem temple. Judgment on "Shiloh" recurs in the Old Testament: Jeremiah, a priest from the descendants of Eli at Anathoth (Jer. 1:1; cf. 1 Kgs. 2:26-27), warned that what had happened to Eli and Shiloh would be repeated in the destruction of Solomon's temple and removal of its unfaithful priests (Jer. 7:12-14). As in the first instance, however, this warning came with the promise of a restored house and a

---

his "vocational" reading of the term, so long as the priestly resonance is heard. For further discussion, see Lane (1991: 224-225); Attridge (1989: 200); Best (1960: 285-286); Dunnill (1992: 222-224); Purisful (1993: 75-76, 82-84); Scholer (1991: ch. 5).

new priestly family, fulfilled in the restoration temple and the High Priest Joshua (Zech. 3).

As we have seen in chapter 3, "Shiloh" has its place in the typological imagination of the early church. In the early chapters of Luke, John and Jesus are twin Samuels announcing the coming judgment upon the temple and its corrupt leadership. If they warn of the destruction of "Shiloh," however, they also promise the formation of a new priesthood and the construction of a new house. This typology is operating in Hebrews 2-3. 2:17 contains a virtual quotation from 1 Samuel 2:35, describing Jesus as a "faithful" High Priest, and 3:6 indicates that He is the Son over the "house" of those sons who have been brought to glory. Since Jesus is a sanctified priest, it follows that His household is a priestly house. He is a new Zadok, who, not coincidentally, bears the name of the High Priest of the restoration. From the very first chapters of Hebrews, the establishment of a new priesthood, a new house of housekeepers, is presented as the goal of Jesus' ministry. When the author later reminds his readers that they have a ἱερέα μέγαν ἐπὶ τὸν οἶκον (10:21), he is assuring them they may enter the house since they have become a holy brotherhood (3:6) through and under their High Priest.[7] For the writer of this letter, the "apocalyptic" costume change of heaven and earth involves a change not only of νόμος and διαθήκη, but of priesthood.

Hebrews 7 provides another cornerstone of the argument by showing that this new priestly house is no longer confined to a single tribe

---

[7] Pelser (1974: 49); Floor (1971: 75); Dahl (1951: 406), all interpret οἶκος in 10:21 as "household"; *contra* Lane (1991: 276).

or class but encompasses the whole people of God. Throughout the discussion of the mysterious figure of Melchizedek, the focus of the writer, despite some traditional etymologizing of his name and titles, is fixed on the superiority of this priest to Aaron. He teases this conclusion out of Genesis 14 in several ways. In stressing Melchizedek's lack of genealogy, the author is not being "playful" (*pace* Attridge 1989: 187), nor is he offering a glaringly fallacious *argumentum ex silencio*. Silences *are* significant in the midst of surrounding noise; holes in the text are noteworthy if one expects higher ground. And silence concerning the ancestry of a priest is, for both Jew and Greek, nothing short of revolutionary, for "fleshly" descent from the founder of the house was required for many priesthoods of the ancient world (Hughes 1977: 248-249). Dispensing with the genealogical qualification challenges the whole system of graded holiness.

The author also supports his brief for the superiority of Jesus' priesthood by referring to Abraham's payment of tithes to Melchizedek. Because Abraham is the "patriarch" and acknowledged head of all Israel, his homage through gift to Melchizedek indicates that Levi and Aaron too are subordinate to the Melchizedekan priest. This much is on the surface of the text, but the harmony beneath the surface comes from the narrative of Numbers 16-18, in which Korah, Dathan, and Abiram attempt to seize Aaron's priesthood (Num. 16), Yahweh confirms Aaron's election as priest by causing his staff to bear fruit in His presence (Num. 17), and He institutes a tithe system in which the Levites collect a tenth from Israel and passed on a tenth of their tenth to the priests (Num. 18). The tithe system in Hebrews 7:5, then, was set up to confirm the Aaronides' exclusive standing in the holy place. Institutionalized gift-giving traced the contours of religious and social order, and the tithe system also reinforced gradations in food rights, for only Levites could eat from Israel's tithes and only priests from the tithes of the Levites (Num. 18:10, 18). Tithing fortified the partitions separating Israelite from Israelite, showing that some from Abraham's loins were closer to Yahweh's house and table than others from the same loins (Heb. 7:5, 10).[8] The argument of Hebrews 7 is less fanciful and more daring than some have dreamed, for by leveling distinctions within Abraham's seed, the writer seems to take his stand with Korah against the priestly privileges of Aaron.

Consensus concerning the book of Hebrews is difficult to come by, but I suspect that scholarly opinion is unanimous that Korah did not write Hebrews. Yet, this background clarifies the implications of Melchizedek's reappearance. The "change in law" is, in Hebrews 7, mainly a change in qualifications for priestly standing (cf. νόμος in 7:12, 16). Under the Old system, priestly privilege was dependent on genealogy, but the Melchizedekan priest is qualified by resurrection (7:16), and therefore voids the fleshly "law." Christ holds a priesthood that transcends ancient distinctions, a priesthood to which not only lay Israelites but even Abraham paid homage. When Melchizedek appears, all the seed of Abraham bows in and with the patriarch; before Melchizedek, the seed of Abraham is one and undivided. It follows that access to and ministry in the house, once a privilege of those who received tithes, is now extended

---

[8]Attridge (1989: 195) rightly points out that the division in view is that between the tribe of Levi and the rest of Israel, rather than that between priests and Levites.

to all who join Abraham in giving gifts to Melchizedek.

Given the structural analogy of temple and people in the Old system, one would expect that an undifferentiated priesthood would minister in an undivided sanctuary. This is precisely what we find. Hebrews 10:19 states that those who have sprinkled hearts and washed bodies are permitted confidently (ἔχοντες . . . παρρησίαν) to draw near to τὰ ἅγια. Τὰ ἅγια corresponds to the Most Holy Place, since verse 20 encourages the readers to enter by the way that Jesus has made through the καταπέτασμα.[9] Thus, the baptized are now in the position of the High Priest. Continuing to think of "Holy" and "Most Holy," however, misses the point of chapter 9, which hinges on the contrast between the "first" and "second," terminology that, applied to the chambers of the tabernacle, is unique to this author (Lane 1991: 219). This distinction is initially applied not to the tabernacle but to the covenant (8:7, 13). Though translators are correct to supply διαθήκη in 9:1, this emendation misses the subtlety of the author's presentation. ἡ πρώτη in 9:1 prepares for the same phrase in 9:2, this time applied to the σκηνή: "First" tent rhymes with "first" covenant (cf. D'Angelo 1979). This creates a fruitful ambiguity at 9:18, where the

---

[9] In the Mosaic tabernacle, a veil separates the Holy Place from the courtyard, but several considerations make it certain that 10:20 refers to the "second" veil that separated the two portions of the tent. Elsewhere in the letter the word is used to refer to the "second veil." In 6:19, the Christian hope is an anchor for the soul that passes behind the καταπέτασμα where Jesus has entered, and it is clear that Jesus has entered as High Priest into the true Most Holy Place, fulfilling ἅπαξ the annual entry of the Aaronic High Priest (9:7, 11). Moreover, in 9:3, the writer has explicitly referred to the "second veil" (δεύτερον καταπέτασμα). Finally, Attridge points out that though καταπέτασμα sometimes refers to the first veil in the LXX, the inner veil is always translated with this word (Attridge 1989: 184).

author asserts that even ἡ πρώτη was not inaugurated without blood. Again, most translations emend "covenant," but the Greek raises the question, "the first *what*?" and the author's answer is that the initiation of the "first" involves both cutting a covenant and constructing a sanctuary (cf. 9:19-21).[10] We should also take note of the rare verb ἐγκαινίζω, used in the New Testament only in Hebrews 9:18, where it describes the "inauguration" of the covenant, and in 10:20, where it refers to the "opened" way into the sanctuary (cf. Pelser 1974: 47, 49). Covenant and sanctuary are inseparable: A new covenant remodels the holy place.

Having established this homology between covenant and sanctuary, the writer is prepared to offer his summary of the significance of the Mosaic tabernacle. It shows that the way into the ἅγια has not been manifested ἔτι πρώτης σκηνῆς ἐξούσης στάσιν (9:8). In context, the "first tent" is the "holy place" (vv. 2, 6), but through the play on "first" and "second" in the preceding verses, the first tent becomes a παραβολή for the entire dissolving first covenant (Lehne 1990: 100). This is so because the Mosaic tabernacle (and the similarly structured Solomon temple of Solomon) architecturally embodied the exclusion of the "sons" from glory. While the first tent had standing, only those qualified by fleshly descent from Aaron might draw near to stand to serve. Hebrews announces that the "first" no longer has standing, since the "second" has

---

[10]Hebrews 9 combines the inauguration of the covenant (Exod. 24) with the erection of the tabernacle (Exod. 40), though according to the chronology of Exodus these events were separated by the better part of a year (Exod. 19:1; 40:17). Theologically, however, the author is quite correct that the inauguration of the Sinai covenant includes the erection of the tabernacle. See Attridge (1989: 258); Dunnill (1992: 127); Hughes (1977: 374-377); see above, p. 86.

appeared and the "time of reformation" has begun at the consummation of the ages.[11] While the first tent blocked the ὁδός, the Melchizedekan Priest has eliminated the first tent and made a ὁδός, so that the new undifferentiated priestly fellowship might minister in an undivided house.

12:28-13:17 spells out the nature of New Testament "housekeeping" as love for brothers, hospitality, sexual purity, generosity, offering praise, and eating the Eucharistic flesh denied to Aaronic priests, and Hebrews makes clear that these facets of ecclesial life have a priestly character. Christ's blood cleanses the conscience from dead works in order to prepare for "service" (λατρεύειν) to the living God (Heb. 9:14). While the LXX distinguishes consistently between λειτουργία ("priestly ministry") and λατρεία ("worship" in a general sense, including both priests and people), in Hebrews this distinction is effaced and the λατρ- word group is normally used to describe priestly service in the tabernacle (8:5; 9:1, 6). Thus, when 9:14 uses this terminology to refer to Christian service, it means that Christ's blood cleanses consciences specifically to qualify for priestly ministry (Strathmann 1967: 59-65). The new priesthood is not a wholly undifferentiated community. In the Pauline image of the body, the church is harmony of difference rather than a blank unity. Each member ministers to Christ in His house, but housekeeping is multifaceted. Nor is the priestly community not egalitarian in every respect, for among the necessities of housekeeping are ministries of government, administration,

---

[11]In the background, doubtless, is the rending of the veil that, according to the synoptic accounts, took place at the time of Jesus' death, which in principle ended the divided sanctuary and therefore the divided Israel the sanctuary represented (Matt. 27:51; Mark 15:38; Luke 23:45; cf. Brown 1961: 386; Bruce 1964: 246).

and leadership (Heb. 13:7, 17). No member, however, may lay claim to privileged entry rights into the house or exclusive rights at the table. Every member equally stands to serve, hands filled to sacrifice and to feast.

Baptismal induction to priesthood is the ritual enactment of the gospel of Hebrews. Through His unique sacrifice and His entry into the heavenly sanctuary, Jesus has shaken the Old Covenant house, and baptism temporally and geographically extends His disruption of heaven and earth. By its very form, baptism conjugates the Old rite, administering the once-for-all priestly bath to those outside the lineage of Aaron, and thus enacts the promise and threat of Shiloh: formation of a new priestly house crowned and enthroned together with Melchizedek, the dissolution of priestly gradations within the seed of Abraham, the end of genealogical qualification for priests, and the replacement of the divided sanctuary. As first-century Jewish converts, once divided into priests and laymen (cf. Acts 6:7), were baptized, a homogeneously priestly people emerged. Baptism formed a new Israel out of the old, molding her into the eschatological race of the Last Adam, the kingdom of priests. It is the efficacious sign of the clothing change of heaven and earth, destroying antique Israelite order and remapping the terrain. It is the "washing of παλιγγενεσία."

And to the Greek

J. Louis Martyn has pointed out that Galatians 6:15 sets "new creation" not over against "circumcision" but over against an order founded on the duality of "circumcision/uncircumcision." Similarly, 3:28 announces the end of a world structured by "pairs of opposites," which many ancients believed were the building blocks of the physical and social universe (1985: 410-424; cf. Lloyd 1966: chs. 1-2). Male/female in Galatians 3:28 alludes to Genesis 1:27 (Hays 1983: 232), and like male/female, Jew/Greek and slave/free are dualisms of the world now engulfed and dissolved in the baptismal flood. In Hebrews 10:19-22, baptism announces the rending of the veil between priests and people; in Galatians 3:27, baptismal investiture ruptures the dividing wall between Jew and Greek. Obliteration of the latter distinction, like the dissolution of the former, is an aspect of an "apocalyptic" παλιγγενεσία.

Galatians 3:28 provides rich material for a theological sociology, but here I focus only on questions of priesthood. I argued in chapter 3 that Galatians 3:27 describes baptism with a metaphor most likely borrowed from the ordination rite. Assuming this to be the case, I wish now to investigate more carefully how an allusion to priestly investiture fits into Paul's argument and illuminates the significance of baptism. To do this, I examine the Jew/Greek dichotomy, a key theme of Galatians that concerns the "sociological" question of defining the boundaries of the covenant people.

Though opinions differ concerning the degree to which the Judaizing "troublers" in Galatia (1:7; 5:12) wished to bring Gentile Christians under the law,[12] it is clear they were demanding submission to Jewish ceremonies before accepting Gentiles as full members of the New Israel. At Antioch,

---

[12]Dunn (1990: 137-147, 151-159, 221); Thielman (1994: 121).

the issue was table fellowship, and the Jew/Gentile question is still Paul's concern in chapters 3-4, where, however, he does not pose the question as, Who is a table fellow? but, Who is Abraham's seed? (Beker 1980: 48; Dunn 1990: 131), an emphasis highlighted by the references to Abraham that form an *inclusio* around these chapters (3:6-8, 4:21-31). For both Paul and his opponents, however, these questions are virtually equivalent, for all parties in the dispute agree that all Abraham's seed is welcomed at table.

For Paul, this touches the heart of the gospel. He severely rebuked Peter for withdrawing from meals with Gentiles, calling it a threat to the gospel and an attack on justification by faith (2:11-21; cf. Stendahl 1963). According to 3:8, the Lord προευηγελίσατο to Abraham when He promised that "All the nations will be blessed in you." There are two dimensions to the gospel blessing. In verse 8, the Gentiles are promised a share in Abraham's justification, while 3:14 promises the gift of the Spirit.[13] As defined for Paul's purposes here, the gospel proclaims the dissemination of the Abrahamic blessings of the Spirit and righteousness to all nations (Hays 1983: 203; 1989: 106). If any single nation claims exclusive rights to this blessing, the promise is jeopardized, and the gospel announcing its fulfillment is no gospel.

Consideration of the theme of the "one" illuminates Paul's discussion (Wright 1991: ch. 8).[14] In 3:16, Paul insists, in what appears to

---

[13]References to the reception of the Spirit bracket 3:1-14 (Stanley 1990: 492-493; Hays 1989: 110), highlighting the fact that the promise of the Spirit is the content of the Abrahamic covenant.

[14]For critical comments on Wright's reading of Galatians 3, see Thatcher (1997: 405) and Donaldson (1997: 151-160).

be a strained argument, that Yahweh gave the promises τῷ σπέρματί, not τοῖς σπέρμασι. Though often taken as a direct reference to Jesus, this interpretation fails to meet the crucial test of relevance: No one disputes the "oneness" of the Messiah. What the troublers threaten is the "oneness" of the Messiah's church (Wright 1991: 159). Wright's interpretation is therefore more satisfying. He points out that ἐν σπέρμα is used in a collective sense in 3:28-29. If 3:16 refers to the "collective Christ," Paul's argument is that God did not promise righteousness and the Spirit to many distinct lines of descendants but to a single people, coagulated from many nations. Wright finds support in the use of σπέρμα in the LXX of Genesis 15:13; 17:7-8; 22:17-18, and in the light of 1 Corinthians 12:12, the "Christ" of Galatians 3:16 could refer to the *totus Christus*, Head and body (Wright 1991: 158). Maintaining Jew/Greek distinctions violates the gospel that promises the Abrahamic blessings to ἐν σπέρμα.

Wright's interpretation also clarifies the enigmatic verse 20: ὁ δὲ μεσίτης ἑνὸς οὐκ ἔστιν, ὁ δὲ θεὸς εἷς ἐστιν, a crux made more difficult by mistranslations. Paul is not offering an axiom in a general theory of mediation, as most translations suggest, but is making a point about the specific mediator he has just mentioned, Moses. The best translation is: "Now (he) is not the mediator of the one; but God is One" (Wright 1991: 163). Moses was not the mediator of one *what*? Evidently, this refers to verse 16, but on the usual understanding of that verse, verse 20 would make the weird claim that Moses did not mediate Jesus. On Wright's interpretation, Paul is saying that Moses is not the mediator of the unified people promised to Abraham; he is not the mediator of the *totus Christus.* This is basic to Paul's explanation of why the law cannot be the final form of God's covenant. God promised the Spirit and justification to the "one seed" of Abraham but the law institutes practices that necessarily divide and segregate. These divisions, while *aptum* in their time, have to be temporary, for throughout the period of the law, the blessings promised to "one seed," given 430 years earlier, remained in force (3:17). Ultimately, the reason why God cannot be satisfied with a world or church divided into Jew and Greek is something every Jew knew and confessed daily -- that Yahweh our God is One Lord. Thus, as Wright puts it, Paul uses "the Shema to relativize the Torah" (1991: 171). So, it is central to Paul's gospel that Jew/Greek give way to "one seed"; or, to say the same thing, that the dualism of "circumcision/ uncircumcision" give way to "new creation."

Literature on Galatians, however, gives surprisingly little attention to the nature of the distinction that Paul is overthrowing. Jew/Gentile was not a racial difference, since any man might be circumcised into Israel. Nor was it necessarily a distinction between true worshipers and idolaters, for God-fearing Gentiles worshiped Yahweh without being circumcised or, apparently, observing dietary and cleanliness laws (cf. Acts 10:1-2). Rather, the segregation of Israel from the nations instituted by Torah was a division with respect to priestly privileges and tasks, with respect to proximity to and responsibility for Yahweh's house (cf. Thielman 1994: 55-57). Indicative of this, as Hamerton-Kelly points out, the temple was the place where, in Paul's day, "there was an explicit system of exclusion," and Paul's reference to breaking down and building up (Gal. 2:18) perhaps refers to the dividing wall between Jewish and Gentile chambers (1990:

107-108). Moses was thus not the mediator of the "one," but of the distinct, separated "holy nation" and "royal priesthood" (Exod. 19:6).[15]

Paul's claims about the "law" must be understood in this context. Though often implicitly interpreted in terms of modern conceptions of legal or moral systems, νόμος refers to the whole constitution of worship and national life instituted at Sinai (Belleville 1986: 71). A chief purpose of the law's pedagogy (Gal. 3:24) was to enable Israel to live safely with the dangers of the sanctuary. Uncleanness had to be identified and eliminated, sin confessed and atoned, sacrificial food offered, the house maintained, so that Yahweh would not break out in wrath or abandon the house, leaving it desolate (Num. 18:5). To be ὑπὸ νόμον was to be under the strict regulations governing those near the holy house. The specific issues at stake in Galatians revolve around Israel's priestly standing. Peter's withdrawal from table fellowship with Gentiles arose from a rigorist interpretation of the Torah's dietary restrictions, which were part of the system of graded holiness introduced by the Sinai covenant (Lev. 11:44-45), and circumcision set the boundaries of the Old priestly people. Judaizers who enforced food laws and required circumcision were implicitly claiming that Jews continued to have a standing that Gentiles did not have.[16]

---

[15]I do not mean that the divisions of Jew and Gentile instituted by the Torah were identical to those practiced in the first century. Contrary to Peter's practice, the Old Testament permitted table fellowship with Gentiles, even at some religious feasts (cf. Deut. 16:9-15). Israel's purpose, moreover, was evidently evangelistic; they were to call the nations to worship Yahweh. Yet, the Sinai covenant, by setting up Yahweh's house in the midst of Israel and arranging Israel around the house, instituted a separation of Israel from the nations.

[16]With regard to the double Abrahamic promise of righteousness and the Spirit,

This helps also to specify the sense in which the dualisms of Galatians 3:28 are dissolved by baptism. He certainly did not believe "there is neither male nor female" *tout court* (cf. 1 Tim. 2:12-15), he assumed that slavery would continue (Eph. 6:5-9), and Donaldson persuasively argues that even the Jew/Greek distinction remained relevant for Paul's mission (Donaldson 1997: 158). At the center of the gospel, however, is the declaration that there is no more Jew/Greek (or male/female, slave/free) with respect to access to God, standing in His house as sons, seating at His table, or inheritance of Abrahamic righteousness and the Spirit. Hence, Paul wraps Jew and Greek in common *priestly* robes. Since the distinction of priestly Jew and non-priestly Gentile forms a fundamental coordinate of antique religious topography, Paul's gospel of the "one" seed, symbolized and enacted in baptism, announces the beginning of a new creation. Here, again, baptism is the "washing of παλιγγενεσία."

Jew, Gentile, Barbarian, Greek

Though Israel alone was ὑπὸ νόμον, Paul warns that the Gentile

---

Albert Vanhoye helpfully notes that "justification" is linked to communion with God; those who believe are reckoned righteous and therefore may draw near for fellowship. Vanhoye cites Psalms 15 and 24, both of which demand righteousness of those who wish to ascend of the hill of the Lord and enter His house (1993: 101, 107). The promise to Abraham is thus that the right standing necessary for entry into the house and access to the Spirit will be granted to all in Abraham's seed. In terms of our discussion, the promise to Abraham is that all nations will in Christ become a nation of ministers in the house of the Lord who is Spirit (cf. Sam K. Williams 1987: 91-100; Hays 1983: 210-212).

Galatians, having been redeemed from slavery, are in danger of reverting (πάλιν, 4:9) to a similar subjection under the στοιχεῖα τοῦ κόσμου (4:3, 9). Though scholars debate the relation of the law and the στοιχεῖα,[17] it is evident they have a strong family resemblance, so that life in subjection to τὰ στοιχεῖα was for the Gentiles what life under the law was for Israel. If we follow Martyn's suggestion that for Paul the new creation replaces a world built upon binary oppositions, and if, as I have argued, the opposition of priest/non-priest is a fundamental structure of the world system whose termination Paul announces, and if subjection under the stoixei/a is parallel to life ὑπὸ νόμον, then one can hypothesize that Gentile socio-religious organization was, like the Jewish, a system of "graded holiness," organized around the opposition of priest/non-priest. If this is the case, redemption from the "elementary principles," like redemption from the curse of the law, forms a community where this distinction no longer operates. Baptism to priesthood breaks through the boundaries of Gentile order as well as Hebrew.

The classic studies of the ancient Greco-Roman city by Max Weber and Fustel de Coulanges support this hypothesis.[18] In his unfinished

---

[17]Hays (1983: 230) identifies them, while Donaldson (1986: 96-97) says they are not equivalent but are on a similar level. Belleville (1986: 54, 67, 69-70), defining the term as "rudimentary principles," provides a chiastic outline of 3:21-4:11 in which ὑπὸ νόμον corresponds to ὑπο τὰ στοιχεῖα, thus supporting her claim that the two forms of subjection are similar kinds of experience. According to Wright, adherence to tribal and ethnic loyalties is a kind of reversion to στοιχεῖα (1991: 165, 170). Though I am developing a less racially tinged understanding of the phrase, I agree with Wright that "elementary principles" concern cultural mythologies, structures, and loyalties, as well as spiritual powers.

[18]Supporting evidence is found in the addendum to this chapter.

treatise on the city, included at the end of *Economy and Society,* Weber examines the economic, political-administrative, and military dimensions of the ancient city, but he suggestively notes that "The truly fundamental element in the formation of a polis. . . . was always thought to be the fraternization of the sibs into a *cult* community," the *sunoikismos* or "settling together," which involved "the replacement of the *prytaneia* of individual families by a common *prytaneion* of the city in which the prytans took their common meals" (1978: 1286). Admission to cultic citizenship was strictly controlled, so that "the term denoting a 'citizen' is at times directly identical with the word for a member of the patrician 'families'" descended from the founding clans (1978: 1288).

Thus, "in historical times only a member of the patriciate (*patricius ,* *eupatrides*) could validly communicate, as priest or official, with the gods of the polis through conducting the sacrifices or consulting the oracles (*auspicia*)" (1978: 1288). Ancient cities were "religiously exclusive" to those outside, and because the clans or *gentes* that were an "indispensable feature" of even democratic cities were themselves exclusive cultic organizations, the system was divided "internally against everyone who did not belong to one of the confederated sibs -- that is, against the plebeians" (1978: 1242). Freed slaves were also denied access to priesthoods (1978: 1357-58). Patrician/plebeian was therefore originally a religious divide, and the "struggle of the Orders" was a conflict over the distribution of priestly privilege within the ancient city. Over time, the patrician-plebeian distinction became less important, and as religious divisions gave way to stratification by wealth, "status conflict" gave way to "class struggle" (1978: 1308-9).

205

In certain respects, Fustel de Coulanges's history of the ancient city follows the same lines. According to his evolutionary scheme, ancient religion began as domestic religion, focused on honor for dead ancestors. Archaic religions taught that the souls of the dead lived on under ground, and that the dead were divine. Tombs therefore became places of worship, where the living offered blood and food. Each house, moreover, had its own domestic cult, centered on the hearth fire, which symbolized the continuing life of the ancestors. The fire had to be maintained and worshiped, and it received the first portion of all meals. Since the cult was offered to ancestors, only blood relations might participate as priests, though other members of the household might join in through their mediation. From this construct, Fustel extrapolates primitive conceptions of marriage (a woman's initiation into the cult of her husband's family) and property (based on the association of departed ancestors with the soil).

When families organized into a city, they preserved many elements of domestic religion, projected onto a larger screen. Each *gens* of a city had its own ancestral religion, and the *gentes* banded together to form a civic order by adopting a common worship, usually that of the most powerful families. Like the domestic, the civic cult centered on daily offerings at the hearth in the prytaneion, dedicated to the founder of the city or to the eponymous deity. The chief ceremony of the civic religion was the common meal, which the priests ate daily but which occasionally involved all citizens, whose festive dress, at least in Athens, was reminiscent of priestly garments. Every city was "holy," a "sanctuary," and only the citizens could enter its temples and sacred spaces (1980: 117, 133, 142-

206

143, 147-149).

Also living in the city's territory were the "plebs," excluded from the religion of the city because they lacked genealogical connection with the founding clans. Segregation of patrician and plebeian was sometimes geographic:

> Originally a Greek city was double; there was the city, properly so called – πόλις, which was built ordinarily on the summit of some hill; it had been built with the religious rites, and enclosed the sanctuary of the national gods. At the foot of the hill was found an agglomeration of houses, which were built without any religious ceremony, and without a sacred enclosure. These were the dwellings of the plebeians, who could not live in the sacred city (1980: 223).

Foreigners to the civic religion and geographically thrust to the margins, the plebs had no political rights, for citizenship required membership in a clan and participation in the cult. At base, what separated pleb from patrician was the former's lack of religion: Plebs might not hold a priesthood (1980: 225). Over several centuries, the archaic city witnessed a series of revolutions that ended with the plebs' entry into the city. Having gained their share of wealthy men, soldiers, and their own priests, the plebs made a bid for equality with the patricians. In Rome, the struggle climaxed when the plebeians secured the right to priesthoods previously reserved for patricians.

The formal similarities between the antique order of Greece and Israel are striking. Both were internally structured by the distinction between priest and non-priest. In the Greek city, the citizens exercised "priestly" functions and enjoyed priestly privileges, while non-citizens were excluded. Originally (and always mythically) citizenship was inherited from founding clans. Within Israel, the Aaronic priests alone served in the house of Yahweh and only the circumcised participated fully in the community and its worship. In both Israel and Greece, the gradations of priesthood extended to encompass the entire political world: Greek/barbarian echoes Jew/Gentile. In both, the divisions within the community were displayed in access to or exclusion from sacred places and holy food. On the other hand, both Greece and Israel anticipated to some extent a wider distribution of priesthood. After the struggle of the orders, priesthood and citizenship were extended to those outside the hereditary ranks, and already at Sinai Israel became a priestly nation.

It was, however, the rise of Christianity that finally destroyed the hereditary principle of priesthood and with it the graded holiness of antique order. Medieval cities were, Weber argues, still "cultic," but clan ties no longer dominated social order (though this transformation was more complete in Northern than in Southern Europe; 1978: 1243-1247). Remarkably, for Weber, it was Paul who first challenged the ancient city and pointed the way to the medieval, when, in the event of Galatians 2, he insisted that Peter return to table fellowship with Gentiles. Paul grounded his reformation of table fellowship in the priestly investiture of baptism. Baptism of the Greek city reconstructed its foundations, rearranged the seating at the civic table, and remodeled its social order.

So we return to Paul, and Galatians 3:27. For Gentile converts to submit to Jewish regulations of holiness would be to revert to a variation of the same old dualistic system ὑπὸ τὰ στοιχεῖα.[19] In baptism, the

---

[19]Paul strikes a similar note in his condemnation of factions and rivalry at the

Galatians have become citizens of a new *polis* where all wear the Priest who has gone through the veil to destroy the excluding system of graded holiness. In Galatians, baptism announces and creates a new *polis* where the "one seed" of Jew and Greek share the Abrahamic blessing, where none are forced outside the city walls, where the marginal are welcomed to the *agora* and its joyful assembly.

Conclusion

From these exegetical considerations, several speculative conclusions of a more theoretical nature follow -- more points for further reflection than "assured results." According to Paul, Christ has fulfilled the Abrahamic promise of the Spirit to the "one seed," and the Spirit wars against the enmities, strife, jealousy, disputes, dissensions, factions, envy of the flesh (Gal. 5:19-21). Given the use of "flesh" elsewhere in Galatians, it seems that Paul considers life both ὑπὸ νόμον and ὑπὸ τὰ στοιχεῖα as "fleshly" forms of existence that promote rivalry and dissension (3:3; 6:12). Our discussion suggests that the priest/non-priest dichotomy is one feature of both forms of the fleshly organization of life, and that the Spirit opposes the flesh by removing the veil that establishes this dualism. That is, the Spirit's work condenses into enduring institutional structures that inhibit the flourishing of fleshly life. As the hovering Spirit formed the divisions of the original creation, so the Spirit

---

Lord's table in Corinth (1 Cor. 11:18-22), where pagan divisions threaten to fracture the one loaf.

of Pentecost destroys old religious and cultural boundaries, draws new lines, and makes the world new. Against this background, baptismal induction to priesthood is one of the Spirit's weapons to destroy vanity, enmities, and factions. Several specific points can be made in this regard.

First, a somewhat Girardian point concerning Christianity's exposure and destruction of the mechanisms of mimetic rivalry and violence. From Cain and Abel, through Korah, to the conflicts of Jesus with His Jewish adversaries (cf. Wright 1996: 523, 525-526, 606), the Bible shows that violence arises from contests over *sancta*. Paul says in Galatians 4:17 that by "shutting out" the Galatians who do not observe Jewish holiness regulations, the Judaizers hope to foster a desire to "get in." Paul's response is that the Galatians are not in fact "shut out" of anything -- clothed as they are by baptism as heirs and ministers in the Spirit's house. Because it destroys the divided sanctuary and its prohibited spaces, opening the door and rending the veil, the baptismal city undermines one of the bases of rivalry; for when the sanctuary is open, access to *sancta* unrestricted, and the supply of holy food inexhaustible, no one need fight for entry to the inner ring. By eliminating the possibility of "shutting out," baptismal induction to priesthood also dissipates the mimetic desire to "get in."

The same mimetic dynamics were at work in the Greco-Roman city.[20] Ballanche, like Weber and Fusel de Coulanges, argues that the ancient city was divided among patrician "initiateurs" and plebeian "initiables." Under

---

[20]Frazer opens his *Golden Bough* with the myth of the title, which involves the priest of Aricia, whose successors murder him to take control of his sanctuary (Frazer 1950: 1).

the conditions of antique order, the excluded plebeians gained entry only through violent confrontation but Christianity initiates without violence, transforming ancient solidarity into Christian charity (1981: 15, 172 fn. 3). Importantly, the baptismal assembly no longer ritually enacts conflict among orders, as Greek feasts often did (Vernant 1988: 31-32) but shares a sacred meal where faction is strictly forbidden (cf. 1 Cor. 11:18-34). Thus, our typology provides a gloss on Augustine's "deconstructive" reading of pagan virtue.[21]

From the third century, an agonistic element is present in baptismal renunciations and exorcisms and later appears in decorations on medieval fonts and baptisteries.[22] Formation of the baptismal polity of the church thus did not imply either quietism toward evil or a dissolution of all boundaries. Internal grades of priesthood are entirely eliminated, but baptism itself radically partitions the baptized priesthood from the world. To pass through the waters is to die to fleshly life whether ὑπὸ νόμον or ὑπὸ τὰ στοιχεῖα, and to be enrolled in the army of the Spirit who makes war against the flesh (Gal. 5:17). Baptismal consecration to priesthood encourages imitation of the zeal of the Levites (Exod. 32) and of Phinehas

---

[21]During the Punic wars, Augustine points out, Rome was united only by common fear, and once Carthage's power was broken, the inner divisions broke into internecine civil strife that ended with the Empire (*De civitatis Dei* 2.18; 3.26-30; 1984: 68-9, 126-132). Rome was unified only when faced with a common enemy or an overwhelming power. Milbank (1987: 208) calls Augustine's reading "deconstructive."

[22]On exorcisms, see Stenzel (1958: 78, 98-104); Kelly (1985); Cramer (1993: 136-155). On combat imagery in baptismal architecture and art, see J.G. Davies (1962: 80-83).

211

(Num. 25). The water incorporates the oil of soldiers as well as of priests (cf. Finn 1992a: 78); the garments of baptismal investiture are also the armor of God.

Related to this, the elimination of sacred space through Christ's work, extended in baptism, decenters the religious world. According to book of Hebrews, the world is still centered on the sanctuary, but the sanctuary is now in heaven and wherever heaven and earth meet through the Spirit. Wherever there is a body washed or a community gathered around the word and sacrament, there is a temple of the Holy Spirit. While a central earthly sanctuary existed, a spatial gradation from near to far was inevitable, for it is physically impossible for everyone to be equally near the house of Yahweh in Jerusalem. Heaven is, however, equidistant from all terrestrial points, so a heavenly sanctuary eliminates the distinction between near and far. Again, the socio-religious shape of the New Covenant undermines a basis for rivalry and pride.

Societies organized by principles of graded holiness have a centripetal cultural force: Everything moves toward the center. All roads led back to Rome, Athens, Jerusalem. Exile from the land sanctified by the sanctuary or by the graves of dead ancestors was abnormal, tragic. Radcliffe notes the irony of Hebrews 13:13, which redescribes movement through the veil as movement out of the camp, to the place of reproach and shame (1987: 500). If N.T. Wright is correct that Jesus proclaimed the end of Israel's exile (Wright 1996), it must be said that this "return" has an ironic twist, for the last word of the gospels is not "gather" or "wait" but "go." By eliminating the "center," baptism to priesthood reverses the direction of cultural force, which now leads centrifugally to the four corners of the earth. As Ballanche put it, the *ville des expiations* formed by baptism stands between immobile civilizations of antiquity and the progressive civilizations of the *Anno Domini.*

The baptismal dissolution of antique order also challenges the Greek antipathy to manual labor and mechanics. Behind Plato and Aristotle's subordination of artisans and tradesmen to citizens are religious motives, including fears of contagion. Though the primary place of Christian "housekeeping" is the church, the enthroned Christ also "fills all things" (Eph. 1:21-23), consecrating a cosmic house. For the baptized, therefore, all lawful labor is ministry to Christ, and thus labor becomes a sphere for the exercise of *virtus* and a form of λειτουργία. Weber points out that the medieval city of the baptized ruled by tradesman, merchants, and producers would have been unimaginable for the Greeks. Baptism to priesthood grounds a theology of labor and vocation, much as Ruskin attempted to restore the dignity of craft labor by allegorizing it as "royal" and "noble" (cf. Milbank 1990: 199-200).

Finally, with a nod to Durkheim, one might suggest the destruction of sacred configurations of society registered in forms of consciousness. Without claiming that "dual classification" was the sole or even dominant mode of Greek thought, G.E.R. Lloyd's *Polarity and Analogy* (1966: 15-171) provides extensive evidence of the prevalent use of "paired opposites" (e.g., hot/cold, moist/dry, right/left, which last was still used by Aristotle) in Greek cosmology and the argumentative strategies of the philosophers. Lloyd also suggests that natural dualities acquired cosmological significance partly because they were "the symbolic manifestation of fundamental religious or spiritual categories," so that dual classification

213

"may reflect, and itself form a part of, a system of religious beliefs which expresses the ideal of society, and by which the whole life of the society is regulated" (1966: 80). Cosmological uses of political and social imagery are also relevant. Plato's "authoritarian bias" in politics reproduces his cosmological monarchy of reason, and Heraclitus's belief that war is "father of all and king of all" reflects "the social upheavals of the late sixth century" (Lloyd 1966: 97, 222-224). Drawing together polarity and analogy, we might suggest that the dualistic tendency of thought registers the dual ordering of society, the priestly division of citizen/non-citizen.[23] By decentering the socio-religious world, the cross and baptism transformed not only ancient society but the topography of the ancient mind, opening vistas never before glimpsed. Patterns of thought and argument dominated by paired opposites reproduce the *agon* of antique order, so that a dissolution of those agonistic structures dethrones dialectic as the sole or primary mode of reaching truth and replaces it with persuasion of a rhetorical, musical, aesthetic, poetic, or liturgical character (cf. Milbank 1990).

Baptism is in these ways the water that effects a παλιγγενεσία of the social, cultural, and political cosmos – the water that washes away the old sacerdotal distinctions and recreates social space, which is also religious

---

[23]Levi-Strauss (1963: 132-163) raises the question whether any society is really ordered dualistically, but Lloyd points out that even in societies that are actually more complex in operation "*the members of the society themselves* describe their own social organization in terms of a simple dualist structure" (1966: 31). So, we are operating at least in part in the realm of social imagination rather than actual social order; but it must remembered that social order always has an imaginative component.

The Priesthood of the Plebs

space. A new order is born from the fecund waters of baptism. The font is the womb not only of the church but of the world.

Addendum

Though recent work has questioned or discredited certain details of Weber's and Fustel's analyses (cf. Finley 1977: 305-327; Momigliano 1977: 325-344), scholarship vindicates their emphasis on the religious nature of the *polis* and its structures.[24] Christine Sourvinou-Inwood writes,

---

[24]My focus is on Greece, but Rome is for my purposes very similar. On the fundamentally religious character of Roman public and political life, see Liebeschuetz (1979: esp. 1-3, 197-198); Gordon (1990a: 179-180); Wardman (1982: 1-20). On the stratification of Roman social order, see MacMullen (1974: 88-120) and Alföldy (1985). On the religious dimensions of the struggle for orders, see Liebeschuetz (1979: 21) and Alföldy (1985: 15), and for the continuation of religion's role in social and political struggles of the second century B.C., see Rawson (1991: 149-168). On priesthood in Rome, see Beard (1990: 17-48), who emphasizes the supreme role of the aristocratic Senate in Roman religion, especially in comparison with the advisory role of the priestly colleges; and Gordon (1990a: 177-198; 1990b: 199-231; 1990c: 233-255) who emphasizes, in Maussian fashion, the use of priestly benevolence in the accumulation of symbolic capital and thus highlights the close connection between membership in the priestly colleges and high social and political position. Links of philanthropy and priesthood, Gordon claims, indicate that the god-mortal relation is "implicitly offered as a model of the relationship between the élite and the rest of the community" (1990b: 229). Dumezil provides this explanation for the importance of the central circular *aedes Vestae* in Rome: The arrangement makes sense "if one considers the whole of the city, within its *pomerium* -- the Romans themselves invited this view -- as an immense unitary and permanent sacrificial area, within which the quadrangular *templa* and the round *aedes*, with their respective fires, are mystically articulated." On this view, "the life of Rome may be considered as an immense permanent liturgy, unitary in its distribution throughout the year, in which each priest or college plays a distinctive part" (1970: 579; cf. 314: "the city regarded itself in certain respects as a vast and immovable *templum* within which the dwellings of men and those of the gods were

215

Each *polis* was a religious system which formed part of the more complex world-of-the-*polis* system, interacting with the religious systems of the other *poleis* and with the Panhellenic religious dimension; thus direct and full participation in religion was reserved for citizens, that is, those who made up the community which articulated the religion. One belonged to the religious community of one's own *polis*, (or *ethnos*); in the *sacra* of others, even in Panhellenic sanctuaries, one could only participate as a *xenos*. On at least some occasions a *xenos* could take part in cult only with the help of a citizen, normally the *proxenos* of his city, who acted as "intermediary" (Sourvinou-Inwood 1990: 295-6, cf. 304).[25]

Details of Greek social and political life confirm this judgment. Meetings of the assembly (*ekklesia*) were opened with the sacrifice of a pig, a curse and a prayer (Garland 1990: 87). For Xenophon, citizenship was defined, among other things, by "taking part together in the ceremonies ... of the cult."[26] One became a citizen by offering sacrifice at the city-hearth of *Hestia* in the prytaneion, the political counterpart to the domestic

---

conjoined"). Gordon (1990b: 215) cites Aelius Aristides to the effect that "the Empire has become a single city." Given this conception, citizenship, full participation in the city, is simultaneously membership of the civic temple-house, i.e., a priesthood.

[25]See de Polignac (1995: 77-79) and Zaidman and Schmitt Pantel (1992: 90-91). The point holds whatever the merits of de Polignac's controversial emphasis on the role of extraurban sanctuaries located at the margins of the city's territory (see the critical comments in Sourvinou-Inwood 1993:1-5). Martin Nilsson says that in organizing classical Athens Solon founded a "sacral legislation" (Nilsson 1949: 225), and Claude Vatin claims that citizenship in the Greek world consisted of common participation in the cult, fighting together, and seeking the interests of the group (1984: 13). See Parker (1996: 56-66).

[26]*Hellenica* 2.4.20, quoted in Loraux (1986: 328).

hearth-altar (Nilsson 1949: 243).[27]   New colonies were formed by the transfer of hearth and fire to a new location (Miller 1978: 14; Detienne and Vernant 1989: 3-4). Within the polis, each subdivision – its tribes, demes, phratries – was also a religious organization with its own cults and festivals (Martha 1882: 9).

In the narrow sense, a Greek ἱερεύς was, like his Ancient Near Eastern counterparts, a minister to the image of a god in a sanctuary, to which he often had exclusive access (Martha 1882: 7-8, 45-54, 88-89; Garland 1990: 77-78), and like other priests he exercised authority over "religious" matters. Yet, an exclusive focus on such forms of priesthood misses Fustel's insight into the "sacred" character of the entire Greek city. Thus, for example, Robert Garland examines the religious authority of Greek priests, and concludes that no exclusive priestly "class or caste" existed in classical Athens, that most priesthoods (excluding the older "gentilic" priesthoods that were the preserve of a single *gens*) were "available to all Athenians," and that there was no ordination rite (1990: 75-77). Yet this occludes the fact that "all Athenians" means "all Athenian *citizens*" – still a restrictive category in democratic times – and that to become a citizen, one passed through the rite of entry at Hestia's hearth in the prytaneion (Zaitmann and Schmitt Pantel 1992: 65-67; Miller 1978: 14).[28]   Garland himself recognizes the "priestly" character of the

---

[27]Despite the fiction of blood descent from founding families, citizenship was not a closed rank. From the mid-fifth century B.C., benefaction to Athens could lead to an offer of citizenship (Osborne 1981-83: 1.5-6; 4.139-184).

[28]Manville (1990), operating with an Aristotelian understanding of the city, almost completely ignores its religious dimensions. He describes how Solon constructed Athenian citizenship by drawing cultural boundaries between Athens and not-

217

entire Athenian democracy when he summarizes by saying that "it would be valid to think of the Athenian *dêmos*, sitting in *ekklêsia* (assembly), as a focus of communication between men and gods," and this applies also to the *boulê* (1990: 86-87).

"Social" divisions within the Greek city were gradations of priestly rank.[29] This is true in the sense that some formal priesthoods were reserved to certain families and that ποίητοι citizens and χένοι were excluded from holding the archonate or priesthoods, apparently to prevent defilement of these offices by foreign blood.[30] Again, in a more important sense citizenship was itself a priestly privilege. With its hearth-fire burning to Hestia in the prytaneion, the polis was a civic house, and every citizen had the right and duty of "house keeping" and was permitted to participate in sacrifice. Those who were not citizens, by contrast, were not part of the house, nor did they share its table.[31] As de Polignac points

---

Athens, including restrictions on the access that non-citizens would have to the agora and common sacrifices and feasts, but he fails to realize the extent to which all boundary marking in Greece was a religious act (cf. Parker 1983). On the connection of sacrifice at the prytaneion with citizenship, see Miller (1978: 14, 169-70), where Miller includes several texts that indicate that this sacrifice was part of one's registration as a citizen (θύσαντες ἐν ταῖς ἐγγραφαῖς ἐν τῶι πρυτανείωι ἐπὶ τῆς κοινῆς ἑστίας τοῦ δήμου).

[29]There are, of course, other dimensions to the social configuration of Greek cities, as for example the ranking of slave and free. But religious or priestly privileges are, with the right to bear arms and the right of political participation, the features that distinguished citizens from all others -- whether slaves or free non-citizens.

[30]Sourvinou-Inwood (1990: 320); Martha (1882: 24-25); Osborne (1981-1983: 4.173-4).

[31]According to Ballanche, the dualism of ancient civic order extended even to the

out, the *polis* was the preserve of rightly ordered relations between gods and men, and right order required proper distancing and separation and also appropriate forms of intimacy (1995: 35-36). These separations encompassed the world outside the city walls. Delphi was considered the center of the world, as reflected in the order of consultation with the oracle and the organization of the Delphic games:

> Greeks came before barbarians; among the Greeks, the Delphians before all other Greeks; after the Delphians and before the other Greeks came the other ethnic groups and *poleis* who were members of the Delphic Amphictiony [League]. . . . the same articulation pertains in the Panhellenic Games as in the order of the oracular consultation: the Delphic *polis* at the centre, the Amphictiony forming the inner circle, the other Greeks the outer one. Here the barbarians were excluded from competition -- for this was one of the rites defining membership of the group "Greeks" (Sourvinou-Inwood 1990: 298-299).

Both institutions mapped out the ethnic and religious terrain, as seen from Delphi. Confusion of these divisions was a possible source of pollution. Robert Parker writes,

> The danger that demanded constant vigilance was not so much that of attack from below as infiltration [of the citizen body]. Shortly after the expulsion of the Peisistratids, citizens who were 'impure in descent' were rejected. (The timing, of course, suggests that this was a purification from tyranny as well as a

---

name, for each city had a secret and an open name, one for the initiated, one for everyone else (1981: 24). He also suggests that this dualism was supported by a myth of soul-migration according to which the souls of the guilty were more attracted to plebeians, those of the innocent to patricians (1981:101).

219

cleansing of the citizen body.) Pericles' law of 451/0, excluding the children of non-Athenian mothers, rendered the citizen body, in principle, a sealed and impenetrable unit. Penalties for infiltration were savage, and it is clear from comedy and oratory that the possibility was one that was constantly present in many people's minds. The language of 'purity' is sometimes found in this context (1983: 262-263).

According to Marcel Detienne, for the Greeks "political power cannot be exercised without sacrificial practice," and sacrificial meals formed alliances between cities. Within the sacrificial community, distribution of meat marked out political and religious rankings. Unequal cities received unequal portions of the alliance-forming sacrifice. Durand describes the procedure in detail:

> the animal's body is completely taken apart, as if it has exploded in such a way as to coincide with the very limits of the society of men in the city organized around it. The trajectory assigned to the animal's body, beginning with the splanchnic center, slice after slice, reaches out to the whole social body. The ultimate raison d'etre of the edible body is to be blended with the civic space, conforming ultimately to an exact geometry. . . . Shares of meat are placed on the table in oblation to the gods; later the priest disposes of them. Along with the inedible shares that have been completely consumed by the flames, the gods thus receive shares eaten by the ministers of the cult. The priest has a special relationship to the divine. Like the god who receives the total oblation of the animal with its death, the priest receives the part that made for its wholeness in the beginning, the vital wrapping: the hide, the only evidence of what once was, left at the end of the rite. The status of the *hiereus* is indicated by samples taken from the center out of the men's share, even before the question of finding a place in the animal's body that honors men arises (Durand 1989: 104).[32]

---

[32]For further on what Ballanche called the "dietetic regime" of the Greeks, see Gernet (1981: 13-47).

Still in the Hellenistic period, feasts distinguished between citizens and non-citizens:

> Le festin est avant tout celui des citoyens (citoyens, cité, *dêmos*) et parfois même des seuls notables (citoyens membres des assemblées et des corps de magistrats). Ces derniers sont toujours invités au repas. L'ouverture plus ou moins grande de la fête concerne les autres catégories de population: les habitants de la cité, qui se confondent souvent avec les étrangers domiciliés, les voisins, les étrangers de passage, les Romains. Plus on est proche, dans la vie quotidienne, des citoyens, plus on a de chance d'être convié au banquet. . . . Ces non-citoyens n'ont normalement pas leur place au banquet public, sinon dans des repas qui leur sont réservés, dans des lieux distincts (Schmitt Pantel 1981: 92).

By contrast to the archaic city, with its highly restrictive policies regarding sacrificial banquets, Hellenistic civic feasts were sometimes offered to all free inhabitants (Schmitt Pantel 1981: 93). Into the Roman period, however, fellowship among different social classes occurred only in private religious fraternities, many of which came from the East (Gager 1975: 99; Beaujeu 1964: 74-75).

Greek political philosophy masks the religious character of its gradations but traces of the gradations survive to be defended on a different basis. Plato patterns his ideal republic after the hierarchy of the faculties of the human mind (or vice versa), but the classes of his city are fairly homologous with those of Athenian society. The community of philosophers, who have mystical insight into the real, are like priests who have contact with the gods.[33] Aristotle's *politeia* is essentially a discourse about citizenship: Constitutional types register different distributions of political participation and power, and even more than Plato he suppresses the religious dimension (cf. Mossé 1967: 17-21). Occasionally, however, Aristotle reveals something of the religious background of the *polis*, as when he excludes mechanics (*banausos*) and farmers from holding priestly offices, arguing that only citizens should worship the gods (*Politics* 1329a; 1981: 416). In other respects also, his politics may be linked to graded priesthood: his use of *koinonia* terminology in definitions of the *polis* (e.g., the city is a "political association," *Politics* 1252a; 1981: 54), since this word-group was used, among other things, with reference to fellowship with the gods in sacrificial banquets; the limitation of civic feasts to citizens, and the connection of common meals and temples (*Politics* 1330a, 1331a; 1981: 419-420, 424-425); the exclusion of mechanics and tradesmen from the agora and the separation of the city center into two agoras, one for trade and one for *schole* (*Politics* 1331a; 1981: 425-426); the emphasis on being "well-born" as a precondition for the life of virtue (cf. *Nic Ethics* 1099a; 1976: 80; cf. Wood and Wood 1978: 219-222); the fundamental distinction between "parts" (*meroi*) of the political *koinonia* and other residets who function as a *conditio sine qua non* of the citizens' happiness; and the inclusion of religion among the functions of the citizen body (cf. *Politics* 1328a-b; 1981: 412-413).

---

[33]Cornford (1952: 62-126) traces links between mythology and cosmological speculation and shows the similarities of shaman, poet, seer, and philosopher.

CHAPTER SIX

O Foolish Galatians! Who Has Bewitched You?

In a classic passage, Augustine intimates that baptismal chrism implies a radical restructuring of ecclesial life:

> *Et solus tunc ungebatur rex, et sacerdos: duae istae illo tempore unctae personae. In duabus personis praefigurabatur futurus unus rex et sacerdos, utroque munere unus Christus, et ideo Christus a chrismate. Non solum autem caput nostrum unctum est, sed et corpus ejus non ipsi. Rex autem est, quia nos regit et ducit; sacerdos, quia pro nobis interpellat (Rom. viii, 34). E quidem solus ille sacerdos talis extitit, ut ipse esset etiam sacrificium. Sacrificium obtulit Deo non aliud quam seipsum. Non enim inveniret praeter se mundissimam rationalem victimam, tanquam agnus immaculatus fuso sanguine suo redimens nos, concorporans nos sibi, faciens nos membra sua, ut in illo et nos Christus essemus. Ideo ad omnes Christianos pertinet unctio: prioribus autem Veteris Testamenti temporibus ad duas solas personas pertinebat. Inde autem apparet Christi corpus non esse, quia omnes ungimur: et omnes in illo et Christi et Christus sumus, quia quodammodo totus Christus caput et corpus est.*[1]

A temporal contrast between what was the case *tunc* and what is true *nunc* structures this entire passage. The newness of the New is a relocation of royal and priestly privilege, marked by anointing. *Tunc* only king and priest received the unction, and Augustine seems initially to be heading toward an affirmation that *nunc* it is more widely administered. Instead, surprisingly, he first notes a restriction: The *duae personae* of the Old Testament prefigured the *futurus unus rex et sacerdos*. The two point to One

---

[1] *Ennaratio in Psalmum* 26, II.2 (PL 36, 199-200). Dabin (1950: 99) comments that this passage "est si fondamental qu'il est repris, sous une forme ou sous un autre, par les representants les plus autorisés de la tradition occidentale."

who combines the two, and that One alone rules and leads, sacrifices and intercedes. Nonetheless, the limitation is ultimately for the purpose of extension, since "not only our head is anointed but also his body, we ourselves," or, more briefly, because the One has made the many *concorporans sibi*. The unity of head and members is remarkable: *in illo* (i.e., in the Head) *et nos Christus essemus* and *omnes in illo et Christi et Christus sumus*. *Quodammodo* in the final clause signals Augustine's desire to protect the priority and uniqueness of the priestly kingship of the Head but the proclamation of *totus Christus* is powerful. What *tunc* pertained to only two, *nunc* is granted to *omnes Christianos*.

The eschatological dimension of this passage is no less important: To the *tunc* and *nunc*, there is added a *futurus*, of which the present is a figure. The whole passage is a comment on the title of Psalm 26, which, in Augustine's Latin Bible was, "Of David, before he was anointed." Augustine thus sees the Psalm as the anointed believer's desperate cry for the presence of God. Believers, already anointed *in sacramento*, are, like David, in a sense yet to be anointed; though wearing already the tent-garment, they long for the weight of a glorious house. Unction does not confer a static position but impels forward, leading the anointed ones toward a future fullness of the oil of gladness. Augustine hears the same cry in Psalm 118 (119:81), where the *regale sacerdotium* strains *avidissime ac vehementissime* toward a good not yet seen or granted (*Enarratio in Psalmum* 118 (119); PL 37, 1557).

In Augustine's view, Christ's priesthood consists preeminently in His self-offering, and since the church's priesthood is a participation in that of

224

the Head, her ministry takes the same form.[2] Through the Only-begotten Priest, the church offers her multifaceted sacrifice in the whole of her corporate life: by defending the truth to the point of shedding blood, by cultivating the fires of holy and pious love, by keeping appointed feasts as a memorial of Christ's saving work, by humility and praise.[3] At the close of *De civitate Dei* 10.6, Augustine adroitly moves from the general sacrifice that encompasses the whole life of the church to its ritual expression in the Eucharist. Christ offered Himself as a servant, and Augustine cites Romans 12:1-6 to prove that the church's living sacrifice likewise involves "not thinking of yourself more highly than you ought." True sacrifice is humble promotion of the unity of the body, as each seeks not his own but the other's good: *Hoc est sacrificium Christianorum:* **multi unum corpus in Christo**, and this unity is liturgically embodied in sharing one loaf in the Eucharistic feast, where the church both offers and is offered (*De civitate Dei* 10.6; Augustine 1984: 379-380; PL 41, 283). The Eucharist is not a propitiatory sacrifice, but it is sacrificial in that it liturgically condenses the whole-life self-offering of the church.

Augustine insists that sacrifice is the work of the whole people, yet he

---

[2]On sacrifice in Augustine, see Lécuyer (1954: 905-914); Quinot (1962: 129-168).

[3]*Cum ad illum sursum est, ejus est altare cor nostrum: ejus Unigenito eum sacerdote placamus: ei cruentas victimas caedimus, quando usque ad sanguinem pro ejus veritate certamus: ei suavissimum adolemus incensum, cum in ejus conspectu pio sanctoque amore flagramus: ei dona ejus in nobis, nosque ipsos vovemus, et reddimus: ei beneficiorum ejus solemnitatibus festis et diebus statutis dicamus sacramusque memoriam, ne volumine temporum ingrata subrepat oblivio: ei sacrificamus hostiam humilitatis et laudis in ara cordis igne fervidae charitatis. Ad hunc videndum, sicut videri potest, eique cohaerendum, ab omni peccatorum et cupiditatum malarum labe mundamur, et ejus nomine consecramur* (*De civitate Dei* 10.3; Augustine 1984: 375; PL 41, 280).

does not discount the importance of ordained leadership.[4]   Pastors exercise their authority not *in se* but *in corpore Pastoris*, so that even evil bishops have the right to be obeyed (Jourjon 1954: 166, 173-174). Without pastors, men neither become Christians nor live Christian lives (Pellegrino 1968: 73). Despite his emphasis on order and authority in pastoral office, however, Augustine writes little about the privileges of the ordained, and presidency at the Eucharist does not play a large role in his thought. Pastors exercise the authority of service, as expressed in his repeated episcopal motto: *praesumus, sed si prosumus* (cf. Pellegrino 1968: 59ff). Augustine's focus is thus on the different ways ordained and non-ordained participate in the one priesthood of Christ. Pastors do not stand guard to exclude the baptized from the house but lead the whole community in procession up to the altar. Bishops are perhaps chief priests but they preside over and train a thoroughly priestly community (Hofmann 1933: 413-420).

Already in the New Testament, analogies are occasionally drawn between Old Testament priests and ministers of the gospel (1 Cor. 9:13-14). These scattered references were systematically developed in the patristic period. Clement of Rome compared the Old Testament priestly orders to those of the church (1 Clement 40:1-3) and Jerome developed this into the classic correlation matching Israel's High Priest, priests, and Levites with the church's hierarchy of bishop, presbyter, deacon (PL 22, 1195). Yet, as Aidan Kavanagh points out, it was especially under the

---

[4]On Augustine's view of the ordained priesthood, see Pellegrino (1968); Jourjon (1954: 151-178); Cowdrey (1969: 449-454). On the importance of *auctoritas* in Augustine, see Brown (1967: 216, 238, 278, 310-311).

"medieval polity" that "religious vows and priestly ordination took on much of the aura once possessed by baptism," and this has led to an ecclesiology in which baptism creates "a Christian proletariat while holy orders creates something called 'first-class citizenship' in the Church" (1995: 4). In this final chapter, I explore the liturgical evidence for Kavanagh's claim, and discuss some wider ramifications for the *ecclesia* that was Western Christendom. Though the following discussion is scarcely exhaustive, it shows that the eclipse of the New Testament's radical reconfiguration of antique order is an undercurrent of modern church history, and plays a role in the rise of secularism.

Follow the Oil

The story of the introduction of anointing into initiation rites provides a cautionary tale of *lex orandi* leading *lex credendi* into a ditch. Though not inevitable, the development possesses a powerful logic: Anointings were added very early to the primitive rite of water baptism; priestly meanings were attached to the oil; and, as the oil migrated from initiation to other ritual sites, priestly meanings migrated with it. Once this happened, trying to reattach a fully Augustinian significance to baptism, that is, trying to recover the full power of the gospel, was like trying to gather water in a sieve. The Reformers might be excused a knowing smirk: Had water alone been left to bear the multiple significances of initiation, no such migration would have been possible.

Though the church never surrendered the priestly dimensions of initiation, the oil did flow, with priestly dignity following in its trail. The earliest liturgical shift was the temporal separation of chrismation/confirmation from initiation, which seems to have arisen as something of an accident in fifth-century Gaul and by the eighth century in Germany.[5] Hugh of St. Victor in the twelfth century said the baptismal candidate was anointed on the chest and back so that *fortitudinem accipiat ad portandum onus Domini* (2.6.11; PL 176, 457C-D). As with some earlier theologians, investiture is the specifically priestly act of initiation, and for Hugh, the priestly *anointing* takes place at confirmation.[6] Priestly dignity thinned as it was stretched to encompass both baptism and confirmation, and a question mark appeared over the "merely baptized."

Oil flowed further with the introduction of anointing into ordination. Early ordination liturgies, both Eastern and Western, consisted of election or acclamation by the people, a series of prayers, the laying on of hands, and various incorporative gestures (e.g., a kiss) between the newly ordained and the people. Though the Leonine Sacramentary speaks of "the dew of heavenly unction" (Bradshaw 1990: 216), there is no evidence of an actual chrism in Western ordination at the time. Similarly, Gregory Nazianzus's ordination sermon begins with references to the unction he

---

[5]See Fisher (1965: esp. 120-147); Wainwright (1969: 29-38); Cramer (1993: 179-184).

[6]*Chrismatis unctionem jam ab antiquo in Veteri Testamento institutam legimus, qua tunc quidem reges solum et sacerdotes liniebantur. Quorum unctione singularis ille unctus praefigurabatur, qui prae cunctis participibus suis unctus est [Heb. I], ut cum illo participerant in nomine, qui participes illius esse mererentur in unctione. A christmate enim Christus dicitur, et a Christo Christianus nominatur. Propterea ex quo nomen omnes communicare coeperunt, omnes unctionem accipere debuerunt quia in Christo omnes genus electum sumus, et regale sacerdotium [I Pet. II] (De sacramentis 2.7.1; PL 176, 459D).*

received, and alludes to the Aaronic ordination, but the text does not necessarily imply rites of anointing and investiture (Lécuyer 1983: 83-84). The earliest undisputed evidence appears *c.* 700-730 among the Visigoths of Aquitaine, who anointed the hands of presbyters at their ordination.[7] Anointing of episcopal candidates on the head did not arise for several more decades, and then in North-Central France, at the time that Pope Stephen anointed Pepin. The Roman Sacramentary did not include episcopal anointing, so when Charlemagne imposed it on the empire he in effect suppressed the practice. It revived during the later Carolingian period and after, inspired by the posthumous influence of Amalarius and the False Decretals, and Rome adopted the rite in the mid-tenth century.[8]

Hands were anointed to consecrate them for Eucharistic ministry. Thus, both Ivo of Chartres and Hugh of St. Victor explicitly connect the anointing of the hands with the *gratia consecrandi* (Bligh 1956: 38-40). For Thomas, ordination imprinted an indelible character in the *traditio* of chalice and paten, yet he states that the unction consecrates *ad aliquod sacramentum tractandum* and is reserved for priests alone, since they *propriis*

---

[7]There is some disagreement about the interpretation of the text. There are two prayers, the first of which is labeled *"Consecratio Manus"* and the second *"Item Alia."* Ellard (1933: 20) interprets this as a double anointing of the hands of the ordinand to priesthood; Bradshaw's arrangement implies that the second is an alternate prayer (1990: 227); Chydenius and Bligh believe the first prayer applied to presbyterian ordination, the second to episcopal ordination, and that they were placed together under the heading of presbyterial ordination by mistake (Chydenius 1965:42; Bligh 1956: 129). Of these, Bradshaw's is the least speculative explanation.

[8]Ellard (1933: 16-21; 30-33; 34-50, 67-68, 97-98); Kantorowicz (1958: 63); Porter (1967: 79-80).

manibus corpus Christi tangunt. Chalice and paten are anointed for similar reasons (quoted in Bligh 1956: 42-43). Significantly, the prayer accompanying anointing in some liturgies asks that whatever the priest consecrates will be consecrated and whatever he blesses will be blessed, and it is immediately followed by the *traditio* of chalice and paten. By ordination, the priest received permission to touch holy objects and power to perform sacred actions prohibited to or impossible for the unordained.

From the first, ordination anointings were interpreted by Old Testament typology. In the earliest texts, the anointing of the hands is accompanied by a prayer recalling Samuel's anointing of King David,[9] and Amalarius and tenth-century English ordination rites directly connect ordination anointing with Aaron's.[10] Chydenius suggests that the Old Testament typology was the source of both presbyterial and episcopal chrismation. Aaron was anointed on the head at his ordination, and *consecrabis manus*, the Latin translation of the technical Hebrew phrase יד מלא, might have produced hand-anointing (Chydenius 1965: 41). Even if episcopal anointing copied the Carolingian royal rite, as Kantorowicz claims, the ultimate inspiration was still from the Old Testament, since the Frankish kings fancied themselves heirs of the *regnum Davidi* rather than of the Roman *imperium* (Kantorowicz 1958: 56-57, 63).

---

[9] *Unguantur manue istae de oleo sanctificato et crismate sanctificationes sicut uncxit samuhel david in regem et prophetam* (quoted in Ellard 1933: 20; English translation Bradshaw 1990: 227).

[10] *Ungo has manus oleo sanctificato, et crismate unctionis purificato. sicut unxit moyses uerbo oris sui manus sancti aaron germani sui* (quoted in Ellard 1933: 81). In his *Liber officialis*, Amalarius writes that *Presbyteri deputantur in loco filiorum Aaron . . . . Hunc morem tenent episcopi nostri: manus presbyterorum ungunt de oleo* (quoted in Bligh 1956: 38).

Eucharistic sacrifice eventually became defined by consecration,[11] which was a monopoly of the ordained. As a result, later medieval and counter-Reformation Catholic theologians assume that only the Eucharistic consecration is "true sacrifice," and accordingly reduce lay sacrifices of praise, virtue, contrition, and repentance to "figurative" status.[12] A similar inversion of terminology occurs with priesthood: Parallel to the change in the use of *mysticum* and *verum* uncovered by de Lubac (1949: ch. 9), Congar finds a limitation of *verus sacerdos* to the ordained (Congar 1985: 188, fn. 2). While for Augustine anointing was a sign of the priestly dignity of the baptized, for later writers the oil of ordination highlights the privileges of the hierarchy and confines the laity to a "metaphorical" priesthood.[13]

---

[11]Two intertwined changes were involved: first, in the meaning of "sacrifice" and, second, in the role of the church in the Eucharistic offering. On the first point, Jungmann sees an "unmistakable shift of emphasis" in Isidore's definition of sacrifice as "that which is made holy" by the prayer of consecration (Jungmann 1976: 59). On the second point there was a move away from the primitive view that Eucharistic sacrifice is an act of the whole church, which was reflected in the first person plural, *offerimus*, in Hippolytus's *Apostolic Tradition* (Jungmann 1959: 16-17).

[12]Commenting on 1 Peter 2:5, William Estius (1542-1613) explained that "Sont appelés prêtres au sens particulier et propre, ceux qui ont pour office d'offrir le sacrifice propre et particulier, par rite externe et immolation en quelque façon. Dans l'Église, il n'y en a pas d'autre que le sacrifice non sanglant du corps et du sang du Seigneur. Au sens impropre et general sont appelés prêtres ceux qui offrent a Dieu des sacrifices au sense figuré, c'est-a-dire tout ceux qui exercent les œuvres bonnes et saintes, soit de religion, soit de misericorde, soit de toute vertu" (quoted in Dabin 1950: 382).

[13]See Gabriel Biel *Canonis Misse Expositio* lectio V (Oberman and Courtenay 1963-67: 1.40-42). Cajetan wrote that *Dignitas namque sacerdotalis non sic est populi, ut quilibet sit pars sacerdotii ... sed sacerdotalis dignitas sic est populi ut habeat ex suis aliquos*

The Return of Antique Order

Ordination anointing had by the tenth century introduced a sharp liturgical cleavage within the Christian priesthood. Ideological support was provided, above all, by the theorists of the eleventh-century Gregorian Reform and papal theorists of the following centuries.[14] To be sure, the Gregorian party did not create the gap between clergy and laity (Oakley 1979: 83-84). Already in the aftermath of the barbarian invasions of the sixth century, a cultural and social chasm had opened, which widened during the Carolingian period. Many of the most egregious offenses against the laity, moreover, were committed in centuries following the Gregorian reform (Congar 1983: ch. 5, 324-332). I do not endorse in an unqualified way the system that Gregory dismantled, nor do I wish to deny the salutary effects of his program, including its substantial contribution to the twelfth-century Renaissance and his efforts to protect the church and clergy from entanglements in sticky social and political webs. But his reform did more than this: When Gregory defrocked the

---

sacerdotes (quoted in Bodem 1971: 62, fn. 83). John Fisher pointed to the unction of the ordination rite as proof of the superiority of the ordained priesthood over the laity: *Adde, quod in illo populo hi, qui templo prefuerunt, non modo sacerdos ipse maximus, verum etiam et minores quoque sacerdotes ungebantur in eorum ordination. Quamobrem sic quaret umbre veritas, ut et certe quadrare debet, oprtet eos, qui pastores ecclesie per maiorum manus ordinantur, unctione spirituali gratie interius deliniri; nam gratia Spiritus unctio quedam spiritualis est* (Fisher 1925: 38-39; 1935: 56-57).

[14]On the history of the Gregorian reform, see Tierney (1964); Tellenbach (1993); Morris (1989: esp. 98-103). For evaluations of its place in Western history, see Berman (1983: 85-119) and Rosenstock-Huessy (1993: 516-561).

emperor and other political leaders, he removed most of the laity's remaining priestly vestments and confirmed the clerical monopolization of "real" priesthood.[15] Whatever the immediate fortunes of Gregory's claims for the papacy, this aspect of his program endured. Gregory's revision of the Augustinian (and biblical) conjugation of ordination was a powerful undercurrent of later Western political, social, and intellectual history. I cannot attempt a full portrait of the post-Gregorian West, but a brief caricature can capture some of the important features.

According to the early medieval conception the Christian empire was the *ecclesia*, a single family ruled by papal and imperial parents (Congar 1968: 81, 258, 291). Conflicts within the Carolingian world were tensions, as Congar puts it, between rival monisms; all agreed that the *ecclesia* had a single finality, with no division of natural and supernatural (Congar 1968: 286, 307). In keeping with this, in France, England, and among the German emperors after Otto I, princes had, by virtue of their anointing and a hand-laying rite that resembled the ordination for priests, a quasi-clerical status and allegedly "magical" powers.[16] Since a bishop anointed the ruler, the argument could be and was made that the king's political power was mediated through the church (Ullmann 1975: 86-87); nonetheless, the king was a member of the *ordo clericalis*, or, in the

---

[15]On the struggles of the eighth through eleventh centuries, see Congar (1968; 1983: ch. 5, 309-316); Leclercq (1970: 59-60). On the place of clergy/lay distinctions in Gregory's reform, Tellenbach (1993: 339); Berman (1983: 88, 98, 110, 114, 575-577, fn. 1); Duby (1980: 198-199).

[16]Gaudemet (1967: 566-568); Bloch (1983: 65-75, 460-477); le Goff (1988: 268); Congar (1968: 272, 281-286).

terminology applied to Charlemagne, *rex et sacerdos*.[17]

Gregory's was a triumph of dualism, not merely of *sacerdotium* and *imperium* within a single *ecclesia* but of two societies, *ecclesia* and *imperium* (Congar 1983: ch. 4, 94). Gregory and his party sought to strip political leaders of their sacred character, at times deploying rhetoric that suggested the political order was virtually diabolical (Bloch 1983: 122). The liturgical dimension of this struggle focused on the status of the royal anointing, and in the twelfth century the Gregorian position institutionalized its victory when the royal unction was downgraded from a full sacrament to a sacramental (Ullmann 1975: 87).

This was not, as Gaudemet suggests (1967: 568), merely a result of growing precision in the definition of sacraments, but part of a conscious program at whose center was a redefinition of "layman." Etymologically, a layman is a member of the *laos*, and in this sense "layman" is perfectly compatible with the Augustinian theology of priesthood. Following the Gregorian reform, "layman" began to take on a derogatory connotation. Albert the Great could dismiss lay requests for the spiritual bread of the clergy and religious with *Non est bonum sumere panem fiiliorum et mittere canibus* (quoted in Congar 1983: ch. 5, 329). Clerical supremacy in the church was legitimated by claims to a special form of priesthood. Gregory reintroduced the ancient dualism between priestly patricians and non-priestly plebs, a principle that Paul scorned as among τὰ στοιχεῖα, at the heart of the Christian *polis*.

---

[17]Bloch (1983: 74). Le Goff points out that applied to Charlemagne, *sacerdos* referred to "the priest's ability to preach, not his charismatic functions" (1988: 268), but even so the point stands.

Closely related to this were changes in Eucharistic liturgy that took place over several centuries. The cup was withdrawn from the laity, and their infrequent participation in Eucharistic bread highlighted their subordination to the clergy. As I argued above, both ancient Israel and the Greek city-state were *koinoniai* in sacrificial food; citizen and table companion were synonymous, and both terms described a priestly dignity. Christ introduced a new seating arrangement at the table, which remodeled the church and eventually the city. With the restriction of commensality to the clergy, archaic distributions of sacrificial food reappeared and architectural and other liturgical changes reinforced clerical sacredness. Cloisters and choirs were marked off for clergy, the priest celebrated the Eucharist silently with his back to the congregation and often with no congregation present, the people no longer brought forward the bread and wine, and the host was changed from the bread of the "lay" table to specially prepared wafers.[18] Communal offering *per sacerdotes* became a sacerdotal sacrifice *pro populo* (Jungmann 1976: 64-70). In the end, the one loaf exploded into its many grains, as the laity's role devolved from "doing" to "seeing/hearing" to individual "feeling/thinking" (Dix 1948: 249, 616), a shocking ecclesial "atomization" that originated with the fission of priest and people at the Mass. In this retrogression toward passivity, we see one dimension in the development of modern consciousness. Spatial separation of sanctuary and nave impressed itself on the worshiper, whose active eyes and mind

---

[18]See Le Goff (1988: 257); White (1995: 6-9); Harper (1991: 33-36, 40-41); Dix (1945: 480-482, 594, 598-599); Bouyer (1968: 367-379). On lay communion, see Dix (1945: 597-598); Bossy (1985: 70).

were encumbered by a passive body. Thomas à Kempis, with his emphasis on interior communion, anticipated not only Zwingli but Descartes.

By the eleventh century, these shifts in practice were having their impact on sacramental theology. Conflict over Berengar's "figurative" understanding of the Eucharist arose, significantly enough, in the same period as the Gregorian Reform (Sheedy 1980), and Berengar was savagely treated because he threatened the reform party's vision of order, centered on the priest's ability to confect the sacrament (Rubin 1991:19, 35, 49-51; cf. Troeltsch 1931: 1.232, 235). According to Gregory's own defense of his deposition of Henry IV (1081), the superiority of priesthood to royalty is evident in the priest's sacramental powers. Even the exorcist, among the lowest orders of clergy, is superior to the king since he commands spirits, not men. No king can "snatch a Christian from the devil" through baptism or confirm with the oil of chrism. Supremely, "who among [royalty] is able by his own word to create the body and blood of the Lord?" -- this being the "greatest thing in the Christian religion." Gregory concludes, "From this it is apparent how greatly superior in power is the priestly dignity" (Tierney 1964: 69-70). Berengar, by suggesting that the priests were doing "nothing more" than manipulating "signs," endangered clerical dignity.

Modifications in the meaning of *corpus mysticum* are relevant here. Following de Lubac, Michel de Certeau (1992: 82-84) displays the changing "punctuation" of Eucharistic dogma by graphing various ways in which theology transmutes the threefold body of Christ to binary form. Let H = historical body, S = sacramental body, C = ecclesiastical body, ^

236

= conjunction, and / = separation. The earlier relation can be diagramed as, H / (S ^ C): the sacrament performance by the whole church continues or reproduces in some way the temporally distinct events of Christ's history. Importantly, sacrament and church are on the same side of the partition. In later medieval theory, the relation is, (H ^ S) / C: the historical body is mystically present in the priest's sacramental actions and materials, now screened off from the ecclesial body. This exactly reproduces Gregorian hierarchy: On this theory, the priest stands alone within the veil confecting God, as the plebs outside strain for a glimpse of the marvel.

Emphasis on the priestly miracle of consecration eventually created a crucial watershed in medieval culture. William Courtenay points out that for Bernard in the twelfth century, symbols as such have "power," but by the time of the high scholastics, this power was limited to a few rites done in the church. On this view, non-sacramental signs only symbolize or declare an action or event that occurs by other means. Sacramental magic thus interrupts the chain of cause and effect that binds natural and cultural life (1972: 208-209). Courtenay suggests this twelfth- and thirteenth-century development is a more significant change in the medieval world view than anything achieved by Gregory, but he fails to realize that a sharp distinction between ecclesiastical and cultural semiotic processes relies on a prior distinction between *ecclesia* and *societas*. This duality did not exist in the Carolingian empire but was a product of the Gregorian reform. Restriction of symbolic "magic" to the church, that is, to the clergy, begins to carve out a "sacred" sphere set off from a "secular" counterpart. More on this below.

237

Dignitas in the quotation from Gregory is also important. In the Latin fathers and early medieval theologians, the word is commonly found in discussions of baptismal anointing. A *Tractatus* attributed to Maximus of Turin contrasts the royal and sacerdotal anointings of the Old Covenant to the baptismal anointing of the New: the latter *chrisma, id est haec unctio quae vobis imposita est, illius sacerdotii contulit dignitatem* (*Tractatus* 3; PL 57, 777D-779A). Rabanus Maurus likewise says that baptismal unction and investiture confer a "sacerdotal dignity" (PL 107, 313D), and for Peter Damien the whole church shares a *regia dignitas* (PL 144, 556 CD; 755 AB). Already in the late eighth century, Theodulf of Orleans exhorted the clergy to *semper memores esse tantae dignitatis* (Bligh 1956: 130). Disputing Peter Damien, Cardinal Humbert, a leading member of the Gregorian party, condemned the exaltation of worldly power in a way that would minimize the "dignity of the church." Employing a traditional analogy he argued that "as the soul excels the body and commands it, so too the priestly dignity excells the royal or, we may say, the heavenly dignity the earthly" (Tierney 1964: 40-42; cf. Gierke 1987: 130, fn. 72). Humbert was not so accurate as the thirteenth-century canonist Hostiensis, who estimated that the "priest's dignity is 7,644 ½ times higher than the royal," since that is the "proportion between sun and moon" according to Ptolemy (quoted in Rosenstock-Huessy 1993: 546). If so high is the priest above the king, I suspect medievals lacked adequate technology to calculate the proportionate dignity of priest and commoner.

The Gregorian program was supported by an explicit appeal to the principles of archaic binary order. On the one hand, a flattened typology obscured the centrality that the *totus Christus* had played in Augustine's

238

biblically-grounded hermeneutics. Isidore had expanded Jerome's use of Old Testament hierarchy to encompass other orders of the church (PL 83, 781-790), and in this he was followed by Pseudo-Alcuin, a tenth-century writer (PL 101, 1231), whose treatment was picked up by twelfth-century scholastics (Chydenius 1965: 23-26, 56-58, 86-89). A similar hermeneutics grounded Carolingian political theory: Charlemagne, not the *totus Christus*, became the new David (Morris 1972: 25), even, in a sense, the new *rex-sacerdos*, Melchizedek. During the Gregorian period and after, regulations governing the holiness of the Aaronic priesthood were applied to the Christian clergy. Priests had to avoid the contagions of simony and sex so as not to pollute the Lord's body. When Leo IX defends clerical celibacy by asking rhetorically, "if you commit incest with your spiritual daughter, with what conscience do you dare to handle the mystery of the Lord's body?" (quoted in Morris 1989: 103; cf. Bossy 1985: 37), one hears a distant echo of Levitical prohibitions. Humbert's defense of the superiority of the clergy to laity is supported by quotations from Numbers that emphasize the fearful danger of laymen touching sacred objects (1891: 212-213). In the century after Gregory, Bernard called for a more contemplative papacy but he had no doubt that the Pope was "by [his] dignity, an Aaron" (Tierney 1964: 93). Though the Augustinian typology was never wholly abandoned, in the later medieval period, and even more in Counter-Reformation Catholicism, the grammar linking Aaronic priests to the ordained absorbed Augustine's more radical conjugation.[19]

---

[19]The *Catechism of the Council of Trent* took up the distinction between the "internal" priesthood of the faithful and the "external" priesthood of the ordained clergy, defending it by   reference to the Old Testament: "the Almighty appointed the entire tribe of Levi to the ministry of the temple, and forbad by an express law

On the other hand, the post-Gregorian papacy adorned itself with the trappings of the ancient city. From the time of Urban II, the Roman clergy began to style itself a "curia," a term that originally referred to a union of clans in archaic Rome (Alföldy 1985: 6) and which for medieval papalists "evoked the ancient Roman senate" (Le Goff 1988: 271). Though not referring to antique Roman order, Urban drew elaborate analogies between medieval society and the hierarchical structure of the church (Reynolds 1978: 2, fn. 6); instead of presenting an alternative configuration of social life, the church simply imaged the segmentations of worldly society. Several centuries and a Reformation later, Johannis Maldonati (1534-1583) argued that a division between priests and people characterizes all human society: As Rome was divided between patricians and plebeians and Israel into the ordained and the circumcised, so the church has its classes of clergy and laity (1965: 93, 290, 391-392, 398; Book 2, *De Ordine*, 1. 3, part 2). Maldonati saw the archaic binary order of priest/non-priest, whose destruction by the cross and baptism is part of the apostolic gospel, as a permanent, natural feature of social order.

---

that any member of a different tribe should dare to intrude himself into that function. Wherefore king Osias, stricken by God with leprosy for having usurped the Sacerdotal office, was visited with the heaviest chastisement for his arrogance and sacrilege. . . . we find the same distinction of internal and external Priesthood in the Evangelical Law" (Donovan 1839: 314). Nicolaus Herborn (1480-1535) argued in a similar way from the Aaronic unction: *Ut igitur non omnes ad carnale sacerdotium Aaronicum uncti sunt Iudei, ita neque omnes Christiani ex aequo sacris mysteriis depututi sunt* (1927: 64-66). In his *Malleus in haeresim lutheranam* 1.2, John Faber (1478-1541) argues that baptized Christians are priests only allegorically, spiritually, and figuratively (quoted in Dabin 1950: 339-40). The Presbyterian Westminster Confession's Directory of Government compares ministers to Aaronic priests.

The Gregorian Construction of Modernity

Reintroduction of gradations of priesthood reignited the ancient "struggle of the orders" (cf. Le Goff 1988: 265, 271), and much of later medieval and modern church history recounts permutations of this struggle. Throughout the later Middle Ages, the Gregorian church faced a series of sectarian or heretical revolts, many of which expressly attacked the clerical monopoly of *sancta*. Orthodox movements, such as those of Hus and Wycliff, took aim at the Eucharistic practice of the Roman church, urging utraquism and frequent communion (Bossy 1985: 80-82). Luther's early polemics have as much to do with the location of priestly privilege as with justification by faith: To Gregory's 27 theses in *Dictatus Papae* Luther opposed his 95, challenging the system of papal indulgences. Though Luther emphatically affirmed the "priesthood of the baptized" in a fully Augustinian sense, later Reformers suppressed this theme (Avis 1981: 95-96, 102). Corporate and sacramental dimensions of priesthood especially were stifled. "Priesthood of believers" (not, "of the baptized") came to mean that each can make his individual approach to God, the key anti-Gregorian slogan ironically aiding and abetting the very atomization Gregory did so much to foster. Anabaptist and Spiritualist reactions to the Reformation were further attempts to secure, through "private inspiration," the *dignitas* and ministry of the *laicus*, but these too ended in failure, not least because "believer's baptism" perpetuated a semi-Gregorian dichotomy of priest/non-priest within the church. Within Roman Catholicism, Gregory so raised the stakes that the papacy became an object of rivalry, ultimately resulting in schism (Oakley 1979: 32-73). In response to the Reformation, Trent formalized the Gregorian system in a rigorous form, and the reforms of Vatican II, welcome and even radical as they are, perpetuate an "essential distinction" between the priesthood of the clergy and of the baptized (Flannery 1980: 361). These opposition movements, inchoate and even heretical as they sometimes were, contested the Gregorian demotion of the laity. Finding themselves excluded from the city constructed to welcome them, the plebs again stormed the gates.

Resentment against clerical privilege manifested itself also in post-Gregorian theology. Reventlow traced the intricate links between medieval and early modern anti-clerical movements and the rise of biblical criticism (1984), and I have briefly noted how hostility to priesthood has distorted theology, philosophy, and sociology (cf. p. 41). Since clerical privilege was defended by resort to Old Testament models, attacks on the former modulated into Marcionite renunciation of the latter. And, since the clergy clung to its monopoly of sacraments, anti-clericalism was often accompanied by a rejection of sacrament and ritual *per se*. Liberal theology is largely a sophisticated continuation of these currents of anti-priestly animus, preaching a Christ stripped of layers of priestly -- i.e., Old Testament -- cult and dogma.

Anti-clericalism took a severe form in the Enlightenment, but by this time it had made a volatile alliance with secularism. The latter too was a development to which Gregory unwittingly contributed. At the verbal level, during the Gregorian period, the meaning of *saeculum* changed significantly and permanently (Berman 1983: 109-110). In earlier Christian theology, *saeculum* could refer to the time between fall and eschaton in which both church and state participated (Milbank 1990: 1). From the twelfth century, the line between secular and spiritual ran *through* the ranks of clergy rather than bounding off the clergy from the laity. Gregory's reform drew the line elsewhere: Humbert urged laymen to refrain from interference in *ecclesiastica*, since their proper concern is with *saecularia* (1891: 208),[20] and Hugh of St. Victor in the following century employed the term in the same sense. As the soul is superior to the body, Hugh argues, so those devoted to *spiritualia* are *dignior* than those who are dedicated to *terrena*. Thus, *spiritualis potestas terrenam sive saecularem potestatem honore, ac dignitate praecedit* (PL 176, 417-418). By confining the laity to *terrena* while maintaining a clerical monopoly of *spiritualia* and *ecclesiastica*, the Gregorian program destroyed the unity of the Carolingian arrangement. Gregory, to be sure, distinguished to dominate, but the way the distinction was drawn initiated the process that eventually led to the retreat of the church from terrestrial affairs into the private sphere of soul cure. Plebs, excluded from the sanctuary and table, determined to construct a new city, and found they could get along well enough with no

---

[20]Contrary tendencies were at work in Gregory and later medieval society, of course. Gregory, like all medievals, believed that political powers are ordained of God, and he never imagined that the secular power would dare to ignore the counsel of the church. Yet, Bloch is correct that prior to the Gregorian Reform the "sacred and profane had been almost inextricably mixed" (quoted in Brown 1982: 305), and Brown adds that the Gregorian program was a leading impetus behind the "disengagement of the two spheres." It is better to say, however, that Gregory's program was an important moment in the construction of the secular rather than an unveiling of a distinction always below the surface (Milbank 1990: 1).

help from the priests. By the eighteenth century, the "struggle of the orders" was no longer a protest on behalf of the plebs but brought forward the secular claim that the entire *ancien regime* was a smokescreen of priestly deception, a conclusion then retroactively used to reconstruct the history of ancient Israel.

In the Carolingian model, society was *ecclesia*, so that Gregory's bifurcation of priest and layman introduced a fundamental division within the social body as much as in the ecclesial body. The marginalized that, according to Paul, received special honor in the new Israel were re-marginalized in Gregorian order. Post-Gregorian clergy became the first "new class," whose monopoly of potent symbols and specialized language, whose common aims and protective instincts provided a model for other modern elites (Berman 1983: 108-109). Gregory did much to initiate the divergence of specialized elite and marginalized majority that gathered pace over the following centuries. It is a commonplace of modern sociology, and a correct one, that the post-Gregorian church was the prototype of the modern bureaucratic state.

Shifting relations between clergy and laity influenced the development of political thought, providing an impetus for contractual models of authority. Manegold of Lautenbach, a papal apologist, distinguished, in Ullmann's terminology, the "descending" character of papal and clerical authority from the "ascending" trajectory of royal authority: The king is such at the behest of the people, but if he breaks the popular *pactum* he has no legitimacy (Tierney 1964: 75; Gierke 1987: 38-39, 146 fn. 138). For Manegold, the king is little more than an exalted pigherd, and if he fails to take good care of the pigs, they can dismiss him

(Bloch 1983: 121). Thus, efforts to protect papal superiority modulate into a secular democratic foundation for political authority. Royalists, for a time, defended the king's supremacy to other laity and clergy by accentuating the significance of royal anointing.[21] This, of course, was an inversion within an essentially Gregorian framework: Clerical and royalist theories converged in the judgment that the plebs are not priests. Eventually, political theorists determined, correctly, that relying on sacramental or Christological models played into the hands of papal apologists, and they began to imagine a political theory on purely secular or natural grounds. The Gregorian system made another indirect contribution to secular politics. Following the Reformation, the "struggle of the orders" spilled over the boundaries of the church into a century of violence through much of Europe, until politicians, sickened with blood, concluded that purging theology from political life was the price of peace.

The influence of spatial conceptions on political thinking is important here as well (cf. Milbank 1997: 268-292). Baptismal ordination to priesthood, as we have seen, radically decentered antique order, or, more accurately, located the center in heaven rather than any earthly point. Baptism thus implies and, if its implications are followed through, brings

---

[21]Wido of Osnabruck, writing in defense of Henry IV in 1084-85, claimed that "the king must be set apart from the mass of laymen, for since he is anointed with consecrated oil, he partakes of the priestly ministry." In 1143, Louis VII said that both in the Old Testament and New, "only kings and priests are consecrated by anointing with holy chrism. It is fitting that those who, among everyone, are placed at the head of God's people, united among themselves by holy unction, should obtain for their subjects temporal as well as spiritual goods, and that kings and priests should obtain these for each other" (quoted in Le Goff 1988: 268-269).

into being a complex ecclesiastical arrangement, and, insofar as the *ecclesia* serves as model for the larger society, a complex political space, concretely realized in a proliferating host of institutions and practices mediating between political authorities and the individual. The Gregorian reform reintroduced a binary system, undermining the basis for mediating structures; thus the theory that takes ecclesiastical form as Pope/church and clergy/laity takes political form in a dualism of state/individual.

Modern social science normally presumes a Gregorian world, divided between spiritual and political institutions. Troeltsch admitted that his theories applied only to a society where "differentiation" of "value spheres" had already occurred (Milbank 1990: 89), and the fountainhead of this process in the Christian West was the dichotomy of cleric/layman. For Weber, this differentiation was the dormant genius of biblical religion, though it came to fruition mainly in the modern West (Milbank 1990: 93). In the same vein, Comte, Durkheim, Parsons, and Eliade consider the sacred/profane distinction to be the ahistorical essence of society and religion (Milbank 1990: 60, 63, 129). These theorists, like Johannis Maldonati, take Gregorian space as a given, rather than as a contingent re-assembly of priesthood. Against this, one should "out-Marx Marx" by insisting that the church *created* the gap of sacred and profane in its modern form (and so created "class"). Insofar as the social sciences are "sciences of conflict" (Milbank 1990: 23), they presume the dialectical oppositions that proliferated from the Gregorian settlement. It does not seem fanciful to ponder whether and to what extent the potentially violent dualisms of modern thought and society – capital/labor, interior/exterior, public/private, society/individual, state/individual – are transmutations of priest/non-priest.

Conclusion

Baptism is the beginning of the gospel because it announces Christ's boundary-transgressing work, because it extends the redistribution of priestly privilege and ministry that began with the cross and Pentecost, because it symbolizes and effects the opening of the house, altar, and table to Jew and Greek, male and female, slave and free, because it forms the eschatological city peopled by the royal priesthood in the midst of the pre-eschatological world.

Within a few centuries, and more grossly after Gregory's papacy, the church returned to something like life ὑπὸ τὰ στοιχεῖα, which, being a form of fleshly existence, could only produce the fruits of rivalry, violence, strife, and schism endemic in the modern world. Unfortunately, even the greatest of protests against the Gregorian regime, the Reformation, did not consistently hit the nail on the head. Luther was right that the gospel was at stake in his protest, but wrong about the central message of the gospel: The good *news* is *not* justification by faith, for that, as Paul insists, is a truth as old as Abraham. Luther was closer to the heart of Paul's gospel when he attacked the Babylonian Captivity of the church and exulted in the "clerical" status of the baptized.

As we near the end of the second millennium of the new creation, we have some cause to hope that the momentum of the Gregorian detour is decreasing and that the church is prepared to proclaim without embarrassment a gospel that begins with baptism, one that makes good on the promise of a priesthood for the plebs.

Whether or not this lies on the immediate horizon, it is thrilling and sobering in equal measure to reflect that much of the evangelical work of building the city imagined in baptism remains to be done.

Summary and Areas of Future Research

In the first chapter, I identified a persistent theological framework for sacramental theology, which I labeled "semi-Marcionite." According to this paradigm, the New Covenant begins an ascent out of the economy of signs and rites that makes up human cultural life. Therefore, the sacraments of the New Covenant function differently from those of the Old; while the Old sacraments were bound up with a materialistic and ritualistic form of religion, the New sacraments aim to effect spiritual and internal transformations. After offering several examples of this tendency, I turned to Augustine for an alternative. In a number of works, Augustine describes the New Covenant sacraments as "conjugations" of the Old, which implies that signs and rites have the same corporate function in both Old and New, and that the signs of the New can only be understood properly against the background of the rites of ancient Israel. The beauty of liturgy and of liturgical theology, on Augustine's rendering, depends on a polyphonic interlacing of Old and New.

Based on this conclusion, the second chapter turned to my specific thesis that baptism is a conjugation of, among other things, the Aaronic ordination rite. Chapter 2 examined priesthood and the ordination rite in the Old Testament. Several lines of evidence were presented to show that Israel's priests were essentially "attendants to Yahweh in His house," and I continued by exploring some features of the ordination rite, not only to support this understanding of priesthood but also to set out some of the rite's symbolisms. Turning to the New Testament in chapter 3, I offered *prima facie* Christological, ecclesiological, and ritual-liturgical arguments for the hypothesis that baptism inducts into the Christian priesthood, and I supported this conclusion with extended exegetical studies of Luke's account of Jesus' baptism and 1 Corinthians 1:21-22. To prove the stricter hypothesis that baptism fulfills and replaces ("conjugates") the ordination rite, I examined three other New Testament passages, Hebrews 10:19-22, 1 Corinthians 6:11, and Galatians 3:27. From the first two, I concluded that baptism in the church does what the ordination did in Israel, making priests, conferring sanctuary access, and consecrating "saints." The conclusions from Galatians 3 were more tentative, but I suggested that the idea of baptismal "investiture" with Christ is rooted in the ordination and therefore it supports the typology.

In chapter 4, I applied the typology to questions of baptismal liturgy and theology. Patristic and medieval writers interpreted baptismal anointings and investitures in terms of the priestly typology, but I contended that these enhancements of baptism were unnecessary and potentially misleading. Since Aaronic priests and their households ate sacrificial food denied to laymen, I argued typologically that the baptized, including infants, should be permitted to eat the church's sacrificial food, the Eucharist. Concerning baptismal theology, the typology of priestly ordination implies that baptism "causes what it symbolizes," effectively making priests *ex opere operato*. The structure of the ordination texts in Exodus and Leviticus also suggests that Aaron and his sons were made "new creations" through the rite of ordination, and this led me to a doctrine of baptismal regeneration. I defended my formulation against the objection that it was "purely juridical" by arguing that roles and narratives constitute personal identity and by arguing that baptism effects a transition in the "regard of God" upon us, which is the deepest ground of who we are. I closed chapter 4 arguing for a "poetic" account of baptismal causality; as the church enacts God's creative word in baptism, she participates with Him in His creation of new people, a priesthood.

Chapter 5 broadened the scope of the discussion. The Aaronic ordination changed not only Aaron and his sons, but the entire socio-liturgical system of Israel and the world, and I suggested baptism also renews socio-religious order. The covenantal change announced by the New Testament is described in many passages in "apocalyptic" terms; new covenant brings new creation. Against this background, an investigation of Hebrews 10:19-22 led to the conclusion that baptism is the sign of the end of Israel's system of graded holiness, both announcing and effecting the formation of a new priesthood without grades of access or divisions in food rights. From Galatians, I argued that baptism also effectively marks the end of the priestly division between Jew and Gentile, forming the "one seed" of Abraham. Since the division of priest/non-priest was also one coordinate of Greco-Roman social order, I further argued that the baptismal community of priests challenges antique Gentile order divided between patricians and plebs. In these ways, baptism is the "washing of cosmic regeneration."

Chapter 6 is a story of decline. Already in the church fathers, and especially in the aftermath of the Gregorian reform, the priestly significance and symbolisms associated with baptism were transferred to ordination. While the church never completely denied that the baptized are priests, clergy claimed exclusive food rights and exclusive rights of access to "holy" spaces. This reintroduced archaic divisions of patrician/plebian, priest/nonpriest in the heart of the new *polis* of the church, and was sometimes explicitly defended by appeal to principles of antique order. In this way, Gregory reinitiated the ancient struggle of the orders, so that Gregorian dualistic order is also implicated in the rise of modern secular thought and culture.

For Further Investigation

Nearly every stage of my argument would benefit from further study, but a few specific areas of research suggest themselves:

1) My study of baptismal priesthood needs to be supplemented by a theology of ordination and pastoral ministry. Paul himself drew analogies between New Covenant apostle and Old Testament priest (1 Cor. 9:13-14). How do these analogies fit into the typology I have defended? If, as I have argued, one cannot make a complete and direct transfer from the authority of the Aaronic priests to that of the Christian pastor, on what biblical/theological basis might this authority be founded? What is the significance of the ordination rite of laying on of hands? What Old Testament rite does it "conjugate"? More specifically, what implications does the typology of baptismal priesthood hold for women's ordination? Does the typology undermine the basis for the clerical monopoly in the administration of sacraments?

2) A second set of concerns centers on the cultural implications of my thesis. More study of the forms of Greco-Roman civic religion is necessary, with more detailed attention to the links between Greco-Roman religion and philosophy. A fuller comparison of the competing *poleis* of

Aristotle and Paul would be illuminating. It would be of interest to investigate in detail the impact of the baptismal priesthood as it permeated Greco-Roman civilization during the first few centuries A.D. I also need to fill out the impressionistic narrative of chapter 6, for I suspect that sacramental theology is deeply implicated in the rise of modern thought and culture.

3) Finally, the Levitical system has been the basis of much of this thesis, but I have only begun to plumb the resources available there for theological reflection. I hope I have made a plausible case for my belief that Levitical patterns are at work behind the scenes in a good deal of the New Testament, but I need to offer a more systematic defense of this prejudice. Beyond that, study of the Levitical system would shed considerable light on Eucharistic theology and also contribute to ecclesiology. The church is now the "sanctuary" consecrated by the presence of the Spirit, and the Pentateuch provides the most detailed biblical information about the significance of the sanctuary, its maintenance, and the proper conduct of its ministers. Because the sanctuary is also a social model, study of its significance, in conversation with cultural anthropology, could serve as a basis for a theological sociology.

If I complete one-ten-thousandth of this work in what remains of my life, I shall be content.

BIBLIOGRAPHY

Abba, R. (1962). "Priests and Levites" in *The Interpreter's Dictionary of the Bible* (5 vols.; New York: Abingdon) 3.

Abba, Raymond (1978). "Priests and Levites in Ezekiel," *VT* 28.

Adam, Karl (1932). *Saint Augustine: The Odyssey of his Soul* (trans. Dom Justin McCann; London: Sheed and Ward).

Adams, Jeremy Duquesnay (1971). *The Populus of Augustine and Jerome: A study in the Patristic Sense of Community* (New Haven: Yale).

Aland, Kurt (1963). *Did the Early Church Baptize Infants?* (Library of History and Doctrine; trans. G. R. Beasley-Murray; London: SCM).

Albright, W.F. (1938). "What Were the Cherubim?" *BA* 1.

Alföldy, Géza (1985). *The Social History of Rome* (trans. David Braund and Frank Pollock; London: Croom Helm).

Allo, P.E.B. (1956). *Saint Paul: Seconde Épitre aux Corinthiens* (Études Bibliques; 2d ed.; Paris: Gabalda).

Anderson, E. Byron (1995). "Performance, Practice and Meaning in Christian Baptism," *Worship* 69.

Aristotle (1976). *The Ethics of Aristotle: The Nicomachean Ethics* (rev. ed.; trans. J.A.K. Thomson; London: Penguin).

Aristotle (1981). *The Politics* (rev. ed.; trans. T.A. Sinclair; London: Penguin).

Armerding, Carl Edwin (1975). "Were David's Sons Really Priests?" in Gerald F. Hawthorne, ed., *Current Issues in Biblical and Patristic Interpretation: Essays in Honor of Merrill C. Tenny Presented by His Former Students* (Grand Rapids, MI: Eerdmans).

Arrington, French L. (1977). *New Testament Exegesis: Examples* (Washington, DC: University Press of America).

Asad, Talal (1993). *Genealogies of Religion: Discipline and Reasons of Power in Christianity and Islam* (Baltimore: Johns Hopkins).

Attridge, Harold W. (1986). "The Uses of Antithesis in Hebrews 8-10," in George W.E. Nickelsburg with George W. MacRae, eds., *Christians among Jews and Gentiles: Essays in Honor of Krister Stendahl on his Sixty-fifth Birthday* (Philadelphia: Fortress).

Attridge, Harold W. (1989). *The Epistle to the Hebrews* (Hermeneia; Philadelphia: Fortress).

Augustine (1872). *On the Merits and Forgiveness of Sins* in Peter Holmes, trans., *The Anti-Pelagian Works of Saint Augustine, Bishop of Hippo* (3 vols.; Edinburgh: T&T Clark) 1.

Augustine (1951-56). *Letters* (6 vols.; trans. Sister Wilfrid Parsons; New York: Fathers of the Church).

Augustine (1953). *Confessions* (Fathers of the Church; trans. Vernon J. Bourke; Washington, DC: Catholic University of America Press).

Augustine (1958). *On Christian Doctrine* (trans. D.W. Robertson, Jr.; Indianapolis, IN: Bobbs-Merrill).

Augustine (1968). *The Teacher; The Free Choice of the Will; Grace and Free Will* (The Fathers of the Church; trans. Robert P. Russell; Washington, DC: Catholic University of America Press).

Augustine (1970). *The Trinity* (trans. Stephen McKenna; Washington, DC: Catholic University of America Press).

Augustine (1974a). *Reply to Faustus the Manichaean* in Philip Schaff, ed., *A Select Library of Nicene and Post Nicene Fathers* (first series; 14 vols.; Grand Rapids, MI: Eerdmans) 4.

Augustine (1974b). *On Baptism, against the Donatists* in Philip Schaff, ed., *A Select Library of Nicene and Post-Nicene Fathers* (first series; 14

vols.; Grand Rapids, MI: Eerdmans) 4.

Augustine (1984). *Concerning the City of God Against the Pagans* (trans. Henry Bettenson; London: Penguin).

Auneau, J. and Beaude, Pierre-Marie (1985). "Sacerdoce" in *Supplement au Dictionnaire de la Bible* (12 vols.; Paris: Letouzey & Ané) 10.

Avis, Paul D. L. (1981). *The Church in the Theology of the Reformers* (London: Marshall, Morgan & Scott).

Baldwin, Joyce (1988). *1 and 2 Samuel: An Introduction and Commentary* (Tyndale Old Testament Commentaries; Leicester: Inter-Varsity).

Ballanche, Pierre-Simon (1981). *La Ville des Expiations et autres textes* (Lyon: PressesUniversitaires de Lyon).

Barrett, C.K. (1968). *A Commentary on the First Epistle to the Corinthians* (Black's New Testament Commentaries; London: Adam and Charles Black).

Barrett, C.K. (1973). *A Commentary on the Second Epistle to the Corinthians* (Black's New Testament Commentaries; London: Adam and Charles Black).

Barth, Karl (1948). *The Teaching of the Church Regarding Baptism* (trans. Ernest A. Payne; London: SCM).

Barth, Karl (1969). *Church Dogmatics IV/4: The Christian Life (Fragment): Baptism as the Foundation of the Christian Life* (trans. G.W. Bromiley; ed. G.W. Bromiley and T.F. Torrance; Edinburgh: T&T Clark).

Barth, Markus (1951). *Die Taufe -- Ein Sakrament? Ein exegetischer Beitrag zum Gespräch über die kirchliche Taufe* (Zürich: Evangelischer Verlag).

Baudissin, Wolf Wilhelm Grafen (1889). *Die Geschichte des alttestamentlichen Priesterthums* (Leipzig: S. Hirzel).

Beard, Mary and North, John, eds. (1990). *Pagan Priests* (London: Duckworth).

Beard, Mary (1990). "Priesthood in the Roman Republic," in Mary Beard and John North, eds. *Pagan Priests* (London: Duckworth).

Beardslee, John W. III, ed. and trans. (1965). *Reformed Dogmatics: J. Wollebius, G. Voetius, F. Turretin* (Library of Protestant Thought; New York: Oxford University Press).

Beasley-Murray, G.R. (1973). *Baptism in the New Testament* (Grand Rapids, MI: Eerdmans).

Beaujeu, Jean (1964). "La religion de la classe sénatoriale à l'époque des Antonius," in Marcel Renard and Robert Schilling, eds., *Hommages à Jean Bayet* (Collection Latomus #70; Bruxelles Berchem: Latomus).

Beet, Joseph Agar (1889). *Holiness as Understood by the Writers of the Bible* (London: Hodder and Stoughton).

Beker, J. Christiaan (1980). *Paul the Apostle: The Triumph of God in Life and Thought* (Philadelphia: Fortress Press).

Bell, Catherine (1992). *Ritual Theory, Ritual Practice.* (New York: Oxford University Press).

Belleville, Linda L. (1986). "'Under Law': Structural Analysis and the Pauline Concept of Law in Galatians 3.21-4.11," *JSNT* 26.

Belleville, Linda L. (1989). "A Letter of Apologetic Self-Commendation: 2 Cor. 1:8-7:16," *NovT* 31.

Belleville, Linda L. (1996). "Paul's Polemic and the Theology of the

Spirit in Second Corinthians," *CBQ* 58.

Bergman, J., Ringgren, Helmer and Dommershausen, W. (1995). "כהן" in G. Johannes Botterweck, Helmer Ringgren, Heinz-Josef Fabry, eds., *Theological Dictionary of the Old Testament* (7 vols.; trans. David E. Green; Grand Rapids: Eerdmans) 7.

Berman, Harold J. (1983). *Law and Revolution: The Formation of the Western Legal Tradition* (Cambridge, MA: Harvard University Press).

Berman, Joshua (1995). *The Temple: Its Symbolism and Meaning Then and Now* (Northvale, NJ: Jason Aronson).

Best, Ernest (1960). "Spiritual Sacrifice: General Priesthood in the New Testament," *Int* 14.

Betz, Hans Dieter (1979). *Galatians: A Commentary on Paul's Letter to the Churches in Galatia* (Hermeneia; Philadelphia: Fortress).

Blenkinsopp, Joseph (1976). "The Structure of P," *CBQ* 38.

Blenkinsopp, Joseph (1977). *Prophecy and Canon: A Contribution to the Study of Jewish Origins* (University of Notre Dame Center for the Study of Judaism and Christianity in Antiquity #3; Notre Dame: University of Notre Dame Press).

Blenkinsopp, Joseph (1992). *The Pentateuch: An Introduction to the First Five Books of the Bible* (London: SCM).

Bligh, John (1956). *Ordination to the Priesthood* (London: Sheed and Ward).

Bligh, John (1964). "The Structure of Hebrews," *HeyJ* 5.

Bligh, John (1966). *Chiastic Analysis of the Epistle to the Hebrews* (Oxon: Heythrop).

Bligh, John (1969). *Galatians: A Discussion of St Paul's Epistle* (Householder Commentaries #1; London: St. Paul Publications).

Bloch, Marc (1983). *Les Rois Thaumaturges: Étude sur le caractère surnaturel attribué à la puissance royale particulièrement en France et en Angleterre* (new ed.; Bibliothèque des Histoires; Paris: Gallimard).

Bloch, Maurice (1989). *Ritual, History and Power: Selected Papers in Anthropology* (London School of Economics Monographs on Social Anthropology #58; London: Athlone).

Blum, Erhard (1990). *Studien zur Komposition des Pentateuch* (Beiheft zur Zeitschrift für die alttestamentliche Wissenschaft #189; Berlin: Walter de Gruyter).

Bodem, Anton (1971). *Das Wesen der Kirche nach Kardinal Cajetan: Ein Beitrag zur Ekklesiologie im Zeitalter der Reformation* (Trierer Theologische Studien, #25; Trier: Paulinus).

Böhlemann, Peter (1997). *Jesus und der Täufer: Schlüssel zur Theologie und Ethik des Lukas* (Cambridge: Cambridge University Press).

Bonner, Gerald (1986). "Augustine's Conception of Deification," *JTS* n.s. 37.

Borg, Marcus J. (1984). *Conflict, Holiness, and Politics in the Teachings of Jesus* (Studies in the Bible and Early Christianity #5; Lewiston, NY: Edwin Mellen).

Borg, Marcus J. (1993). *Jesus, A New Vision: Spirit, Culture, and the Life of Discipleship* (London: SPCK).

Bossy, John (1985). *Christianity in the West, 1400-1700* (Oxford: Oxford University Press).

Bourdieu, Pierre (1991). *Language and Symbolic Power* (ed. John B. Thompson; trans. Gino Raymond and Matthew Adamson;

Cambridge: Polity Press).

Bourgeois, Henri (1994). "Bulletin de théologie sacramentaire," *RSR* 82.

Bourgeois, Henri (1996). "Bulletin de théologie sacramentaire," *RSR* 84.

Bouyer, Louis (1968). *Eucharist: Theology and Spirituality of the Eucharistic Prayer* (trans. Charles Underhill Quinn; Notre Dame, IN: University of Notre Dame Press).

Bouyer, Louis (1955). *Liturgical Piety* (Notre Dame, IN: University of Notre Dame).

Bovon, François (1991). *L'Évangile selon Saint Luc (1, 1-9, 50)* (Commentaire du Nouveau Testament 3a; Genève: Labor et Fides).

Bradshaw, Paul F. (1990). *Ordination Rites of the Ancient Churches of East and West* (New York: Pueblo).

Bradshaw, Paul F. (1992). *The Search for the Origins of Christian Worship: Sources and Methods for the Study of Early Liturgy* (New York: Oxford University Press).

Brinsmead, Bernard Hungerford (1982). *Galatians, Dialogical Response to Opponents* (SBL Dissertation Series #65; Chico, CA: Scholars Press).

Brock, Sebastian (1977). "The Syrian Baptismal Ordines (with special reference to the anointings)," *StudLit* 12:4.

Brock, Sebastian (1978). "Baptismal Themes in the Writings of Jacob of Serugh," *OCA* 205.

Brock, Sebastian (1982). "Clothing Metaphors as a Means of Theological Expression in the Syriac Tradition," in Margot

Schmidt and Carl Friedrich Geyer, eds., *Typus, Symbol, Allegorie bei den östlichen Vätern und ihren Parallelen im Mittelalter* (Philosophie und Theologie, Eichstätter Beiträge #9; Regensburg: Friedrich Pustet).

Bromiley, Geoffrey W. (1979). *Children of Promise: The Case for Baptizing Infants* (Edinburgh: T&T Clark).

Brown, David and Loades, Ann, eds. (1996). *Christ: The Sacramental Word* (London: SPCK).

Brown, John (1961). *An Exposition of Hebrews* (London: Banner of Truth Trust).

Brown, Peter (1967). *Augustine of Hippo: A Biography* (London: Faber and Faber).

Brown, Peter (1982). *Society and the Holy in Late Antiquity* (London: Faber and Faber).

Brown, Raymond E. (1993 (1977)). *The Birth of the Messiah: A Commentary on the Infancy Narratives in the Gospels of Matthew and Luke* (Anchor Bible Reference Library; updated ed.; New York: Doubleday).

Brown, Francis, et. al., eds. (1959). *A Hebrew and English Lexicon of the Old Testament* (Oxford: Clarendon Press).

Bruce, F.F. (1964). *Commentary on the Epistle to the Hebrews* (The New London Commentary on the New Testament; London: Marshall, Morgan & Scott).

Bruce, F.F. (1982). *The Epistle of Paul to the Galatians: A Commentary on the Greek Text* (New International Greek Testament Commentary; Exeter: Paternoster Press).

Brunner, Emil (1944). *The Divine-Human Encounter* (trans. Amandus W. Loos; London: SCM).

Brunner, P. (1964). "The Significance of the Old Testament for Our Faith," in Bernhard W. Anderson, *The Old Testament and Christian Faith* (London: SCM).

Büchsel, Friedrich (1964). "γίνομαι" in Gerhard Kittel, ed., *Theological Dictionary of the New Testament* (10 vols.; ed. and trans. Geoffrey Bromiley; Grand Rapids, MI: Eerdmans) 1.

Bultmann, Rudolf (1985). *The Second Letter to the Corinthians* (trans. Roy A. Harrisville; Minneapolis: Augsburg).

Burnett, Fred W. (1984). "Philo on Immortality: A Thematic Study of Philo's Concept of παλιγγενεσία" *CBQ* 46.

Burrows, Eric (1940). *The Gospel of the Infancy, and Other Biblical Essays* (ed. Edmund F. Sutcliffe; Bellarmine Series VI; London: Burns Oates & Washbourne).

Burton, Ernest de Witt (1921). *A Critical and Exegetical Commentary on the Epistle to the Galatians* (ICC #35; Edinburgh: T&T Clark).

Calvin, John (1853). *Commentaries on the Epistle of Paul the Apostle to the Hebrews* (trans. John Owen; Edinburgh: Calvin Translation Society).

Calvin, John (1960). *Institutes of the Christian Religion* (2 vols.; LCC #20-21; ed. John T. McNeill; trans. Ford Lewis Battles; Philadelphia: Westminster Press).

Calvin, John (1958). "An Admonition Showing the Advantages which Christendom Might Derive from An Inventory of Relics," in Henry Beveridge, trans., *Tracts and Treatises on the Reformation of the Church* (3 vols.; Edinburgh: Oliver & Boyd) 1.

Casel, Odo (1962). *The Mystery of Christian Worship and Other Writings* (ed. Burkhard Neunheuser; Westminster, MD: Newman Press).

Cassidy, Ronald (1971). "Paul's Attitude to Death in II Corinthians 5:1-10," *EvQ* 43.

Cassuto, Umberto (1967). *A Commentary on the Book of Exodus* (Perry Foundation for Biblical Research Publications; trans. Israel Abrahams; Jerusalem: The Magnes Press, The Hebrew University).

Castelot, John J. and Cody, Aelred (1990). "Religious Institutions of Israel," in Raymond E. Brown, Joseph A. Fitzmyer, and Roland E. Murphy, eds., *The New Jerome Biblical Commentary* (2d ed.; Englewood Cliffs, NJ: Prentice Hall).

de Certeau, Michel (1992). *The Mystic Fable: Volume 1: The Sixteenth and Seventeenth Centuries* (trans. Michael B. Smith; Chicago: University of Chicago Press).

Chance, J. Bradley (1988). *Jerusalem, the Temple and the New Age in Luke-Acts* (Macon, GA: Mercer University Press).

Chauvet, Louis-Marie (1995). *Symbol and Sacrament: A Sacramental Reinterpretation of Christian Existence* (trans. Patrick Madigan and Madeleine Beaumont; Collegeville, MN: Liturgical Press).

Chemnitz, Martin (1978). *Examination of the Council of Trent, Part II* (trans. Fred Kramer; St. Louis: Concordia).

Chenu, M.-D. (1968). *Nature, Man, and Society in the Twelfth Century: Essays on New Theological Perspectives in the Latin West* (trans. Jerome Taylor and Lester K. Little; Chicago: University of Chicago Press).

Childs, Brevard S. (1974). *Exodus: A Commentary* (London: SCM).

Chydenius, Johan (1965). *Medieval Institutions and the Old Testament* (Societas Scientiarum Fennica, Commentationes Humanarum Litterarum, 37.2; Helsinki: Helsingfors).

Clements, R.E. (1965). *God and Temple* (Oxford: Blackwell).

Clifford, Richard J. (1971). "The Tent of El and the Israelite Tent of Meeting," *CBQ* 33.

Cody, Aelred (1969). *A History of Old Testament Priesthood* (Analecta Biblica #35; Rome: Pontifical Biblical Institute).

Cody, Aelred (1984). *Ezekiel, with an Excursus on Old Testament Priesthood* (Old Testament Message #11; Wilmington, DE: Michael Glazier).

Congar, Y. M.-J. (1968). *L'ecclésiologie du Haut Moyen âge: De Saint Grégoire le Grand à la désunion entre Byzance et Rome* (Paris: Éditions du Cerf).

Congar, Yves (1970). *L'Église de saint Augustin à l'époque moderne* (Histoire des Dogmes, #3; Paris: Éditions du Cerf).

Congar, Yves (1983). *Etudes d'ecclésiologie médiévale* (London: Variorum Reprints).

Congar, Yves M. J. (1985). *Lay People in the Church: A Study for a Theology of Laity* (rev. ed; trans. Donald Attwater; London: Geoffrey Chapman).

Congar, Yves (1994). *Église et papauté: regards historiques* (Cogitatio Fidei; Paris: Editions du Cerf).

Connolly, R. Hugh (1929). *Didascalia Apostolorum: The Syriac Version Translated and Accompanied by the Verona Latin Fragments* (Oxford: Clarendon Press).

Conzelmann, Hans (1975). *1 Corinthians* (Hermeneia; trans. James W. Leitch; Philadelphia: Fortress).

Cook, Stephen L. (1995). "Innerbiblical Interpretation in Ezekiel 44 and the History of Israel's Priesthood," *JBL* 114.

Cooke, Bernard J. (1990). *The Distancing of God: The Ambiguity of Symbol in History and Theology* (Minneapolis: Fortress).

Cornford, F.M. (1952). *Principium Sapientiae: The Origins of Greek Philosophical Thought* (Cambridge: University Press).

Courtenay, William J. (1972). "The King and the Leaden Coin: The Economic Background of 'sine qua non' Causality," *Traditio* 28.

Courtenay, William J. (1984). *Covenant and Causality in Medieval Thought: Studies in Philosophy, Theology, and Economic Practice* (London: Variorum Reprints).

Cowdrey, H.E.J. (1969). "The Dissemination of St. Augustine's Doctrine of Holy Orders during the Later Patristic Age," *JTS* n.s. 20.

Cramer, Peter (1993). *Baptism and Change in the Early Middle Ages c. 200-c. 1150* (Cambridge Studies in Medieval Life and Thought, 4th series, #20; Cambridge: University of Cambridge Press).

Crites, Stephen (1971). "The Narrative Quality of Experience," *JAAR* 39.

Cross, Frank M. (1947). "The Tabernacle: A Study from an Archeological and Historical Approach," *BA* 10:3.

Crouter, Richard (1988). "Introduction" to Friedrich Schleiermacher, *On Religion: Speeches to Its Cultured Despisers* (Cambridge: Cambridge University Press).

Cullmann, Oscar (1950). *Baptism in the New Testament* (Studies in Biblical Theology #1; trans. J. K. S. Reid; London: SCM).

Cyprian (1964). *Letters* (Fathers of the Church; trans. Rose Bernard Donna; Washington, DC: Catholic University of America Press).

Dabin, Paul (1950). *Le Sacerdoce Royal des Fideles dans la Tradition Ancienne et Moderne* (Brussels: L'Editions Universelle).

Dahl, Nils A. (1951). "A New and Living Way: The Approach to God according to Hebrews 10:19-25," *Int* 5.

Dahl, Nils Alstrup (1955). "The Origin of Baptism" in *Interpretationes ad Vetus Testamentum Pertinentes Sigmundo Mowinckel* (Oslo: Forlaget land og kirke).

D'Angelou, Mary Rose (1979). *Moses in the Letter to the Hebrews* (SBL Dissertation Series #42; Missoula, MT: Scholars Press).

Danielou, Jean (1960). *The Bible and the Liturgy* (London: Darton, Longman, & Todd).

D'Argenlieu, B. Thierry (1929a). "La doctrine de Saint Thomas d'Aquin sur le caractère   sacramentel dans les 'Sentences,'" *RevTh* 34 (n.s. 12).

D'Argenlieu, B. Thierry (1929b). "La doctrine du caractère sacramentel dans la 'Somme,'" *RevTh* 34 (n.s. 12).

Davidson, Richard M. (1981). *Typology in Scripture: A Study of Hermeneutical TYPOS Structures* (Andrews University Seminary Doctoral Dissertation Series, #2; Berrien Springs, MI: Andrews University Press).

Davies, G. Henton (1962). "Tabernacle" in *Interpreter's Dictionary of the Bible* (5 vols.; New York: Abingdon) 4.

Davies, J.G. (1962). *The Architectural Setting of Baptism* (London: Barrie and Rockliff).

Davis, Charles Thomas (1982). "The Literary Structure of Luke 1-2," in David J.A. Clines, David M. Gunn, and Alan J. Hauser, eds., *Art and Meaning: Rhetoric in Biblical Literature* (JSOT Supplement

#19; Sheffield: JSOT Press).

DeGuglielmo, Antonine (1955). "Sacrifice in the Ugaritic Texts," *CBQ* 17.

Delling, Gerhard (1963/4). *Die Taufe im Neuen Testament* (Berlin: Evangelische Verlagsanstalt).

Denzinger, Henricus, ed. (1957). *The Sources of Catholic Dogma* (from the 30th ed.; trans. Roy J. Deferrari; St. Louis: Herder).

Denzinger, Henricus, ed. (1965). *Enchiridion Symbolorum: Definitionum et Declarationum de Rebus Fidei et Morum* (33d ed.; Freiburg: Herder).

Derrett. J. Duncan M. (1984). "Palingenesia (Matthew 19:28)" *JSNT* 20.

Detienne, Marcel and Vernant, Jean-Pierre, eds. (1989). *The Cuisine of Sacrifice among the Greeks* (trans. Paula Wissing; Chicago: University of Chicago Press).

Dibelius, Martin and Conzelmann, Hans (1972). *The Pastoral Epistles* (Hermeneia; trans. Philip Buttolph and Adela Yarbro; Philadelphia: Fortress).

Didier, J.-C. (1956). "Saint Augustin et le baptême des enfants," *RevEtAug* 2.

Dillmann, August (1880). *Die Bücher Exodus und Leviticus* (2d ed.; ed. August Knobel; Leipzig: S. Hirzel).

Dinkler, Erich (1962). "Die Taufterminologie in 2 Kor. 1 21f," in A.N. Wilder, et. al., *Neotestamentica et Patristica: Eine freundesgabe Herrn Professor Dr. Oscar Cullmann zu seinem 60. Geburtstag überreicht* (Supplements to NovT #6; Leiden: Brill).

Dittoe, John T. (1946). "Sacramental Incorporation into the Mystical

268

Body," *Thom* 9.

Dix, Gregory (1945). *The Shape of the Liturgy* (San Francisco: Harper and Row).

Dix, Gregory (1946). *The Theology of Confirmation in Relation to Baptism* (Westminster: Dacre).

Donaldson, T.L. (1986). "The 'Curse of the Law' and the Inclusion of the Gentiles: Galatians 3:13-14," *NTS* 32.

Donaldson, Terence L. (1997). *Paul and the Gentiles: Remapping the Apostle's Convictional World* (Minneapolis: Fortress).

Donovan, J., trans. (1839). *The Catechism by Decree of the Holy Council of Trent* (Rome: Propaganda Press).

Douglas, Mary (1973). *Natural Symbols: Explorations in Cosmology* (2d ed.; London: Barrie and Jenkins).

Douglas, Mary (1984). *Purity and Danger: An Analysis of the Concepts of Pollution and Taboo* (London: ARK Paperbacks).

Driver, S.R. (1913). *Notes on the Hebrew Text and Topography of the Books of Samuel* (2d ed; Oxford: Clarendon Press).

Duby, Georges (1980). *The Three Orders: Feudal Society Imagined* (trans. Arthur Goldhammer; Chicago: University of Chicago Press).

Dudley, Martin and Geoffrey Rowell, eds. (1993). *The Oil of Gladness: Anointing in the Christian Tradition* (London: SPCK).

Duke, Rodney K. (1987). "The Portion of the Levite: Another Reading of Deuteronomy 18:6-8," *JBL* 106.

Dumézil, Georges (1970). *Archaic Roman Religion* (2 vols.; trans. Philip Krapp; Chicago: University of Chicago Press).

Dunn, James D.G. (1970). *Baptism in the Holy Spirit: A Re-Examination of the New Testament Teaching on the Gift of the Spirit in relation to Pentecostalism today* (Studies in Biblical Theology, 2d series, #15; London: SCM).

Dunn, James D.G. (1990). *Jesus, Paul and the Law: Studies in Mark and Galatians* (London: SPCK).

Dunn, James D.G. (1993). *The Epistle to the Galatians* (Black's New Testament Commentary; Peabody, MA: Hendrickson).

Dunnill, John (1992). *Covenant and Sacrifice in the Letter to the Hebrews* (Society for New Testament Studies #75; Cambridge: Cambridge University Press).

Durand, Jean-Louis (1989). "Greek Animals: Toward a Topology of Edible Bodies" in Marcel Detienne and Jean-Pierre Vernant, eds., *The Cuisine of Sacrifice among the Greeks* (trans. Paula Wissing; Chicago: University of Chicago Press).

Durkheim, Emile (1976 (1915)). *The Elementary Forms of Religious Life* (2d ed.; trans. Joseph Ward Swain; London: George Allen & Unwin).

Eastman, A. Theodore (1991). *The Baptizing Community: Christian Initiation and the Local Congregation* (2d ed.; Harrison, PA: Morehouse Publishing).

Eco, Umberto (1984). *Semiotics and the Philosophy of Language* (London: Macmillan).

Eire, Carlos M. N. (1986). *War Against the Idols: The Reformation of Worship from Erasmus to Calvin* (Cambridge: Cambridge University Press).

Eliade, Mircea (1955). *The Myth of the Eternal Return, Or, Cosmos and History* (trans. Willard R. Trask; London: Routledge and Kegan Paul).

Eliade, Mircea (1959). *The Sacred and the Profane: The Nature of Religion* (trans. Willard R. Trask; San Diego, CA: Harcourt Brace Jovanovich).

Eliade, Mircea (1966). *Rites and Symbols of Initiation: The Mysteries of Birth and Rebirth* (trans. Willard R. Trask; New York: Harper Torchbooks).

Ellard, Gerald (1933). *Ordination Anointings in the Western Church before 1000 A.D.* (Monographs of the Mediæval Academy of America #8; Cambridge, MA: Mediæval Academy of America).

Elliott, John Hall (1966). *The Elect and the Holy: An Exegetical Examination of 1 Peter 2:4-10 and the Phrase* βασίλειον ἱεράτευμα (NovT Supplements #12; Leiden: Brill).

Ellis, E. Earle (1960). "II Corinthians V.1-10 in Pauline Eschatology," *NTS* 6.

Episcopal Church of the United States of America (1990). *Proposed Book of Common Prayer* (New York: Seabury).

Evans, Ernest, trans. (1964). *Tertullian's Homily on Baptism* (London: SPCK).

Evans, Robert F. (1972). *One and Holy: The Church in Latin Patristic Thought* (Church Historical Series #12; London: SPCK).

Fackenheim, Emil L. (1967). *The Religious Dimension in Hegel's Thought* (Bloomington, IN: Indiana University Press).

Fairbairn, Patrick (1870). *Typology of Scripture* (2 vols.; Edinburgh: T&T Clark).

Fee, Gordon D. (1987). *The First Epistle to the Corinthians* (Grand Rapids, MI: Eerdmans).

271

Fee, Gordon D. (1994). *God's Empowering Presence: The Holy Spirit in the Letters of Paul* (Peabody, MA: Hendrickson).

Finley, M.I. (1977). "The Ancient City: From Fustel de Coulanges to Max Weber and Beyond," *CSSH* 19.

Finn, Thomas M. (1992a). *Early Christian Baptism and the Catechumenate: West and East Syria* (Message of the Fathers of the Church #5; A Michael Glazier Book; Collegeville, MN: Liturgical Press).

Finn, Thomas M. (1992b). *Early Christian Baptism and the Catechumenate: Italy, North Africa, and Egypt* (Message of the Fathers of the Church #6; A Michael Glazier Book; Collegeville, MN: Liturgical Press).

Fishbane, Michael (1985). *Biblical Interpretation in Ancient Israel* (Oxford: Clarendon Press).

Fisher, J.D.C. (1965). *Christian Initiation: Baptism in the Medieval West: A Study in the Disintegration of the Primitive Rite of Initiation* (Alcuin Club Collections #47; London: SPCK).

Fisher, J.D.C. (1970). *Christian Initiation: The Reformation Period* (Alcuin Club Collections #51; London: SPCK).

Fisher, Ioannis (1925 (1525). *Sacri Sacerdotii Defensio contra Lutheranum* (trans. Hermann Klein Schmeink; Corpus Catholicorum #9; Munster: Aschendorffschen Verlagsbuchhandlung).

Fisher, John (1935). *The Defense of the Priesthood* (trans. P.E. Hallett; London: Burns Oates & Washbourne).

Fitzmyer, Joseph A. (1981-85). *The Gospel According to Luke* (2 vols.; Anchor Bible; Garden City, NY: Doubleday).

FitzPatrick, P.J. (1993). *In Breaking of Bread: The Eucharist and Ritual* (Cambridge: Cambridge University Press).

Flannery, Austin, gen. ed. (1980). *Vatican Council II: The Conciliar and Post Conciliar Documents* (Northport, NY: Costello).

Flemington, W. F. (1948). *The New Testament Doctrine of Baptism* (London: SPCK).

Flinn, P. Richard (1982). "Baptism, Redemptive History, and Eschatology: The Parameters of Debate," in James B. Jordan, ed., *The Failure of American Baptist Culture* (Christianity and Civilization #1; Tyler, TX: Geneva Divinity School Press).

Floor, L. (1971). "The General Priesthood of Believers in the Epistle to the Hebrews," *NeoT* 5.

Fox, Everett, trans. (1995). *The Five Books of Moses* (The Schocken Bible #1; New York: Schocken).

Frame, John M. (1987). *The Doctrine of the Knowledge of God* (A Theology of Lordship; Phillipsburg, NJ: Presbyterian and Reformed).

Frazer, James George (1950). *The Golden Bough: A Study in Magic and Religion* (abr. ed.; New York: Macmillan).

Fretheim, Terence E. (1991). *Exodus* (Interpretation; Louisville, KY: John Knox Press).

Friedman, Richard Elliott (1992). "Tabernacle," in *The Anchor Bible Dictionary* (6 vols.; New York: Doubleday) 6.

Fuller, Reginald H. (1978). "The Conception/Birth of Jesus as a Christological Moment," *JSNT* 1.

Fung, Ronald Y.K. (1988). *The Epistle to the Galatians* (NICNT; Grand Rapids, MI: Eerdmans).

Furnish, Victor Paul (1984). *II Corinthians* (Anchor Bible; Garden City, NY: Doubleday).

Fustel de Coulanges, Numa Denis (1980). *The Ancient City: A Study of the Religion, Laws, and Institutions of Greece and Rome* (Baltimore, MD: Johns Hopkins University Press).

Gager, John G. (1975). *Kingdom and Community: The Social World of Early Christianity* (Englewood Cliffs, NJ: Prentice-Hall).

Gammie, John G. (1989). *Holiness in Israel* (Overtures to Biblical Theology; Minneapolis: Fortress).

Garland, Robert (1990). "Priests and Power in Classical Athens," in Mary Beard and John North, eds., *Pagan Priests* (London: Duckworth).

Gaudemet, J. (1967). "Anointing in the Middle Ages" in *New Catholic Encyclopedia* (17 vols.; New York: McGraw-Hill) 1.

Gavin, F. (1928). *The Jewish Antecedents of the Christian Sacraments* (London: SPCK).

George, Timothy (1994). *Galatians* (New American Commentary #30; Nashville: Broadman and Holman).

Gernet, Louis (1981). *The Anthropology of Ancient Greece* (trans. John Hamilton and Blaise Nagy; Baltimore, MD: Johns Hopkins University Press).

Gerrish, B.A. (1993). *Grace & Gratitude: The Eucharistic Theology of John Calvin* (Minneapolis, MN: Fortress).

Gerstenberger, Erhard S. (1996). *Leviticus: A Commentary* (trans. Douglas W. Scott; Old Testament Library; Louisville, KY: Westminster John Knox).

Gierke, Otto (1987 (1900)). *Political Theories of the Middle Age* (trans. Frederic William Maitland; Cambridge: Cambridge University Press).

Goody, Jack (1961). "Religion and Ritual: The Definitional Problem," *BJS* 12.

Goody, Jack (1977). "Against 'Ritual': Loosely Structured Thoughts on a Loosely Defined Topic," in Sally F. Moore and Barbara G. Myerhoff, eds., *Secular Ritual* (Assen/Amsterdam: van Gorcum).

Gordon, Richard (1990a). "From Republic to Principate: priesthood, religion and ideology," in Mary Beard and John North, eds., *Pagan Priests* (London: Duckworth).

Gordon, Richard (1990b). "The Veil of Power: emperors, sacrificers and benefactors," in Mary Beard and John North, eds., *Pagan Priests* (London: Duckworth).

Gordon, Richard (1990c). "Religion in the Roman Empire: the civic compromise and its limits," in Mary Beard and John North, eds., *Pagan Priests* (London: Duckworth).

Gordon, Robert P. (1986). *1 & 2 Samuel: A Commentary* (Exeter: Paternoster).

Gorman, Frank H., Jr. (1990). *The Ideology of Ritual: Space, Time and Status in the Priestly Theology* (JSOT Supplement #91; Sheffield: JSOT Press).

Gourges, Michel (1977). "Remarques sur la 'structure centrale' de l'Épitre aux Hébreux," *RB* 84.

Goulder, Michael D. and Sanderson, M.L. (1957). "St. Luke's Genesis," *JTS* ns 8.

Goulder, Michael D. (1989). *Luke: A New Paradigm* (2 vols.; JSNT Supplement #20; Sheffield: JSOT Press).

Grabbe, Lester L. (1995). *Priests, Prophets, Diviners, Sages: A Socio-Historical Study of Religious Specialists in Ancient Israel* (Valley

Forge, PA: Trinity Press International).

Grail, Augustin (1951). "Le Baptême dans l'Épitre aux Galates (III, 26-IV, 7)," *RB* 58.

Gray, George Buchanan (1925). *Sacrifice in the Old Testament: Its Theory and Practice* (Oxford: Clarendon Press).

Grimes, Ronald L. (1995). *Beginnings in Ritual Studies* (rev. ed.; Studies in Comparative Religion; Columbia, SC: University of South Carolina Press).

Grosheide, F.W. (1953). *Commentary on the First Epistle to the Corinthians* (NICNT; Grand Rapids, MI: Eerdmans).

Hafemann, Scott (1989). "The Comfort and Power of the Gospel: The Argument of 2 Corinthians 1-3," *RevExp* 86.

Hafemann, Scott J. (1995). *Paul, Moses, and the History of Israel: The Letter/Spirit Contrast and the Argument from Scripture in 2 Corinthians 3* (Wissenschaftliche Untersuchungen zum Neuen Testament #81; Tübingen: J.C.B. Mohr).

Hamerton-Kelly, Robert G. (1990). "Sacred Violence and the Curse of the Law (Galatians 3:13: The Death of Christ as a Sacrificial Travesty," *NTS* 36.

Hamilton, David S.M. (1990). *Through the Waters: Baptism and the Christian Life* (The Croall Lectures 1987; Edinburgh: T&T Clark).

Hanson, Anthony T. (1988). "The Origin of Paul's Use of παιδαγωγός for the Law," *JSNT* 34.

Haran, Menahem (1960). "The Nature of the *'ohel mo'edh'* in Pentateuchal Sources," *JSS* 5.

Haran, M. (1972). "Priests and Priesthood" in *Encyclopaedia Judaica* (16 vols.; Jerusalem: Keter Publishing House) 13.

Haran, Menahem (1985). *Temples and Temple Service in Ancient Israel: An Inquiry into Biblical Cult Phenomena and the Historical Setting of the Priestly School* (Winona Lake, IN: Eisenbrauns).

Haran, Menahem (1988). "Temple and Community in Ancient Israel," in Michael V. Fox, ed., *Temple in Society* (Winona Lake: Eisenbrauns).

Haring, N. M. (1948a). "Berengar's Definitions of *Sacramentum* and their Influence on Mediaeval Sacramentology," *MedStud* 10.

Haring, N.M. (1948b). "One Baptism: An Historical Study on the Non-Repetition of Certain Sacraments," *MedStud* 10.

Harnack, Adolf (1958). *What Is Christianity?* (5th ed.; trans. Thomas Bailey Saunders; London: Ernest Benn).

Harnack, Adolf (1990 (1924)). *Marcion: The Gospel of the Alien God* (trans. John E. Steely and Lyle D. Bierma; Durham, NC: Labyrinth).

Harper, John (1991). *The Forms and Orders of Western Liturgy from the Tenth to the Eighteenth Century: A Historical Introduction and Guide for Students and Musicians* (Oxford: Clarendon Press).

Harris, Horton (1975). *The Tübingen School* (Oxford: Clarendon Press).

Harris, Murray J. (1971). "2 Corinthians 5:1-10: Watershed in Paul's Eschatology?" *TynBul* 22.

Harrison, R. K. (1980). *Leviticus: An Introduction and Commentary* (Tyndale Old Testament Commentaries; Leicester: Inter-Varsity Press).

Hartman, Lars (1992). *"Auf den Namen des Herrn Jesus": Die Taufe in den neutestamentlichen Schriften* (Stuttgarter Bibelstudien #148;

Stuttgart: Katholisches Bibelwerk).

Hauerwas, Stanley (1981). *Vision and Virtue: Essays in Christian Ethical Reflection* (Notre Dame, IN: University of Notre Dame Press).

Hauerwas, Stanley (1983). *The Peaceable Kingdom: A Primer in Christian Ethics* (Notre Dame, IN: University of Notre Dame Press).

Hauerwas, Stanley and Jones, L. Gregory, eds. (1989). *Why Narrative? Readings in Narrative Theology* (Grand Rapids, MI: Eerdmans).

Hays, Richard B. (1983). *The Faith of Jesus Christ: An Investigation of the Narrative Substructure of Galatians 3:1-4:11* (SBL Dissertation Series #56; Chico, CA: Scholars Press).

Hays, Richard B. (1989). *Echoes of Scripture in the Letters of Paul* (New Haven, CT: Yale University Press).

Hendrix, Ralph E. (1991). *"Miskan* and *'ohel mô'ed*: Etymology, Lexical Definitions, and Extra-Biblical Usage," *AUSS* 29.

Hendrix, Ralph E. (1992). "The Use of *Miskan* and *'ohel mô'ed* in Exodus 25-40," *AUSS* 30.

Heppe, Heinrich (1950). *Reformed Dogmatics: Set out and illustrated from the sources* (trans. G.T. Thomson; ed./rev. Ernst Bizer; London: George Allen & Unwin).

Herborn, Niclaus (1927 (1529)). *Locorum Communium Adversus Huius Temporis Haereses Enchiridion* (ed. P. Patricius Schlager; Corpus Catholicorum #12; Munster: Aschendorffschen Verlagsbuchhandlung).

Herder, J.G. (1969). "Ideas for a Philosophy of History of Mankind," in F.M. Barnard, ed., *J.G. Herder on Social and Political Culture* (Cambridge: Cambridge University Press).

Hertzberg, Hans Wilhelm (1964). *I & II Samuel: A Commentary*

(London: SCM).

Heschel, Abraham J. (1962). *The Prophets* (New York: Harper and Row).

Hettlinger, Richard F. (1957). "2 Corinthians 5.1-10," *SJT* 10.

Hoffman, Lawrence A. (1987). *Beyond the Text: A Holistic Approach to Liturgy* (Bloomington: Indiana University Press).

Hoffman, Lawrence A. (1991). "Reconstructing Ritual as Identity and Culture," in Paul F. Bradshaw and Lawrence A. Hoffman, eds., *The Making of Jewish and Christian Worship* (Two Liturgical Traditions #1; Notre Dame, IN: University of Notre Dame).

Hofmann, Fritz (1933). *Der Kirchenbegriff des hl. Augustinus: In Seinen Grundlagen und in seiner Entwicklung* (München: Max Hueber).

Holifield, E. Brooks (1974). *The Covenant Sealed: The Development of Puritan Sacramental Theology in Old and New England, 1570-1720* (New Haven: Yale).

Holeton, David (1981). *Infant Communion -- Then and Now* (Grove Liturgical Study #27; Bramcote: Grove Books).

Hood, Rodney T. (1961). "The Genealogies of Jesus," in Allen Wikgren, ed., *Early Christian Origins: Studies in Honor of Harold R. Willoughby* (Chicago: Quadrangle Books).

Houssiau, A. (1978). "L'engagement baptismal," *RTL* 9.

Hovda, Robert W. (1976). "Hope for the Future: A Summary" in Murphy Center for Liturgical Research, *Made, Not Born: New Perspectives on Christian Initiation and the Catechumenate* (Notre Dame, IN: Notre Dame University Press).

Hugh of St. Victor (1951). *On the Sacraments of the Christian Faith* (trans. Roy J. Deferrari; Cambridge, MA: Mediaeval Academy of

America).

Hughes, Philip Edgcumbe (1962). *Paul's Second Epistle to the Corinthians*
  (2d ed.; New London Commentary; London: Marshall, Morgan
  & Scott).

Hughes, Philip Edgcumbe (1977). *A Commentary on the Epistle to the
  Hebrews* (Grand Rapids, MI: Eerdmans).

Humbert (1891). *Adversus Simoniacos* in *Monumenta Germanica Historica*
  (ed. Fridericus Thaner; Hannover: Impensis Bibliopolii
  Hahniani) Libelli de lite 1.

Humphrey, Caroline and Laidlaw, James (1994). *The Archetypal Actions
  of Ritual: A Theory of Ritual Illustrated by the Jain Rite of Worship*
  (Oxford Studies in Social and Cultural Anthrpology; Oxford:
  Clarendon Press).

Hyatt, J. Philip (1971). *Commentary on Exodus* (New Century Bible;
  London: Oliphants).

Jagger, Peter J. (1970). *Christian Initiation 1552-1969: Rites of Baptism and
  Confirmation Since the Reformation Period* (Alcuin Club Collections
  #52; London: SPCK).

Jenson, Philip Peter (1992). *Graded Holiness: A Key to the Priestly
  Conception of the World* (JSOT Supplement #106; Sheffield:
  JSOT Press).

Jenson, Philip P. (1995). "Ordination. I: Altes Testament," in
  Theologische Realenzyklopädie (28 vols.; Berlin: Walter de Gruyter)
  25.

Jeremias, Joachim (1960). *Infant Baptism in the First Four Centuries*
  (Library of History and Doctrine; trans. David Cairns; London:
  SCM).

Jeremias, Joachim (1963). *The Origins of Infant Baptism: A Further Study in*

Reply to Kurt Aland (Studies in Historical Theology #1; trans. Dorothea M. Barton; London: SCM).

Jeremias, Joachim (1966). *The Eucharistic Words of Jesus* (New Testament Library; 3d ed.; trans. Norman Perrin; London: SCM).

Jervell, Jacob (1960). *Imago Dei: Gen 1, 26f im Spätjudentum, in der Gnosis und in der paulinischen Briefen* (Forschungen zur religion und Literatur des Alten und Neuen Testaments #76; Göttingen: Vandenhoeck & Ruprecht).

Jewett, Paul K. (1978). *Infant Baptism and the Covenant of Grace* (Grand Rapids, MI: Eerdmans).

Johnson, Marshall D. (1988). *The Purpose of the Biblical Genealogies: With Special Reference to the Setting of the Genealogies of Jesus* (2d ed.; Cambridge: Cambridge University Press).

Johnson, Maxwell E., ed. (1995). *Living Water, Sealing Spirit: Readings on Christian Initiation* (A Pueblo Book; Collegeville, MN: Liturgical Press).

Jones, Cheslyn, et. al. (1992). *The Study of Liturgy* (rev. ed.; London: SPCK).

Jones, David (1959). *Epoch and Artist: Selected Writings* (ed. Harman Grisewood; London: Faber and Faber).

Jones, Gwilym H. (1984). *1 and 2 Kings* (2 vols; The New Century Bible Commentary; Grand Rapids, MI: Eerdmans).

Jones, L. Gregory (1987). "Alasdair MacIntyre on Narrative, Community, and the Moral Life," *MT* 4.

Jones, Paul H. (1994). *Christ's Eucharistic Presence: A History of the Doctrine* (American University Series, Theology and Religion #157; New York: Peter Lang).

281

Jordan, James B. (1984). *The Law of the Covenant: An Exposition of Exodus 21-23* (Tyler, TX: Institute for Christian Economics).

Jordan, James B. (1985). *Judges: God's War against Humanism* (Tyler, TX: Geneva Ministries).

Jordan, James B. (1988). *Through New Eyes: Developing a Biblical View of the World* (Brentwood, TN: Wolgemuth & Hyatt).

Jordan, James B. (1989). *Covenant Sequence in Leviticus and Deuteronomy* (Tyler, TX: Institute for Christian Economics).

Jordan, James B. (1992). *Exodus: taped lectures and study guide* (Niceville, FL: Biblical Horizons).

Josephus (1967). *Jewish Antiquities* (LCL; 6 vols.; trans. H. St. J. Thackeray, Ralph Marcus, Allen Wikgren, and Louis H. Feldman; London: William Heinemann).

Jourjon, Maurice (1954). "L'Évêque et le peuple de Dieu selon saint Augustin," in Henri Rondet, et. al., *Saint Augustin Parmi Nous* (Paris: Xavier Mappus).

Jungmann, J. A. (1959). *The Mass of the Roman Rite: Its Origins and Development* (abr. ed.; trans. Francis A. Brunner; rev. Charles K. Riepe; London: Burns & Oates).

Jungmann, J. A. (1976). *The Mass: An Historical, Theological, and Pastoral Survey* (trans. Julian Fernandes; ed. Mary Ellen Evans; Collegeville, MN: Liturgical Press).

Kant, Immanuel (1960). *Religion Within the Limits of Reason Alone* (2d ed.; trans. Theodore M. Greene and Hoyt H. Hudson; LaSalle, IL: Open Court).

Kantorowicz, Ernst H. (1958). *Laudes Regiae: A Study in Liturgical Acclamations and Mediaeval Ruler Worship* (Berkeley: University of California Press).

Kavanagh, Aidan (1991). *The Shape of Baptism: The Rite of Christian Initiation* (A Pueblo Book; Collegeville, MN: Liturgical Press).

Kavanagh, Aidan (1995). "Unfinished and Unbegun Revisited: The Rite of Christian Initiation of Adults" in Maxwell E. Johnson, ed., *Living Water, Sealing Spirit: Readings on Christian Initiation* (A Pueblo Book; Collegeville, MN: Liturgical Press).

Kearney, Peter J. (1977). "Creation and Liturgy: The P Redaction of Ex 25-40," *ZAW* 89.

Keel, Othmar (1978). *The Symbolism of the Biblical World: Ancient Near Eastern Iconography and the Book of Psalms* (A Crossroad Book; trans. Timothy J. Hallett; New York: Seabury).

Keidel, Christian L. (1975). "Is the Lord's Supper for Children?" *WTJ* 37:3.

Keil, C.F. and Delitzsch, F. (1980). *Commentary on the Old Testament in Ten Volumes, Volume I: The Pentateuch* (3 vols. in 1; Grand Rapids, MI: Eerdmans).

Kellogg, S.H. (1988. *Studies in Leviticus: Tabernacle Worship and the Law of Daily Life* (Grand Rapids, MI: Kregel).

Kelly, Henry Ansgar (198). *The Devil at Baptism: Ritual, Theology, and Drama* (Ithaca: Cornell University Press).

Kelly, J.N.D. (1968). *Early Christian Doctrines* (4th ed.; London: Adam and Charles Black).

Kennedy, A.R.S. (1902). "Tabernacle" in *A Dictionary of the Bible* (5 vols.; Edinburgh: T&T Clark) 4.

Kerby, Anthony Paul (1991). *Narrative and the Self* (Bloomington, IN: Indiana University Press).

Kerr, Alastair James (1988). "ἀρραβών," *JTS* n.s. 39.

Kerr, Fergus (1986). *Theology after Wittgenstein* (Oxford: Blackwell).

Kiesling, Christopher (1963). "The Sacramental Character and Liturgy," *Thom* 27.

Kittel, Gerhard, ed. (1964-1976). *Theological Dictionary of the New Testament* (10 vols.; trans. and ed. Geoffrey W. Bromiley; Grand Rapids: Eerdmans).

Kiuchi, N. (1987). *The Purification Offering in the Priestly Literature: Its Meaning and Function* (JSOT Supplement #56; Sheffield: JSOT Press).

Kline, Meredith G. (1968). *By Oath Consigned: A Reinterpretation of the Covenant Signs of Circumcision and Baptism* (Grand Rapids, MI: Eerdmans).

Kline, Meredith G. (1986). *Images of the Spirit* (S. Hamilton, MA: Meredith Kline).

Knight, George A.F. (1976). *Theology as Narration: A Commentary on the Book of Exodus* (Edinburgh: Handsel).

Kraeling, Carl H. (1951). *John the Baptist* (New York: Charles Scribner's Sons).

Kramer, Samuel Noah (1988). "The Temple in Sumerian Literature," in Michael V. Fox, ed., *Temple in Society* (Winona Lake: Eisenbrauns).

Kraus, Hans-Joachim (1966). *Worship in Israel: A Cultic History of the Old Testament* (trans. Geoffrey Buswell; Oxford: Blackwell).

Kretschmar, Georg (1995). "Recent Research on Christian Initiation," in Maxwell E. Johnson, ed., *Living Water, Sealing Spirit: Readings on Christian Initiation* (A Pueblo Book; Collegeville, MN:

Liturgical Press).

Kurtz, J.H. (1980). *Sacrificial Worship of the Old Testament* (trans. James Martin; Minneapolis, MN: Klock & Klock).

Ladrière, Jean (1984). *L'Articulation du Sens* (2 vols.; Cogitatio Fidei #124-125; Paris: Éditions du Cerf).

Lambrecht, Jan, ed. (1993). *The Truth of the Gospel (Galatians 1:1-4:11)* (Monographic Series of Benedictina, Biblical-Ecumenical Section #12; Rome: Benedicta).

Lampe, G. W. H. (1951). *The Seal of the Spirit: A Study in the Doctrine of Baptism and Confirmation in the New Testament and the Fathers* (London: Longmans, Green, and Co.).

Landgraf, Artur (1933). "Die Gnadenökonomie des Alten Bundes nach der Lehre der Frühscholastik," *ZKT* 57.

Lane, William L. (1991). *Hebrews 9-13* (Word Biblical Commentary, #47B; Dallas, TX: Word).

Lang, G.H. (1951). *The Epistle to the Hebrews: A Practical Treatise for Plain and Serious Readers* (London: Paternoster Press).

Laporte, Jean (1995). "Models from Philo in Origen's Teaching on Original Sin," in Maxwell E. Johnson, ed., *Living Water, Sealing Spirit: Readings on Christian Initiation* (A Pueblo Book; Collegeville, MN: Liturgical Press).

Lash, Nicholas (1968). *His Presence in the World: A Study in Eucharistic Worship and Theology* (London: Sheed and Ward).

Lash, Nicholas (1988). *Easter in Ordinary: Reflections on Human Experience and the Knowledge of God* (London: SCM).

Lash, Nicholas and Rhymer, Joseph, eds. (1970). *The Christian Priesthood* (London: Darton, Longman & Todd).

Lathrop, Gordon W. (1994). "The Origins and Early Meanings of Christian Baptism: A Proposal," *Worship* 68.

Laurentin, René (1957). *Structure et théologie de Luc I-II* (Études Bibliques; Paris: Gabalda).

Lawler, Michael G. (1987). *Symbol and Sacrament: A Contemporary Sacramental Theology* (New York: Paulist Press).

Leach, Edmund (1968). "Ritual" in *International Encyclopedia of the Social Sciences* (New York: Macmillan).

Leach, Edmund (1976). *Culture and Communication: The Logic by which Symbols are Connected: An Introduction to the Use of Structuralist Analysis in Social Anthropology* (Themes in the Social Sciences; Cambridge: Cambridge University Press).

Leclercq, Jean (1970). "The Priesthood in the Patristic and Medieval Church" in Nicholas Lash and Joseph Rhymer, eds., *The Christian Priesthood* (London: Darton, Longman & Todd).

Lécuyer, Joseph (1954). "Le sacrifice selon saint Augustin," *Augustinus Magister* (Paris: Études Augustiniennes) 2.

Lécuyer, Joseph (1983). *Le sacrement d'Ordination: Recherche historique et théologique* (Théologie Historique #65; Paris: Beauchesne).

Leeming, Bernard (1956). *Principles of Sacramental Theology* (London: Longmans, Green, and Company).

Le Goff, Jacques (1988). *Medieval Civilization, 400-1500* (trans. Julia Barrow; Oxford: Blackwell).

Lehne, Susanne (1990). *The New Covenant in Hebrews* (JSNT Supplement #44; Sheffield: JSOT Press).

Leimbach, Karl A. (1936). *Die Bücher Samuel: Übersetzt und Erklärt* (Die

Heilige Schrift des Alten Testamentes, 3.1; Bonn: Peter Hanstein).

Leithart, Peter J. (1992). *Daddy, Why Was I Excommunicated?* (Niceville, FL: Transfiguration Press).

Leithart, Peter J. (1995). "Renewing Circumcision," *Biblical Horizons*.

Leithart, Peter J. (1997). "The Way Things *Really* Ought To Be: Eucharist, Eschatology, and Culture," *WTJ* 59.

Leithart, Peter J. (1998). "The Sociology of Infant Baptism," *Biblical Horizons* 100.

Lenski, R.C.H. (1961). *The Interpretation of St. Paul's Epistles to the Galatians, to the Ephesians, and to the Philippians* (Minneapolis, MN: Augsburg).

Levesque, Joseph L. (1995). "The Theology of the Postbaptismal Rites in the Seventh and Eighth Century Gallican Church," in Maxwell E. Johnson, ed., *Living Water, Sealing Spirit: Readings on Christian Initiation* (A Pueblo Book; Collegeville, MN: Liturgical Press).

Levi-Strauss, Claude (1963). *Structural Anthropology* (Harmondsworth: Penguin).

Levi-Strauss, Claude (1981). *Introduction to a Science of Mythology: Volume 4: The Naked Man* (trans. John and Doreen Weightman; London: Jonathan Cape).

Lewis, Joe O. (1977). "The Ark and the Tent," *RevExp* 74.

Liebeschuetz, J.H.W.G. (1979). *Continuity and Change in Roman Religion* (Oxford: Clarendon Press).

Lillie, William (1977). "An Approach to II Corinthians 5.1-10," *SJT* 30.

Lincoln, Andrew T. (1981). *Paradise Now and Not Yet: Studies in the Role of the Heavenly Dimension in Paul's Thought with Special Reference to his Eschatology* (Cambridge: Cambridge University Press).

Lindbeck, George (1984). *The Nature of Doctrine: Religion and Theology in a Postliberal Age* (London: SPCK).

Lindbeck, George (1997). "The Gospel's Uniqueness: Election and Untranslatability," *MT* 13.

Lloyd, G.E.R. (1966). *Polarity and Analogy: Two Types of Argumentation in Early Greek Thought* (Cambridge: Cambridge University Press).

Longenecker, Richard N. (1990). *Galatians* (Word Biblical Commentary #41; Dallas, TX: Word).

Loraux, Nicole (1986). *The Invention of Athens: The Funeral Oration in the Classical City* (trans. Alan Sheridan; Cambridge, MA: Harvard).

Loughlin, Gerard (1996). *Telling God's Story: Bible, Church and Narrative Theology* (Cambridge: Cambridge University Press).

Louth, Andrew (1989). "Augustine on Language," *Lit&Th* 3:2.

de Lubac, Henri (1949). *Corpus Mysticum: L'eucharistie et l'église au moyen age: Étude historique* (2d ed.; Paris: Aubier).

de Lubac, Henri (1950). *Catholicism: A Study of Dogma in Relation to the Corporate Destiny of Mankind* (London: Burns, Oates, and Washbourne).

de Lubac, Henri (1956). *The Splendour of the Church* (trans. Michael Mason; London: Sheed and Ward).

Luck, Ulrich (1963). "Himmlisches und Irdisches Geschehen im Hebräerbrief," *NovT* 6.

Lull, David J. (1986). "'The Law was Our Pedagogue': A Study in

Galatians 3:19-25," *JBL* 105.

Lundberg, Per Ivar (1942). *La typologie baptismale dans l'ancienne église* (Acta Seminarii Neotestamentici Upsaliensis #10; Leipzig: Alfred Lorentz).

Luther, Martin (1959 (1520)). "The Babylonian Captivity of the Church," in Helmut T. Lehmann, gen. ed., *Luther's Works* (55 vols.; trans. A.T.W. Steinhäuser; Philadelphia: Muhlenberg Press) 36.

Luther, Martin, (1971 (1533)). "The Private Mass and the Consecration of Priests," in Helmut T. Lehmann, gen. ed., *Luther's Works* (55 vols.; trans. Martin E. Lehmann; Philadelphia: Fortress) 38.

MacIntyre, Alasdair (1989). "Virtues, the Unity of a Human Life, and the Concept of a Tradition," in Stanley Hauerwas and L. Gregory Jones, eds., *Why Narrative? Readings in Narrative Theology* (Grand Rapids, MI: Eerdmans).

MacMullen, Ramsay (1974). *Roman Social Relations, 50 BC to AD 284* (New Haven: Yale University Press).

Macy, Gary (1984). *The Theologies of the Eucharist in the Early Scholastic Period: A Study of the Salvific Function of the Sacrament According to the Theologians, c. 1080-c. 1220* (Oxford: Clarendon).

Maldonati, Johannis (1965 (1577)). *Opera Varia Theologica* (Ridgewood, NJ: Gregg Press).

Manville, Philip Brook (1990). *The Origins of Citizenship in Ancient Athens* (Princeton: Princeton University Press).

Marcel, Pierre Ch. (1953). *The Biblical Doctrine of Infant Baptism: Sacrament of the Covenant of Grace* (trans. Philip Edgcumbe Hughes; London: James Clarke).

Marinatos, Nanno and Hägg, Robin, eds. (1993). *Greek Sanctuaries: New*

Approaches (London: Routledge).

Marion, Jean-Luc (1991). *God Without Being: Hors-Texte* (trans. Thomas A. Carlson; Chicago: University of Chicago Press).

Markus, R. A. (1972). "St. Augustine on Signs," in R.A. Markus, ed., *Augustine: A Collection of Critical Essays* (Garden City, NY: Anchor/Doubleday).

Markus, R.A. (1996). *Signs and Meanings: World and Text in Ancient Christianity* (Liverpool: Liverpool University Press).

Martha, Jules (1882). *Les Sacerdoces Athéniens* (Bibliothèque des Écoles Françaises D'Athènes et de Rome #26; Paris: Ernest Thorin).

Martin, Ralph P. (1986). *2 Corinthians* (Word Biblical Commentary #40; Waco, TX: Word).

Martin, Ralph P. (1988). "The Spirit in 2 Corinthians in Light of the 'Fellowship of the Holy Spirit," in W. Hulitt Gloer, ed., *Eschatology and the New Testament: Essays in Honor of George Raymond Beasley-Murray* (Peabody, MA: Hendrickson).

Martyn, J. Louis (1985). "Apocalyptic Antinomies in Paul's Letter to the Galatians," *NTS* 31.

Mauchline, John (1971). *1 and 2 Samuel* (New Century Bible; London: Oliphants).

Mauss, Marcel (1990). *The Gift: The Form and Reason for Exchange in Archaic Societies* (trans. W.D. Halls; London: Routledge).

McCarter, P. Kyle (1984). *II Samuel* (Anchor Bible; Garden City, NY: Doubleday).

McConville, J. Gordon (1983). "Priests and Levites in Ezekiel: A Crux in the Interpretation of Israel's History," *TynBul* 34.

McConville, J. Gordon (1984). *Law and Theology in Deuteronomy* (JSOT Supplement #33; Sheffield: JSOT).

McCormack, Stephen (1944). "The Configuration of the Sacramental Character," *Thom* 7.

McCracken, George E. and Cabaniss, Allen (1957). *Early Medieval Theology* (Library of Christian Classics #9; London: SCM).

McPartlan, Paul (1993). *The Eucharist Makes the Church: Henri de Lubac and John Zizioulas in dialogue* (Edinburgh: T&T Clark).

McPartlan, Paul (1995). *Sacrament of Salvation: An Introduction to Eucharistic Ecclesiology* (Edinburgh: T&T Clark).

McShane, Philip A. (1963). "On the Causality of the Sacraments," *TS* 24.

McWilliam, Joanne, ed. (1992). *Augustine: From Rhetor to Theologian* (Waterloo, Ontario: Wilfrid Laurier University Press).

Mersch, Émile (1936). *Le Corps Mystique du Christ: Études de théologie historique* (2 vols.; 2d ed.; Paris: Desclée de Brouwer et Cie).

Mettinger, Tryggve N.D. (1971). *Solomonic State Officials: A Study of Civil Government Officials of the Israelite Monarchy* (Coniectanea Biblica, Old Testament Series #5; Lund: C.W.K. Gleerup).

Meyer, Heinrich August Wilhelm (1892-1894). *Critical and Exegetical Handbook to the Epistles to the Corinthians* (2 vols.; trans. D. Douglas Bannerman; 5th ed; Edinburgh: T&T Clark).

Milbank, John (1987). "An Essay Against Secular Order," *JRE* 15.

Milbank, John (1990). *Theology and Social Theory: Beyond Secular Reason* (Oxford: Blackwell).

Milbank, John (1991-1992). *The Religious Dimension in the Thought of*

Giambattista Vico, 1668-1744 (2 vols.; Studies in the History of Philosophy #23, 32; Lewiston, NY: Edwin Mellen).

Milbank, John (1997). *The Word Made Strange: Theology, Language, Culture* (Oxford: Blackwell).

Milgrom, Jacob (1970). *Studies in Levitical Terminology, I: The Encroacher and the Levite; The Term 'Aboda* (Berlekey, CA: University of California Press).

Milgrom, Jacob (1983). *Studies in Cultic Theology and Terminology* (Leiden: Brill).

Milgrom, Jacob (1991). *Leviticus 1-16: A New Translation with Introduction and Commentary* (Anchor Bible; New York: Doubleday).

Milgrom, Jacob (1992). "Priestly ('P') Source" in *The Anchor Bible Dictionary* (6 vols.; New York: Doubleday) 5.

Miller, Stephen G. (1978). *The Prytaneion: Its Function and Architectural Form* (Berkeley: University of California Press).

Mingana, A., ed. and trans. (1933). *Commentary of Theodore of Mopsuestia on the Lord's Prayer and on the Sacraments of Baptism and the Eucharist* (Woodbrooke Studies, VI; Cambridge: W. Heffer and Sons).

Mitchell, Leonel L. (1977). *Baptismal Anointing* (Notre Dame, IN: University of Notre Dame Press).

Moffatt, James (1924). *A Critical and Exegetical Commentary on the Epistle to the Hebrews* (International Critical Commentary on the Holy Scriptures of the Old and New Testaments; Edinburgh: T&T Clark).

Moffatt, James (1938). *The First Epistle of Paul to the Corinthians* (Moffatt New Testament Commentary; London: Hodder and Stoughton).

Momigliano, Arnaldo (1977). *Essays in Ancient and Modern Historiography* (Blackwell's Classical Studies; Oxford: Blackwell).

Morris, Brian (1987). *Anthropological Studies of Religion: An Introductory Text* (Cambridge: Cambridge University Press).

Morris, Colin (1972). *The Discovery of the Individual: 1050-1200* (New York: Harper & Row).

Morris, Colin (1989). *The Papal Monarchy: The Western Church from 1050 to 1250* (Oxford History of the Christian Church; Oxford: Clarendon).

Mossé, Claude (1967). "La Conception du citoyen dans La Politique d'Aristote," *Eir* 6.

Müller-Fahrenholz, Geiko, ed. (1982). *. . . and do not hinder them: An Ecumenical Plea for the Admission of Children to the Eucharist* (Faith and Order Paper #109; Geneva: World Council of Churches).

Murphy Center for Liturgical Research (1976). *Made, Not Born: New Perspectives on Christian Initiation and the Catechumenate* (Notre Dame, IN: University of Notre Dame Press).

Murray, John (1980). *Christian Baptism* (Phillipsburg, NJ: Presbyterian & Reformed).

Murray, Oswyn and Price, Simon, eds. (1990). *The Greek City: From Homer to Alexander* (Oxford: Clarendon Press).

Murray, Robert (1975). *Symbols of Church and Kingdom: A Study in Early Syriac Tradition* (Cambridge: Cambridge University Press).

Mußner, Franz (1974). *Der Galaterbrief* (Herders theologischer Kommentar zum Neuen Testamenten #9; Freiburg: Herder).

Nauck, Wolfgang (1960). "Zum Aufbau des Hebräerbriefes," in

Walther Eltester, ed., *Judentum, Urchristentum, Kirche: Festschrift für Joachim Jeremias* (Beihefte zur Zeitschrift für die Neutestamentliche und die Kunde der Alteren Kirche #26; Berlin: Alfred Topelmann).

Neill, Stephen and Wright, Tom (1988). *The Interpretation of the New Testament, 1861-1986* (2d ed.; Oxford: Oxford University Press).

Nelson, Richard D (1993). *Raising up a Faithful Priest: Community and Priesthood in Biblical Theology* (Louisville, KY: Westminster/John Knox).

Neunheuser, Burkhard (1976). "Odo Casel in Retrospect and Prospect," *Worship* 50.

Nicolas, R. P. Marie-Joseph (1974). "La Doctrine de S. Thomas sur le sacerdoce" in *Studi tomistici* (Rome: Pontificia Accademia Romana di S. Tomasso d'Aquino) 2.

Nietzsche, Friedrich (1988). *The Antichrist* (trans. H.L. Mencken; Costa Mesa, CA: Noontide Press).

Nilsson, Martin P. (1949). *A History of Greek Religion* (2d ed.; trans. F.J. Fielden; Oxford: Clarendon).

Nolland, John (1989). *Luke 1-9:20* (Word Biblical Commentary #35A; Dallas, TX: Word).

Noth, Martin (1962). *Exodus: A Commentary* (trans. J.S. Bowden; London: SCM).

Noth, Martin (1966). *The Laws in the Pentateuch and Other Studies* (trans. D.R. St.-Thomas; Edinburgh: Oliver and Boyd).

Oakley, Francis (1979). *The Western Church in the Later Middle Ages* (Ithaca: Cornell University Press).

Oberman, Heiko A. and Courtenay, William J. (1963-67). *Gabrielis Biel Canonis Misse Expositio* (4 vols.; Veröffentlichungen des Instituts für Europäische Geschichte Mainz, #31; Wiesbaden: Franz Steiner).

O'Donovan, Oliver (1982). *"Usus* and *Fruitio* in Augustine, *De Doctrina Christiana*, I," *JTS* 33.

Ogg, George (1959). "The Age of Jesus When He Taught," *NTS* 5.

Old, Hughes Oliphant (1992). *The Shaping of the Reformed Baptismal Rite in the Sixteenth Century* (Grand Rapids, MI: Eerdmans).

Oliver, Harold H. (1964). "The Lucan Birth Stories and the Purpose of Luke-Acts," *NTS* 10.

O'Neill, Colman E. (1963). "St. Thomas on the Membership of the Church," *Thom* 27.

O'Neill, J.C. (1985). "The Study of the New Testament" in Ninian Smart, John Clayton, Steven Katz, and Patrick Sherry, eds., *Nineteenth Century Religious Thought in the West* (3 vols.; Cambridge: Cambridge University Press) 3.

Osborne, Kenan B. (1974). "Methodology and the Christian Sacraments," *Worship* 48.

Osborne, M.J. (1981-1983). *Naturalization in Athens* (4 vols.; Verhandelingen van de Koninklijke Academie voor Wetenschappen, Letteren en Schone Kunsten van België, Klasse der Letteren, #98, 101, 109; Brussels: AWLSK).

Pannenberg, Wolfhart (1993). *Systematische Theologie, Band 3* (Göttingen: Vandenhoeck & Ruprecht).

Pannenberg, Wolfhart (1996). "Baptism as Remembered 'Ecstatic' Identity," in David Brown and Ann Loades, eds., *Christ: The Sacramental Word* (London: SPCK).

Parker, Robert (1983). *Miasma: Pollution and Purification in Early Greek Religion* (Oxford: Clarendon).

Parker, Robert (1996). *Athenian Religion: A History* (Oxford: Clarendon).

Paschasius Radbertus (1969). *De Corpore et Sanguine Domini* (ed. Bedae Paulus; Corpus Christianorum, Continuatio Medievalis, #16; Turnholti: Typographi Brepols Editores Pontificii).

Pate, C. Marvin (1991). *Adam Christology as the Exegetical and Theological Substructure of 2 Corinthians 4:7-5:21* (Lanham, MD: University Press of America).

Payne, E.A. (1959). "Baptism in Recent Discussion" in A. Gilmore, ed., *Christian Baptism: A Fresh Attempt to Understand the Rite in terms of Scripture, History, and Theology* (London: Lutterworth).

Payne, J. Barton (1980). "כהן" in R. Laird Harris, et. al., eds., *Theological Wordbook of the Old Testament* (2 vols.; Chicago, IL: Moody) 1.

Pellegrino, Cardinal Michele (1968). *The True Priest: The Priesthood as Preached and Practiced by St. Augustine* (trans. Arthur Gibson; Langley, UK: St. Paul Publications).

Pelser, G.M.M. (1974). "A Translation Problem: Heb. 10:19-25," *NeoT* 8.

Pesch, Wilhelm (1970). "Zu Texten des Neuen Testamentes über das Priestertum der Getauften" in Otto Böcher and Klaus Haacker, eds., *Verborum Veritas: Festschrift für Gustav Stählin zum 70. Geburtstag* (Wuppertal: Brockhaus).

Peterson, David (1982). *Hebrews and Perfection: An Examination of the Concept of Perfection in the "Epistle to the Hebrews"* (Society for New Testament Studies Monograph Series, #47; Cambridge: Cambridge University Press).

Pfatteicher, Philip H. (1990). *Commentary on the Lutheran Book of Worship: Lutheran Liturgy in Its Ecumenical Context* (Minneapolis, MN: Augsburg).

Philo (1966). *De Vita Mosis* in *Works* (10 vols.; LCL; trans. F.H. Colson; London: William Heinemann) 6.

Pickstock, Catherine (1996). "Necrophilia: The Middle of Modernity. A Study of Death, Signs, and the Eucharist," *MT* 12.

Plato (1967). *Laws* (2 vols.; LCL; trans R.G. Bury; London: William Heinemann).

Plummer, Alfred (1915). *A Critical and Exegetical Commentary on the Second Epistle of Paul to the Corinthians* (ICC; Edinburgh: T&T Clark).

Polignac, François de (1995). *Cults, Territory, and the Origins of the Greek City-State* (trans. Janet Lloyd; Chicago: University of Chicago Press).

Porter, H.B. (1967). *The Ordination Prayers of the Ancient Western Churches* (Alcuin Club Collections, #49; London: SPCK).

de la Potterie, I. (1959). "L'onction du chrétien par la foi," *Bib* 40.

Power, David N. (1984). *Unsearchable Riches: The Symbolic Nature of Liturgy* (A Pueblo Book; Collegeville, MN: Liturgical Press).

Power, David N., et. al. (1994). "Sacramental Theology: A Review of Literature," *TS* 55.

Poythress, Vern Sheridan (1991). *The Shadow of Christ in the Law of Moses* (Brentwood, TN: Wolgemuth & Hyatt).

Poythress, Vern Sheridan (1997a). "Indifferentism and Rigorism in the Church: With Implications for Baptizing Small Children," *WTJ* 59:1.

Poythress, Vern Sheridan (1997b). "Linking Small Children With Infants in the Theology of Baptizing," *WTJ* 59:2.

Prenter, R. (1948). "Metaphysics and Eschatology in the Sacramental Theology of St. Augustine," *StudTh* 1.

Pritchard, James B., ed. (1969). *Ancient Near Eastern Texts Relating to the Old Testament* (3d ed.; Princeton: Princeton University Press).

Pursiful, Darrell J. (1993). *The Cultic Motif in the Spirituality of the Book of Hebrews* (Lewiston, NY: Mellen Biblical Press).

Quinot, Bernard (1962). "L'influence de l'Épître aux Hébreux dans la notion augustinienne du vrai sacrifice," *RevEtAug* 8.

Quinn, Frank C. (1995). "Confirmation Reconsidered: Rite and Meaning," in Maxwell E. Johnson, ed., *Living Water, Sealing Spirit: Readings in Christian Initiation* (A Pueblo Book; Collegeville, MN: Liturgical Press).

Rabe, Virgil W. (1966). "The Identity of the Priestly Tabernacle," *JNES* 25.

Radcliffe, Timothy (1987). "Christ in Hebrews: Cultic Irony," *NewBl* 68.

Rahner, Karl (1963). *The Church and the Sacraments* (trans. W.J. O'Hara; Freiburg: Herder).

Rainey, A.F. (1965). "The Kingdom of Ugarit," *BA* 28.

Rawlinson, George (1906). *II Kings* (The Pulpit Commentary; London: Funk & Wagnalls).

Rawson, Elizabeth (1991). *Roman Culture and Society: Collected Papers* (Oxford: Clarendon).

Rendtorff, Rolf (1985). *Leviticus, I* (Biblischer Kommentar Altes Testament #3; Neukirchen-   Vluyn: Neukirchener Verlag).

Réveillaud, Michel (1968). "Le Christ-Homme, tête de l'Église: Étude d'ecclésiologie selon les *Ennarationes in Psalmos* d'Augustin," *RechAug* 5.

Reventlow, Henning Graf (1984). *The Authority of the Bible and the Rise of the Modern World* (trans. John Bowden; London: SCM).

Reynolds, Roger E. (1978). *The Ordinals of Christ from their Origins to the Twelfth Century* (Beträge zur Geschichte und Quellenkunde des Mittelalters #7; Berlin: Walter de Gruyter).

Ridderbos, Herman N. (1956). *The Epistle of Paul to the Churches of Galatia* (NICNT; Grand Rapids, MI: Eerdmans).

Riley, Hugh M. (1974). *Christian Initiation: A Comparative Study of the Interpretation of the Baptismal Liturgy in the Mystagogical Writings of Cyril of Jerusalem, John Chrysostom, Theodore of Mopsuestia, and Ambrose of Milan* (Catholic University of America Studies in Christian Antiquity #17; Washington, DC: Catholic University of America Press).

Rist, John M. (1996). *Augustine: Ancient Thought Baptized* (Cambridge: Cambridge University Press).

Roman Catholic Church (1986). *Rite of Christian Initiation of Adults: The Final Text with Commentaries* (Dublin: Columba Press).

Robertson, Archibald and Plummer, Alfred (1914). *A Critical and Exegetical Commentary on the First Epistle of St. Paul to the Corinthians* (2d. ed.; ICC; Edinburgh: T&T Clark).

Robinson, Gnana (1993). *Let Us Be Like the Nations: A Commentary on the Books of 1 and 2 Samuel* (International Theological Commentary; Grand Rapids/Edinburgh: Eerdmans/Handsel).

299

Rodríguez, Ángel Manuel (1986). "Sanctuary Theology in the Book of Exodus," *AUSS* 24.

Rosenstock-Huessy, Eugen (1993). *Out of Revolution: Autobiography of Western Man* (Providence, RI/Oxford: Berg).

Rosner, Brian S. (1996). "The Origin and Meaning of 1 Corinthians 6:9-11 in Context," *BZ* n.s. 40.

Rothkoff, Aaron (1972). "Tabernacle" in *Encyclopedia Judaica* (16 vols.; Jerusalem: Encyclopaedia Judaica) 15.

Rubin, Miri (1991). *Corpus Christi: The Eucharist in Late Medieval Culture* (Cambridge: Cambridge University Press).

Ruddick, C. Townsend, Jr. (1970). "Birth Narratives in Genesis and Luke," *NovT* 12.

Sabourin, Leopold (1973). *Priesthood: A Comparative Study* (Supplements to Noumen, Studies in the History of Religions #25; Leiden: Brill).

Sainte Croix, G.E.M. de (1981). *The Class Struggle in the Ancient Greek World: From the Archaic Age to the Arab Conquests* (London: Duckworth).

Sanders, E.P. (1977). *Paul and Palestinian Judaism: A Comparison of Patterns of Religion* (London: SCM).

Sarna, Nahum M. (1986). *Exploring Exodus: The Heritage of Biblical Israel* (New York: Schocken).

Schiffman, Lawrence H. (1985). "Priests" in *Harper's Bible Dictionary* (San Francisco: Harper and Row).

Schillebeeckx, E. (1963). *Christ, the Sacrament of Encounter with God* (trans. Paul Barrett and N.D. Smith; London: Sheed and Ward).

Schillebeeckx, E. (1968). *The Eucharist* (trans. N.D. Smith; London: Sheed and Ward).

Schleiermacher, Friedrich (1928). *The Christian Faith* (2d. ed; trans. H.R. MacIntosh and J.S. Stewart; Edinburgh: T&T Clark).

Schleiermacher, Friedrich (1958). *On Religion: Speeches to its Cultured Despisers* (trans. John Oman; New York: Harper Torchbooks).

Schlier, Heinrich (1962). *Der Brief an die Galater* (Kritisch-exegetischer Kommentar über das Neuen Testament #7; Göttingen: Vandenhoeck & Ruprecht)

Schlette, Heinz Robert (1959). "Die Eucharistielehre Hugos von St Viktor," *ZKT* 81.

Schmemann, Alexander (1974). *Of Water and the Spirit: A Liturgical Study of Baptism* (Crestwood, NY: St. Vladimir's Seminary Press).

Schmemann, Alexander (1986). *Introduction to Liturgical Theology* (3d ed.; Crestwood, NY: St. Vladimir's Seminary Press).

Schmitt Pantel, P. (1981). "Le festin dans la fête de la cité grecque hellénistique," in *La fête: pratique et discours: d'Alexandrie hellénistique à la Mission de Besançon* (Centre de recherches d'histoire ancienne, Annales Littéraires de l'Université de Besançon; #42; Paris: Les Belles Lettres).

Schnackenburg, Rudolf (1964). *Baptism in the Thought of St. Paul: A Study in Pauline Theology* (trans. G.R. Beasley-Murray; Oxford: Blackwell).

Scholer, John M. (1991). *Proleptic Priests: Priesthood in the Epistle to the Hebrews* (JSNT Supplement #49; Sheffield: JSOT Press).

Schoonenberg, Piet (1967). "The Real Presence in Contemporary Discussion," *TD* 15.

Schrage, Wolfgang (1991). *Der erste Brief an der Korinther* (2 vols.; Evangelisch-Katholischer Kommentar zum Neuen Testament; Zürich: Benzinger).

Schrenk, Gottlob (1965). ἱερός, in Gerhard Kittel, ed., *Theological Dictionary of the New Testament* (10 vols.; trans. by Geoffrey W. Bromiley; Grand Rapids: Eerdmans) 3.

Schwartz, Daniel R. (1983). "Two Pauline Allusions to the Redemptive Mechanism of the Crucifixion," *JBL* 102.

Scobie, Charles H.H. (1964). *John the Baptist* (London: SCM).

Scroggs, Robin (1966). *The Last Adam: A Study in Pauline Anthropology* (Oxford: Blackwell).

Searle, John R. (1995). *The Construction of Social Reality* (New York: Free Press).

Searle, Mark (1992). "Ritual" in Cheslyn Jones, et. al., eds. *The Study of Liturgy* (rev. ed.; London: SPCK).

Searle, Mark (1995). "Infant Baptism Reconsidered," in Maxwell E. Johnson, ed., *Living Water, Sealing Spirit: Readings on Christian Initiation* (A Pueblo Book; Collegeville, MN: Liturgical Press).

Sheedy, Charles E. (1980). *The Eucharistic Controversy of the Eleventh Century Against the Background of Pre-Scholastic Theology* (Catholic University of America Studies in Sacred Theology, 2d series, #4; New York: AMS Press).

Silva, Moises (1976/77). "Perfection and Eschatology in Hebrews," *WTJ* 39.

Skorupski, John (1976). *Symbol and Theory: A philosophical study of theories of religion in social anthropology* (Cambridge: Cambridge University Press).

Smart, Ninian, John Clayton, Steven Katz, and Patrick Sherry, eds.
(1985). *Nineteenth Century Religious Thought in the West* (3 vols.;
Cambridge: Cambridge University Press).

Smith, Derwood C. (1982). "Jewish Proselyte Baptism and the Baptism
of John," *ResQ* 25.

Smith, Henry Preserved (1918). "Priest, Priesthood (Hebrew)" in
Encyclopædia of Religion and Ethics (13 vols.; Edinburgh: T&T
Clark) 10.

Smith, Jonathan Z. (1987). *To Take Place: Toward Theory in Ritual*
(Chicago: University of Chicago Press).

Smith, R. Payne (1906). *II Samuel* (The Pulpit Commentary; London:
Funk & Wagnalls).

Smith, William Robertson and Bertholet, A. (1902). "Priest," in
Encyclopedia Biblica (4 vols.; London: Adam and Charles Black)
3.

Smith, William Robertson (1927). *Lectures on the Religion of the Semites:
The Fundamental Institutions* (London: A&C Black).

Soskice, Janet Martin (1985). *Metaphor and Religious Language* (Oxford:
Clarendon Press).

Sourvinou-Inwood, Christine (1990). "What is *Polis* Religion?" in
Oswyn Murray and Simon Price, eds., *The Greek City: From
Homer to Alexander* (Oxford: Clarendon).

Sourvinou-Inwood, Christine (1993). "Early Sanctuaries, the Eighth
Century and Ritual Space: Fragments of a Discourse," in
Nanno Marinatos and Robin Hägg, eds., *Greek Sanctuaries: New
Approaches* (London: Routledge).

Spicq, Ceslas (1966). *L'Épitre de Saint Pierre* (Sources Bibliques; Paris:

303

Gabalda).

Spicq, C. (1969). *Les Épitres Pastorales* (4th ed.; Études Bibliques; Paris: Gabalda).

Spinks, Bryan D. (1995). "Vivid Signs of the Gift of the Spirit? The Lima Text on Baptism and Some Recent English Language Baptismal Liturgies," in Maxwell E. Johnson, ed., *Living Water, Sealing Spirit: Readings on Christian Initiation* (A Pueblo Book; Collegeville, MN: Liturgical Press).

Stanley, Christopher D. (1990). "'Under a Curse': A Fresh reading of Galatians 3:10-14," *NTS* 36.

Stendahl, Krister (1963). "The Apostle Paul and the Introspective Conscience of the West," *HTR* 5.

Stegner, William R. (1985). "The Baptism of Jesus: A Story Modeled on the Binding of Isaac," *BibRev* 1.

Stenzel, Alois (1958). *Die Taufe: Eine Genetische Erklärung der Taufliturfgie* (Innsbruck: Felizian Rauch).

Stockhausen, Carol Kern (1989). *Moses' Veil and the Glory of the New Covenant* (Analecta Biblica #116; Rome: Editrice Pontificio Instituto Biblico).

Strathmann, H. (1967). "λατρεύω, λατρεία" in Gerhard Kittel, *Theological Dictionary of the New Testament* (10 vols.; trans. Geoffrey Bromiley; Grand Rapids, MI: Eerdmans) 4.

Strong, James (1987). *The Tabernacle of Israel: Its Structure and Symbolism* (Grand Rapids, MI: Kregel).

Stroup, George W. (1981). *The Promise of Narrative Theology* (London: SCM).

Swetnam, James (1966). "'The Greater and More Perfect Tent': A

Contribution to the Discussion of Hebrews 9, 11," *Bib* 47.

Swetnam, James (1974). "Form and Content in Hebrews 7-13," *Bib* 55.

Sykes, Stephen (1971). *Friedrich Schleiermacher* (Makers of Contemporary Theology; London: Lutterworth).

Sykes, Stephen (1984). *The Identity of Christianity: Theology and the Essence of Christianity from Schleiermacher to Barth* (London: SPCK).

Sykes, Stephen (1988). "Schleiermacher and Barth on the Essence of Christianity – an Instructive Disagreement" in James O. Duke and Robert F. Streetman, eds., *Barth and Schleiermacher: Beyond the Impasse?* (Philadelphia: Fortress).

Tambiah, S. J. (1979). "A Performative Approach to Ritual," *ProBritAc* 65.

Tarragon, Jean-Michel de (1980). *Le culte à Ugarit: d'Après les textes de la pratique en cunéiformes alphabétiques* (Cahiers de la Revue Biblique #19; Paris: Gabalda).

Taylor, Charles (1989). *Sources of the Self: The Making of Modern Identity* (Cambridge: Cambridge University Press).

Tellenbach, Gerd (1993). *The Church in Western Europe from the Tenth to the Early Twelfth Century* (Cambridge Mediæval Textbooks; trans. Timothy Reuter; Cambridge: Cambridge University Press).

Thatcher, Tom (1997). "The Plot of Galatians 3:1-18," *JETS* 40:3.

Thielman, Frank (1994). *Paul and the Law: A Contextual Approach* (Downers Grove, IL: InterVarsity).

Thiering, Barbara E. (1980). "Inner and Outer Cleansing at Qumran as a Background to New Testament Baptism," *NTS* 26.

Thiering, Barbara E. (1981). "Qumran Initiation and New Testament

Baptism," *NTS* 27.

Thils, G. (1938). "Le pouvoir cultuel du baptisé,"*EphThLov* 15.

Thompson, Andrew D. (1987). "Infant Baptism in the Light of the Human Sciences," in Mark Searle, ed., *Alternative Futures for Worship: Volume 2: Baptism and Confirmation* (A Pueblo Book; Collegeville, MN: Liturgical Press).

Thrall, Margaret E. (1994). *A Critical and Exegetical Commentary on the Second Epistle to the Corinthians* (ICC; 2 vols.; Edinburgh: T&T Clark).

Thurian, Max (1960-1961). *The Eucharistic Memorial* (2 vols. in 1; trans. J.G. Davies; Ecumenical Studies in Worship #7-8; London: Lutterworth).

Thusing, Wilhelm (1965). "'Laßt uns hinzutreten' (Hebr 10, 22): Zur Frage nach dem Sinn der Kulttheologie im Hebräerbrief," *BZ* 9.

Tierney, Brian (1964). *The Crisis of Church and State 1050-1300, with selected documents* (Englewood Cliffs, NJ: Prentice-Hall).

Todorov, Tzvetan (1982). *Theories of the Symbol* (trans. Catherine Porter; Oxford: Blackwell).

Trigg, Jonathan D. (1994). *Baptism in the Theology of Martin Luther* (Studies in the History of Christian Thought #56; Leiden: Brill).

Troeltsch, Ernst (1931). *The Social Teaching of the Christian Churches* (2 vols.; trans. Olive Wyon; London: Allen and Unwin).

Turner, Victor (1966). *The Ritual Process: Structure and Anti-Structure* (Chicago: Aldine).

Turner, Victor (1967). *The Forest of Symbols: Aspects of Ndembu Ritual*

(Ithaca, NY: Cornell University Press).

Turner, Victor (1976). "Ritual, Tribal and Catholic," *Worship* 50.

Ullmann, Walter (1975). *A History of Political Thought: The Middle Ages* (London: Penguin).

United Reformed Church (1988). *Children In Communion? Let's Talk About It* (London: United Reformed Church).

Urie, D.M.L. (1948). "Officials of the Cult at Ugarit," *PEQ* 80.

Van den Eynde, Damian (1951). "Stephen Langton and Hugh of St. Cher on the Causality of the Sacraments," *FS* n.s. 11.

Van Gennep, Arnold (1960). *The Rites of Passage* (trans. Monika B. Vizedom and Gabrielle L. Caffee; London: Routledge & Kegan Paul).

Vanhoye, Albert (1963). *La structure littéraire de l'Épitre aux Hébreux* (Studia neotestamentica #1; Paris: Desclée de Brouwer).

Vanhoye, Albert (1968). "Longue marche ou accès tout proche? Le context biblique de Hébreux 3, 7-4, 11," *Bib* 49.

Vanhoye, Albert (1989). *Structure and Message of the Epistle to the Hebrews* (Subsidia Biblica #12; trans. James Swetnam; Rome: Editrice Pontifico Istituto Biblico).

Vanhoye, Albert (1993). "Pensée théologique et qualité rhetorique en Galates 3, 1-14," in Jan Lambrecht, ed., *The Truth of the Gospel (Galatians 1:1-4:11)* (Monographic Series of "Benedictina," Biblical-Ecumenical Section #12; Rome: St. Paul's Abbey).

Vatin, Claude (1984). *Citoyens et non-citoyens dans le monde grec* (Regard sur l'histoire; Paris: Société d'enseignement supérieur).

de Vaux, R. (1939). "Titres et fonctionnaires Égyptiens à la cour de

David et de Salomon," *RB* 48.

de Vaux, Roland (1961). *Ancient Israel: Its Life and Institutions* (trans. John McHugh; London: Darton, Longman & Todd).

Vernant, Jean-Pierre (1988). *Myth and Society in Ancient Greece* (trans. Janet Lloyd; New York: Zone Books).

Wainwright, Geoffrey (1969). *Christian Initiation* (Ecumenical Studies in History #10; London: Lutterworth).

Wainwright, Geoffrey (1977). "Christian Initiation in the Ecumenical Movement," *StudLit* 12.

Wainwright, Geoffrey (1980). *Doxology: The Praise of God in Worship, Doctrine, and Life: A Systematic Theology* (New York: Oxford).

Wainwright, Geoffrey (1991). "Renewing Worship: The Recovery of Classical Patterns," *TToday* 48:1.

Wallace, Ronald S. (1982). *Calvin's Doctrine of Word and Sacrament* (Tyler, TX: Geneva Divinity School).

Walsh, Liam G. (1974). "Liturgy in the Theology of St. Thomas," *Thom* 38.

Wardman, Alan (1982). *Religion and Statecraft among the Romans* (London: Granada).

Webb, Robert L. (1991). *John the Baptizer and Prophet: A Socio-Historical Study* (JSNT Supplement #62; Sheffield: JSOT Press).

Webb, William J. (1993). *Returning Home: New Covenant and Second Exodus as the Context for 2 Corinthians 6:14-7:1* (JSNT Supplement Series #85; Sheffield: JSOT Press).

Weber, Max (1978). *Economy and Society: An Outline of Interpretive Sociology* (2 vols.; trans. Ephraim Fischoff, et. al.; eds. Guenther Roth and Claus Wittich; Berkeley: University of California Press).

Wedderburn, A.J.M. (1987). *Baptism and Resurrection: Studies in Pauline Theology against its Graeco-Roman Background* (Wissenschaftlichen Untersuchungen zum Neuen Testament #44; Tübingen: J.C.B. Mohr).

Weinfeld, Moshe (1979). *Getting at the Roots of Wellhausen's Understanding of the Law of Israel on the 100th Anniversary of the "Prolegomena"* (Jerusalem: Institute for Advanced Studies at the Hebrew University).

Wellhausen, Julius (1885). *Prolegomena to the History of Israel* (trans. J. Sutherland Black and Allan Menzies; Edinburgh: Adam & Charles Black).

Wenham, G.J. (1975). "Were David's Sons Priests?" *ZAW* 87.

Wenham, Gordon J. (1979). *The Book of Leviticus* (NICOT; London: Hodder and Stoughton).

Wenham, Gordon J. (1981). *Numbers: An Introduction and Commentary* (Tyndale Old Testament Commentaries; Leicester: InterVarsity).

Westcott, Brooke Foss (1920). *Commentary on the Epistle to the Hebrews* (London: Marshall, Morgan & Scott).

Whitaker, E. C. (1960). *Documents of the Baptismal Liturgy* (Alcuin Club Collections #42; London: SPCK).

White, James F. (1995). *Roman Catholic Worship: Trent to Today* (New York: Paulist).

White, R.E.O. (1960). *The Biblical Doctrine of Initiation* (London: Hodder and Stoughton).

Williams, G.O. (1944). "The Baptism in Luke's Gospel," *JTS* o.s. 45.

Williams, Rowan (1987). "The Nature of a Sacrament" in John Greenhalgh and Elizabeth Russell, eds., *Signs of Faith, Hope, and Love: The Christian Sacraments Today* (London: St. Mary's Bourne Street).

Williams, Rowan (1989). "Language, Reality and Desire in Augustine's *De Doctrina*," *Lit&Theo* 3:2.

Williams, Rowan (1996). "Sacraments of the New Society" in David Brown and Ann Loades, eds., *Christ: the Sacramental Word* (London: SPCK).

Williams, Sam K. (1987). "Justification and the Spirit in Galatians," *JSNT* 29.

Wink, Walter (1968). *John the Baptist in the Gospel Tradition* (Society for New Testament Studies Monograph #7; Cambridge: Cambridge University Press).

Winkler, Gabriele (1976). "The History of the Syriac Prebaptismal Anointing in the Light of the Earliest Armenian Sources," *OCA* 205.

Winkler, Gabriele (1995a). "The Original Meaning of the Prebaptismal Anointing and Its Implications," in Maxwell E. Johnson, ed., *Living Water, Sealing Spirit: Readings on Christian Initiation* (A Pueblo Book; Collegeville, MN: Liturgical Press).

Winkler, Gabriele (1995b). "Confirmation or Chrismation? A Study in Comparative Liturgy," in Maxwell E. Johnson, ed., *Living Water, Sealing Spirit: Readings on Christian Initiation* (A Pueblo Book; Collegeville, MN: Liturgical Press).

Witsius, Herman (1990). *The Economy of the Covenants Between God and Man: Comprehending a Complete Body of Divinity* (2 vols.; Escondido, CA: den Dulk Foundation).

310

Wolterstorff, Nicholas (1995). *Divine Discourse: Philosophical reflections on the claim that God speaks* (Cambridge: University of Cambridge Press).

Wood, Ellen M. and Wood, Neal (1978). *Class Ideology and Ancient Political Theory: Socrates, Plato, and Aristotle in Social Context* (Oxford: Blackwell).

Woodhouse, W.J. (1918). "Priest, Priesthood (Greek)" in *Encyclopaedia of Religion and Ethics* (13 vols.; Edinburgh: T&T Clark) 10.

Worgul, George S., Jr. (1980). *From Magic to Metaphor: A Validation of the Christian Sacraments* (New York: Paulist).

Wright, David P. (1992). "Holiness (OT)," in *Anchor Bible Dictionary* (6 vols.; New York: Doubleday) 3.

Wright, G. Ernest and Freedman, David Noel (1975). *The Biblical Archaeologist Reader, I* (Missoula, MT: Scholars Press).

Wright, N.T. (1991). *Climax of the Covenant: Christ and the Law in Pauline Theology* (Edinburgh: T&T Clark).

Wright, N.T. (1992). *The New Testament and the People of God* (Christian Origins and the Question of God #1; London: SPCK).

Wright, N.T. (1996). *Jesus and the Victory of God* (Christian Origins and the Question of God #2; London: SPCK).

Young, Daniel (1983). *Welcoming Children to Communion* (Grove Worship Series #85; Bramcote: Grove Books).

Young, Norman H. (1987). "ΠΑΙΔΑΓΩΓ'ΟΣ: The Social Setting of a Pauline Metaphor," *NovT* 29.

Youngblood, Ronald F. (1992). "1, 2 Samuel" in *The Expositor's Bible Commentary* (12 vols.; Grand Rapids: Zondervan) 3.

Zaidman, Louise Bruit and Schmitt Pantel, Pauline (1989). *Religion in the Ancient Greek City* (trans. Paul Cartledge; Cambridge: Cambridge University Press).

Zizioulas, John D. (1993). *Being as Communion: Studies in Personhood and the Church* (Crestwood, NY: St. Vladimir's Seminary Press).

Zwingli, Ulrich (1953). *On Baptism* in G.W. Bromiley, ed., *Zwingli and Bullinger* (LCC #24; London: SCM).

Printed in the USA
CPSIA information can be obtained
at www.ICGtesting.com
LVHW050719261023
761976LV00005B/130